SOCRATES ON SELF-IMPROVEMENT

What model of knowledge does Plato's Socrates use? In this book, Nicholas D. Smith argues that it is akin to knowledge of a craft that is acquired by degrees, rather than straightforward knowledge of facts. He contends that a failure to recognize and identify this model, and attempts to ground ethical success in contemporary accounts of propositional or informational knowledge, have led to distortions of Socrates' philosophical mission to improve himself and others in the domain of practical ethics. He shows that the model of craft-knowledge makes sense of a number of issues scholars have struggled to understand, and makes a case for attributing to Socrates a very sophisticated and plausible view of the improvability of the human condition.

NICHOLAS D. SMITH is James F. Miller Professor of Humanities and Professor of Classics and Philosophy at Lewis & Clark College. He has written and edited many books on ancient Greek philosophy and contemporary epistemology, including *Plato's Socrates* (with T. C. Brickhouse, 1994), *Socratic Moral Psychology* (with T. C. Brickhouse, Cambridge University Press, 2010), and *Summoning Knowledge in Plato's Republic* (2019).

SOCRATES ON SELF-IMPROVEMENT

Knowledge, Virtue, and Happiness

NICHOLAS D. SMITH

Lewis & Clark College

CAMBRIDGE
UNIVERSITY PRESS

Shaftesbury Road, Cambridge CB2 8EA, United Kingdom

One Liberty Plaza, 20th Floor, New York, NY 10006, USA

477 Williamstown Road, Port Melbourne, VIC 3207, Australia

314–321, 3rd Floor, Plot 3, Splendor Forum, Jasola District Centre, New Delhi – 110025, India

103 Penang Road, #05–06/07, Visioncrest Commercial, Singapore 238467

Cambridge University Press is part of Cambridge University Press & Assessment,
a department of the University of Cambridge.

We share the University's mission to contribute to society through the pursuit of
education, learning and research at the highest international levels of excellence.

www.cambridge.org
Information on this title: www.cambridge.org/9781009012430

DOI: 10.1017/9781009025959

First published 2021
First paperback edition 2023

A catalogue record for this publication is available from the British Library

Library of Congress Cataloging-in-Publication data
NAMES: Smith, Nicholas D., 1949– author.
TITLE: Socrates on self-improvement : knowledge, virtue, and happiness / Nicholas D. Smith,
Lewis & Clark College, Portland.
DESCRIPTION: Cambridge, United Kingdom ; New York, NY, USA : Cambridge University
Press, 2021. | Includes bibliographical references and index.
IDENTIFIERS: LCCN 2021013822 (print) | LCCN 2021013823 (ebook) | ISBN 9781316515532
(hardback) | ISBN 9781009025959 (ebook)
SUBJECTS: LCSH: Socrates. | Plato. | Knowledge, Theory of. | Self-actualization (Psychology) |
Ethics. | BISAC: PHILOSOPHY / History & Surveys / Ancient & Classical | PHILOSOPHY /
History & Surveys / Ancient & Classical
CLASSIFICATION: LCC B317 .S55 2021 (print) | LCC B317 (ebook) | DDC 126–dc23
LC record available at https://lccn.loc.gov/2021013822
LC ebook record available at https://lccn.loc.gov/2021013823

ISBN 978-1-316-51553-2 Hardback
ISBN 978-1-009-01243-0 Paperback

Contents

Contents

vii

Preface

P.1   The Origins of This Project

In Thomas C. Brickhouse's and my 1994 book, *Plato's Socrates*, on p. 37, we said:

> The only cases where Socrates without irony sanctions claims to wisdom are those involving the crafts. The craftsmen, he allows, do have a kind of knowledge that Socrates also lacks ([*Apology*] 22d3–4). So the kind of knowledge that makes one wise is comparable in some way to craft-knowledge.

In this book, I want to follow up on this idea, to a much greater degree than Brickhouse and I actually did in that or any of our subsequent works. Instead, Brickhouse and I focused mainly on the kind of knowledge that is by far more familiar in contemporary epistemology: propositional or informational knowledge – knowledge of *facts*. We articulated a version of what has recently been characterized as a kind of consensus that emerged in the debates about Socrates' knowledge and ignorance, according to which Socrates distinguishes two sorts of cognitive achievement that might be counted as different kinds of knowledge (McPartland 2013: 135). But it is instructive to see what is and is not present in the way the two different sorts of achievement are characterized:

> One sort of achievement is relatively easy to attain and corresponds to weak knowledge – true belief with warrant sufficient for unhedged assertion and full confidence. . . . The second sort of cognitive achievement is extremely hard to come by. The person who manages such an achievement is an expert about a field of inquiry. She possesses definitional knowledge and has an explanatory account of what she knows. Her judgments in her field are authoritative and inerrant, and she has the ability to teach her expertise to others. (McPartland 2013: 135)

McPartland concludes that Socrates does suppose that he and many others can achieve and have achieved "weak knowledge"; but he also

ix

declares that Socrates does not suppose that he has achieved the expertise required for the second sort of cognitive achievement. With a single exception, this has remained the relatively stable and generally accepted scholarly wisdom regarding Socratic epistemology.[1]

This notion of expertise, I now believe, fails to attend adequately to the sort of knowledge on which it is explicitly modeled: craft-knowledge. Unlike knowing *that* something is the case, at least as such knowing is typically analyzed in contemporary epistemology, craft-knowledge is acquired *by degrees* – it is not a matter of either having it or lacking it at any given time. That is not the case with the kind of knowledge contemporary philosophy generally theorizes: propositional or informational knowledge, knowledge that some proposition (*p*) or information (*i*) is the case. McPartland's description of this sort of knowledge seems to recognize only its final and most complete version. But craft-knowledge is not like this: anyone who ever deals with artisans recognizes that not all of them are equal in their expertise. Some are better than others, and at the bottom end, there are some who probably should not even be granted the title "artisan" at all. Even those, however, may be better than anyone who would rightly be regarded as completely innocent or ignorant of the craft.

If craft is constituted by knowledge, then the improvability of one's achievement in a craft entails improvability in the knowledge that constitutes one's level of achievement in the craft. We may then ask what sort of knowledge it is that would allow craft to be improvable in such a way. If we try to apply this insight to McPartland's description, things seem to become either distressingly vague or simply incoherent. An incomplete degree of such knowledge would thus be an inferior sort of "definitional knowledge," for example. But what might that be? On the one hand, if some inferior version of achievement in craft was due to a faulty definition, then on the basis of sentential logic it would appear that such knowledge would be no knowledge at all: propositional knowledge, as we all recognize, has a truth condition. On the other hand, if some less skilled artisan knew the definition at all, and knowing this definition constituted the craft, then how are we to explain the inferiority of this artisan to a better one? It could be, of course, that some artisans with the same knowledge might be more adroit than others in some significant way when it came to

---

[1] Only much more recently (and thus very belatedly) have I discovered an article by someone who made a contribution to this literature that was, I now think, completely on the right track. Unfortunately, no one seems to have picked up on her approach, and it is embarrassing to me to have taken so long to find her excellent paper. For a corrective to the approach I am criticizing here, see Smith 1998.

the execution of their craft. This would have the effect of separating the skill from the knowledge that was supposed to constitute it. Or, to go to a different part of McPartland's description, should we imagine that an inferior artisan would manage judgment that is "inerrant," but somehow the judgment would be less inerrant than what we would be able to get from a true master of the craft? But "inerrant" does not seem amenable to gradation. Is it that the less authoritative artisan would not know as many facts or propositions, and this lack of knowledge would thus make such an artisan more prone to error? If so, then, again, we would not have a degree of inerrancy, but simply an example of its opposite. But if such an artisan is no more prone to error than the true master, in what sense would the lesser one be somehow inferior to the master?

Because so much of this book relies on the craft model of knowledge, some readers may hope (or even expect) that I will provide a thorough analysis of everything Plato has Socrates say about craft. I do not doubt that an entire book dedicated to Socrates' conception of craft would be a useful addition to the literature.[2] But this would be a very different project from the one I have taken on here, and is one that would not be well accomplished with brevity. In this book, I actually seek to avoid any of the important technical aspects of what Socrates might think about crafts, precisely so as not to get lost in those questions. I concede that his references to craft throughout the early dialogues (and also in the way his thought is presented by other Socratic authors) are many and varied. It appears there are different kinds of crafts: some that produce distinct products, for example, and others that do not seem to be productive in the same way (for which see *Charmides* 165d4–166a2). Most crafts make use of things that are produced by other crafts, and in the *Euthydemus*, we find that the value of everything comes from its right use (*Euthydemus* 280c3–d7). But it begins to seem as if virtue might be a craft that makes use of what it produces itself, which would be very different from other crafts. So, too, it seems that *qua* craft, virtue should be what makes the one who has it most of all able to commit wrongdoing, and this seems to be such a puzzle that when it is discussed Socrates and his

---

[2] Not because there haven't already been some such studies. There have been – for example, Roochnik 1996 covers the topic as it appears in all of Plato's works, though not in ways that remain uncontroversial, and also with Plato and Platonic philosophy as the main focus. A better approach, I think, would merge a focus on Plato's early dialogues with remarks about craft in the works of other Socratic writers, especially Xenophon. I am not aware of any book-length study of that sort.

interlocutor both end up in perplexity (see *Hippias Minor* 375e6–376c6).[3] In these and many other puzzles, there are important scholarly questions to be asked and answered. My only excuse for neither asking nor answering such questions herein is that I don't need to do so. All I need to work on the problems that are my focus is the recognition that virtue and knowledge are at least mostly treated in Plato's early dialogues as craft, and then that, whatever kind of craft they may be, as craft they will be achieved in degrees and only improved through certain kinds of practice.

At any rate, as I thought about the very close connections that Plato has Socrates make between knowledge, wisdom, virtue more generally, and happiness, it occurred to me that recognizing a kind of knowledge that either explained or constituted wisdom and virtue, but that was either a kind of craft or at least relevantly like craft that might be achieved *in varying degrees*, would have a very significant impact on how we would need to understand Socratic philosophy.

P.2   Intended Readership and Structure of the Book

Although each chapter provides a different focus than the others, each one also further develops the overall theme of the book, which is what Socrates has to say about self-improvement. Even so, I have designed each chapter so that it can stand alone and be read by someone interested mainly (or only) in the specific topic of that chapter. Partly, this is how I organize my work on these topics, but partly this is a response to the increasingly common practice of publishers to allow electronic access to individual chapters for a lower price than it would cost to access the entire book. This will allow interested users to decide in what order they would like to read things, and even if someone were to read the book's chapters in reverse order, I think the way I have structured it would allow each chapter to be understood well. When I recall something in a later chapter that was explored more thoroughly in an earlier chapter, I note that, so readers who do not choose to read the book from the beginning to the end can know where to find details. The downside of this way of structuring things, however, is that certain main points that affect several chapters are repeated

---

[3] I actually do not accept that there is a difference between other crafts and the craft of virtue in this regard, because I think the impossibility of those with virtue doing what is vicious is not that virtue does not provide the sort of knowledge that would allow the most effective wrongdoing. It does provide such knowledge; the barrier against wrongdoing does not come from the craft of virtue *qua* craft, but from the universal human desire for whatever is best for us. Socrates is convinced that wrongdoing is never in our best interest. For discussion, see Chapter 3.

in each one, though I hope this repetition will not become too burdensome for those who read the book in the traditional way. I have tried not to allow such repetitions to become too lengthy.

This structure, too, seemed to me to be best for the readers I would most like to reach – upper-level undergraduates, graduate students, and younger faculty members who have not yet made up their minds about the things I discuss herein. I hope more senior scholars will also be interested, but I expect that many of them will already be so invested in certain ways of thinking about Socrates (or Plato) that my arguments will not be able to dissuade them from their prior commitments. I have tried to cite as much of the important recent scholarship as I could, and thus to engage with other well-worked-out views about my subjects. But I have tried to structure both the book and my arguments and explanations to make them most suitable to younger scholars and readers who might be able to consider them with fresh eyes and fewer prior commitments.

Despite their relative independence, I did try to structure the chapters to allow my overall argument to be developed in a way that would make each new step to occur in a reasonable order.

I begin in Chapter 1 by paying careful attention to the way in which Plato treats Socrates as an exemplar for us to emulate, and show how his doing so seems to present problems when compared to some of the philosophical views that Socrates is supposed to exemplify. In effect, I argue that what Gregory Vlastos (1971) once called "the paradox of Socrates" can only be resolved if we take seriously that Plato's Socrates must be understood as operating with a very different model of knowledge than the one with which contemporary philosophers are most familiar – again, a model of knowledge based on craft (*technê*).

In Chapter 2, I then turn to a claim that we find Socrates making about himself in the *Gorgias*, a claim that has perplexed many scholars. Socrates says that he has taken up and practices "the true craft of politics" (*Gorgias* 521d6–e1). I review each of the several claims Socrates makes in this passage and show why at least some of them have seemed deeply problematic to scholars evaluating them, but show that, in fact, good sense can be made of each one as something that Socrates actually believes. Once again, it is a peculiar feature of craft that allows me to interpret Socrates' claim as entirely sincere; without this feature, or using the model of knowledge more familiar to contemporary philosophers, Socrates would not be able to make such a claim.

I then, in Chapter 3, turn to another position defended by Socrates in Plato's early dialogues that contributes to what Socrates calls his philosophical "mission" in Athens. Socrates, as most scholars now agree, is a motivational intellectualist, which is to say that he believes that every action done by a human agent indicates and is to be explained in terms of what the agent believes is in their best interest, among the options available and salient to them at the time of action. That means, as Terry Penner has famously claimed, that "for Socrates, when people act badly or viciously or even just out of moral weakness, that will be merely a result of intellectual mistake."[4] In this chapter, I argue for a picture of Socratic moral psychology that explains how and why Socratic intellectualism nonetheless requires for its explication the positing of an etiology of belief-formation that most scholars have missed. Once we see that his intellectualist conception of motivation is influenced by this novel view about belief-formation, we can better understand just how human cognition is associated with virtue and happiness in the particular way it is within Socratic philosophy. It also allows us to understand what some scholars have found so troubling in various Socratic discussions that they have actually made special efforts to deny that Socrates in fact accepts what he seems to be saying: that he thinks there is a place for painful, physical punishments as a way to change the behaviors of certain kinds of wrongdoers. The connection of this chapter's specific focus to the rest of the book will be, I hope, obvious: insofar as there is an etiology of belief-formation that may be considerably less veridically reliable than other etiologies, anyone who is interested in achieving better grades of virtue, skill, and happiness in life will need to be especially vigilant not to allow the less reliable etiology of belief-formation to "do their thinking for them."

In Chapter 4, then, I give a more complete account of Socratic epistemology, and also the way in which Socratic philosophizing (including especially elenctic argumentation) reflects his views about the various etiologies of belief-formation. Most importantly, I show that the way in which Socrates engages in his discussions with certain interlocutors actually shows him attempting to manage the unusual etiology for belief-formation that I discuss in Chapter 5: Socrates sometimes seeks to shame his interlocutors in ways that clearly engage nonrational aspects of their psychologies, but in doing so, he intends to induce in them changes of *beliefs*. In the *Gorgias*, where this process is best exemplified, Socrates even acknowledges quite explicitly that what he is trying to do is to correct Callicles in the way that punishment corrects those who receive it (*Gorgias* 505c3–4). By engaging in the different ways in which people form the beliefs by which they live, Socrates encourages people to become more virtuous, more skilled in the ways that will also afford them greater happiness in life. I finish that chapter by considering how Socrates approaches our need

[4] Penner 2000: 165.

to engage in practical deliberation when none of us are even close to being master artisans in the craft of virtue. Socrates recognizes that all of us have moral decisions to make all of the time. But how are we to practice in such a way as to improve the way in which we make such decisions when we continue to be in a condition of ignorance?

In the final two chapters, I take up the questions of whether or not Socrates accepts either the sufficiency of virtue for happiness (Chapter 5) or the necessity of virtue for happiness (Chapter 6). The principle that virtue is sufficient for happiness entails the preposterous view that virtuous people have such complete control over their lives that nothing can damage their lives and spoil whatever happiness they might otherwise have. In Chapter 5, I argue that Socrates well understood the fundamental frailty and vulnerability of the human condition. The necessity of virtue for happiness has seemed to most scholars to have the effect of showing that no one – including Socrates himself – could ever be happy, since "no one is wiser than Socrates" (*Apology* 21a7), but Socrates says he is "very conscious that I am not wise at all" (*Apology* 21b4–5). Without wisdom, in Socratic philosophy, there can be no virtue. So if virtue is necessary for happiness, then no human being is happy. This unfortunate conclusion, however, can at least be moderated by bringing the craft model of knowledge to bear. If one seeks to improve in the craft (or craft-like) condition of virtue, then one's relative lack of virtue may only entail a relative lack of happiness, rather than a complete lack of it. To put the point more positively, the improvability of virtue allows Socrates to associate our achievements in taking up and pursuing "the true political craft" or wisdom with the achievement of a similar degree of happiness in our lives. Since knowledge, wisdom, and virtue do not have to be achieved in an all-or-nothing way, so too can happiness be achieved in degrees. This way of reconceiving the debates about the sufficiency and necessity of virtue for happiness allows human beings, despite their frailty, to have some genuine hope of success in achieving the happiness that we all want in our lives. I hope my readers will find that this new emphasis on the improvability of knowledge, virtue, and happiness yields a more satisfying and plausible overall view than the one that has often been attributed to Socrates by others.

P.3 Methodological Issues

Developmentalism is the approach to Plato's dialogues that (i) perceives differences between the philosophical views that Socrates either explicitly endorses or at least seems to be committed to in different groups of dialogues, and then (ii) seeks to explain these differences in terms of Plato's own intellectual development.[5] Developmentalism has gone out of fashion among contemporary scholars, and no general defense against the criticisms that have been made of it has been offered recently. When we published our 2010 book (*Socratic Moral Psychology*), Brickhouse and I did offer a kind of rearguard defense of developmentalism by showing that the kinds of arguments normally given in favor of alternative approaches were actually quite poor. We also tried to show that the alternative approaches had not yet managed to confront the very difficult problems they faced themselves. We went on to defend developmentalism as a research program, conceding that while some assumptions of a research program might turn out to be false or misunderstood, the program itself might still provide interesting and valuable results.

I continue to think that the developmentalist approach can and does provide important insights into the interpretation of what may be found in the putatively early dialogues. I also continue to think that the portrait of Socrates that Plato gives in his putatively early dialogues is an intriguing one that is worth our specific attention. As Brickhouse and I complained in our 2010 defense of developmentalism, the other general approaches that have increased in popularity lately have the effect of eliminating the Socrates of Plato's putatively early dialogues from the history of philosophy. Instead, antidevelopmentalists insist that what appears in Plato is Plato's and tells us nothing at all reliable about Socrates or anyone else.[6]

One recent event may have some impact on how we think about Socrates in future generations, and so deserves special notice. In 2019 in Buenos Aires, scholars interested in Socratic studies – that is, in all of the works by many ancient authors in which Socrates appears – created a new academic society, the International Society for Socratic Studies. One specific question was addressed as the group created this new scholarly organization: should works by Plato be included within the focus of this group? The answer was affirmative, and so future years may (and I hope will) include many studies in which the commonalities and differences in the way Socrates was represented in antiquity will be explored. By neither privileging Plato's portrait of

---

[5] In Brickhouse and Smith 2010: 18, we list the relevant works, in alphabetical order, as follows: *Apology, Charmides, Crito, Euthydemus, Euthyphro, Gorgias, Hippias Major, Hippias Minor, Ion, Laches, Lysis, Protagoras,* and *Republic* I. We also noted that the moral psychology in the *Meno* seemed to belong with what we find in this group of early dialogues. I continue to regard these as the relevant group of works and will be citing these in subsequent chapters as evidence for my claims about "Socratic philosophy."

[6] Clear examples of this kind of view, from significantly different perspectives, may be found in Gerson 2013; Kahn 1996; Kamtekar 2017; Nails 1995; Press 2010.

Socrates nor excluding it, new opportunities for understanding this charismatic philosopher from ancient Greece can be engaged. My focus in this book is obviously Plato's portrait. But how that portrait fits with those by other ancient writers is a matter of great interest to me, and to other members of this new organization. I hope that at least some of what I present herein may prove useful to studies of different Socratic authors in antiquity.

P.4 Texts, Translations, Acknowledgments

Citations of text will be from the Oxford Classical Greek texts, including the standard Stephanus page numbers and letters plus line numbers from those texts. Unless otherwise noted, I will use the translations given in Cooper 1997, if only because they are so widely used, but also because I find them mostly reliable and accessible to readers. I often found that I could not entirely agree with these translations, however, and so I have made a note of such when I have made some adjustment. Most of the changes I have made to these translations derive from their use of gendered nouns and pronouns where the Greek does not require them.

When I thought it would be useful to my intended readers, I have included transliterations of specific Greek words or phrases. Since my citations give the line numbers in the Greek text, it will be easy for those who want to find the original Greek for what is given in the translations I offer.

Some of the materials that appear in this book are revised from earlier publications. These are:

"A Problem in Plato's Hagiography of Socrates," *Athens Journal of Humanities and Arts* 5, 2018, 81–103; www.athensjournals.gr/human ities/2018-5-1-5-Smith.pdf, is revised herein as Chapter 1, with permission of the journal.

"Socrates: Apprentice at Politics," forthcoming in T. Angiers, ed., *Skill in Ancient Ethics*, London: Bloomsbury), is revised herein as Chapter 2, with permission of the publisher.

"Ethics in Plato's Early Dialogues," forthcoming in D. Wolfsdorf, ed., *Early Greek Ethics*, (Oxford: Oxford University Press, 2020, 432-454), is revised herein as Sections 3.1–3.4, with permission of the editor and publisher.

"Socrates on Practical Deliberation," *History of Philosophy Quarterly* 30.2, 2013, 93–113, is revised herein as Sections 4.10–4.16, with permission of the publisher.

"Socrates on the Human Condition," *Ancient Philosophy* 36, 2016, 81–95, is revised herein as Chapter 6, with permission of the journal.

In other cases, I have not simply revised but have nonetheless relied so heavily on work done with coauthors that my debt to them must be acknowledged. These works are really just presented in a somewhat different form in the following chapters and sections:

"Socratic Moral Psychology," with T. Brickhouse; in N. Smith, ed., *The Bloomsbury Companion to Socrates* (London: Bloomsbury Press, 2013), 185–209, is the basis of what I present in Sections 3.5–3.13, with permission of the coauthor and publisher.

"Socrates on Knowledge," with J. Lorenço; in N. Smith, ed., *Knowledge in Ancient Philosophy*, vol. 1 in S. Hetherington, gen. ed., *The Philosophy of Knowledge: A History* (London: Bloomsbury Press, 2019), 67–83, is the basis for Sections 4.4–4.9, with permission of the coauthor and publisher.

"Socrates and the Sufficiency Thesis," with Joel Martinez, forthcoming in C. Marsico, ed., *Socratica IV* (publisher not yet named) and "Socrates, Sully, and the Sufficiency Thesis," also with Joel Martinez (paper presented to the American Philosophical Association Pacific Division, 2019), provided the bases for Sections 5.1–5.6, with permission of the coauthor. Our work together on Socrates' aversion to being a victim of wrongdoing (Martinez and Smith 2018) certainly influenced Sections 5.7–5.8, which mostly repeats in very abbreviated form what we argue for more extensively in that work.

I am extremely grateful for the interactions involved in these collaborations, and I am grateful to my coauthors for their insights and contributions to our joint efforts. I am also grateful to Lewis & Clark College for hosting and to the National Endowment for the Humanities for their funding of a Summer Seminar on Socrates that I directed in the summer of 2014, where I got the opportunity to try out many of the ideas in this book and get feedback on them from the participants and guest speakers, which was most helpful. A 2019 Summer Stipend from the National Endowment for the Humanities also helped me to complete the book, and I am especially grateful to Hugh H. Benson and Russell E. Jones for agreeing to serve as referees for the submitted proposal.

I have also had the opportunity to present various parts of this book at a number of different conferences, which allowed me to learn from many comments and criticisms I received. These conferences include: the International Plato Society United States Regional Meeting, Ann Arbor, Michigan, 2012; the conference on "Appetite, Voluntariness and Virtuous Action: A Workshop in Ancient Philosophy" at Uppsala University, 2012; the Northwest Workshop in Ancient Philosophy 2013, 2014, and 2018; the International Plato Society Meeting, Tokyo, Japan, April 2014; the International Conference on *Technê* in Plato, St. Francis Xavier University, Nova Scotia, 2015; the III Congreso Internacional de Filosofia Griega, Lisbon, 2016; the 10th West Coast Plato Workshop 2017; the International Conference on Virtue, Skill, and Practical Reason, Cape Town, South Africa, 2017; the American Philosophical Association Pacific Division meetings, 2017 and 2019; the Hawaii International Conference on Arts and Humanities, 2018; Socratica IV, Buenos Aires, November 2018; the Royal Conference in honor of Paul Woodruff, Austin, 2019; the Fonte Aretusa conference, Siracusa, 2019; and the special joint session of the International Plato Society and the International Society for Socratic Studies held with the American Philosophical Association Central Division Meetings in 2020. Various versions of sections of this book were also presented at specific colloquia at the Universidade Federal de Santa Maria (Brazil); the Universidade Federal do Rio de Janeiro (Brazil); the University of Bergen (Norway); and the Universidad Alberto Hurtado, Santiago, Chile. I am grateful to my hosts and to the audiences at each of these venues for their responses and suggestions.

Last but not least, I am grateful to all of the students at Lewis & Clark College with whom I tried out all of the ideas presented in this book during my triennial seminars on Socrates. I am fortunate to have worked with so many talented and engaged students.

This book is dedicated to Tom (Thomas C.) Brickhouse, with whom I collaborated for over forty years. I hope he will forgive me for the ways in which I have deviated from some of our earlier conclusions, and am convinced that this would be a better book if I had been able to persuade him to work with me on it.

CHAPTER I

Socrates as Exemplar

1.1   An Inconsistency in Plato's Portrait?

Few would doubt that Plato intends to portray Socrates as an exemplar of human excellence. In Plato's *Apology*, Socrates cites the authority of Delphi in support of his claim to be the wisest of human beings[1] (23b2), if only because he is so well aware of his own ignorance. Later in that same dialogue, we learn that Socrates also realizes that he has a reputation for being "superior to the majority of human beings" (35a1) and the context makes clear that the kind of superiority he has in mind is a superiority in virtue (*aretê*: 35a2). In Plato's other dialogues, as well, Socrates seems clearly to be identified as superior with respect to whatever positive trait or virtue is under discussion. In short, Plato seems to miss no opportunities to praise Socrates as a man who is superior to others. Here is how Plato has Alcibiades put it in the *Symposium*:

> You could say many other marvelous things in praise of Socrates. Perhaps he shares some of his specific accomplishments with others. But, as a whole, he is unique; he is like no one else in the past and no one in the present – this is by far the most amazing thing about him. (*Symposium* 221c2–6)

But as plausible as Plato makes such a view about Socrates, he also seems to create problems for that view in other positions he gives to Socrates. One of these is what has come to be known as Socratic "virtue intellectualism" – the view that virtue is a kind of knowledge. The other is that Plato has Socrates persistently disclaim having the knowledge in which virtue

---

[1] Translation slightly modified. As I noted in the Preface, here and elsewhere in this book I will replace translations that use gendered words ("men") when the Greek text does not require them. Socrates' claim here is certainly not that his reputation for superiority only applies in comparison with other *men*.

consists. The problem for Plato's portrait of Socrates, then, can be stated as a trilemma:

(1)   Socrates is an exemplar of virtue.

(2)   Virtue is a kind of knowledge.

(3)   Socrates lacks the knowledge in which virtue consists.

The problem is that if we accept (2) and (3), it seems we must conclude that Socrates *cannot be virtuous*, which plainly conflicts with (1). If we accept (1) and (2), it seems we are forced to conclude that Socrates cannot be telling the truth when he disclaims having the knowledge of virtue (3).[2] If we accept (1) and (3), it seems we cannot accept Socratic virtue intellectualism (2).

The problem thus presented is not a new one to Socratic scholarship. In fact, we find it vividly expressed in Gregory Vlastos' earliest essay on Socrates:

> What would you expect of such a man? To propagate his message, to disseminate the knowledge which is itself the elixir of life. Is this what he does? How *could* he, if, as he says repeatedly in the dialogues, he does not have that knowledge? . . . Could this be true? If it were, then on his own teaching, he too would be one of the damned. (Vlastos 1971: 7)[3]

---

[2] I speculate that Xenophon's view of Socrates would solve the trilemma this way. Evidence for regarding the Xenophontic Socrates as committed to the first two claims in the trilemma can be readily found, but the Xenophontic Socrates appears to be full of the knowledge and wisdom he disclaims having in Plato's texts.

[3] The version of the trilemma I give here is slightly revised from the version originally given in Prior 2006: 158. An earlier version was provided in Graham 1997: 25. Graham argues that Socratic virtue derived from his knowledge of his own ignorance, and both Graham and Prior provide several good arguments for why Socrates' awareness of his own ignorance would be a great ethical advantage. Neither Graham nor Prior explores the relationship between knowledge and craft that I claim solves the problem, so while I am very sympathetic to their arguments, I do not think the answers they give are complete. Gail Fine stipulates that knowledge must be understood as "a truth-entailing cognitive condition that is appropriately cognitively superior to mere true belief" (Fine 2008: 53). In my view, on the contrary, it is the application of this conception of knowledge to the Socratic position that creates the problem. Prior's proposed solution to the problem is somewhat similar to the one for which I argue here, though framed in terms of material from the *Symposium*. In Prior's view, the Alcibiades of the *Symposium* wrongly accuses Socrates of being "simply insincere" (Prior 2006: 159) in his disavowals of knowledge. Plato's more balanced portrait reveals a Socrates who has "inner images of virtue" (Prior 2006: 161) that he gained through "at least a second-hand familiarity with the Form of Beauty" (Prior 2006: 152). This "familiarity" would give Socrates something that could look like a share of the knowledge he claims to lack, while also not giving him so much of it that he would be "simply insincere" in disclaiming knowledge. My own view does not call upon cognitive experience of Forms for explaining what I will claim is a *degree* of knowledge in Socrates. But I see no reason why someone with a more unitarian approach to Plato's dialogues could not make such an application of my argument.

In this chapter, I seek to show that we can actually accept each of the above claims. But in order to do so, we must recognize something about each one of the claims that has not received adequate attention in the scholarly literature. Once we attend to what has gone mostly unattended, however, the three claims can be seen as fully consistent.

Although I do not think that attributing any of the three claims in the trilemma is especially controversial, I will begin by offering at least brief reviews of the kinds of evidence we have for each claim – mainly in order to show the cost involved in attempting to get out of the trilemma by simply denying one of the apparently inconsistent claims. I will then introduce the element that renders the entire set of claims consistent, which can thus allow us to understand more precisely Plato's hagiography of Socrates.

1.2 Plato's Socratic Hagiography: A (Very) Brief Review of the Evidence

In the *Charmides*, for example, where the focus is on temperance (*sôphrosunê*), Socrates' responses to the extraordinarily attractive young Charmides provide a vivid example of self-control in the face of strong temptation (*Charmides* 155b9–156d3).[4] Although perhaps he does not exemplify special courage in the *Laches*, he is recognized by two of Athens' most famous generals as being a subject worthy of recognition as a potential teacher of that virtue (*Laches* 180b7–d3). In the *Apology*, however, Socrates' courage in the face of the threat of death is emphasized repeatedly (see, for example, 28b3–29d5, 32a5–e1, 34b6–e2, 38e2–39b1, 40c5–41d3), and in the *Symposium* his resistance to the hardships of hunger and winter cold and in the face of the enemy in war is vividly depicted (*Symposium* 219e5–221c1). In the *Euthyphro*, Socrates' younger interlocutor is exposed as a confused fraud, thinking he is an expert about piety; the one revealed as pious in the dialogue is Socrates, who actually manages to get Euthyphro to desist from an impious prosecution of his own father – which Euthyphro's other friends and relatives had thus far failed to get him to do.[5] So, too, in the *Apology*, the speech Plato gives to Socrates characterizes the accused man as having gotten into the legal trouble he finds himself

---

[4] I take a closer look at this passage to explore what Socrates' restraint tells us about his vulnerability to factors other than virtue at the end of Section 5.8.
[5] This reading of the effects of the discussion *is* controversial: some have claimed that the discussion with Socrates did not have this effect. But the reading I provide here is one I have defended elsewhere (see Brickhouse and Smith 2004: 14–18), and is also the one defended long ago by Diogenes Laertius (2.29). See also my discussion of the *Euthyphro* in Chapter 4.

in as a result of a mission given to him by the god (23c1, 30a5–7, 30d7–e6, 33c4–7). If so, then it is plainly impious of his prosecutors to seek to rid Athens of Socrates and his divine mission. In that same dialogue, Plato depicts Socrates as a man who always "fights for justice" (31e2–32a3, 32d2–5) and who, at the end of his long life, can say that "I am convinced that I wrong no one" (37b2–3). In the *Gorgias*, Socrates claims to be the only one alive among his fellow Athenians "to take up the true political craft and practice the true politics" and thus to practice justice in what he does (*Gorgias* 521d6–8). So when it comes to justice, too, Socrates is depicted by Plato as an exemplar.

But it is not only that Plato depicts Socrates as a model to emulate; Plato also explicitly has Socrates say things about himself that *only* someone who is virtuous should say. Scholars are well aware of the very close connection Plato's Socrates makes between virtue and happiness – though there are significant disagreements about precisely how this connection should be interpreted. Some have argued that several ancient schools who conceived of themselves as "Socratic" made the connection one of identity: virtue and happiness are simply the same.[6] At least one Platonic text seems to come close to saying this explicitly (*Crito* 48b9), but contemporary scholars have not supported attributing this strong view to Plato's Socrates. Perhaps most scholars, instead, have seen virtue as both necessary and sufficient for happiness in Socratic philosophy.[7] Others claim to find a nomological relationship.[8] In one of my earlier works with Brickhouse,[9] I contended that Socrates' claim to be a "good man" (obviously implied by what he says at *Apology* 41c9–d2) had to be understood in a way that did not entail that he was virtuous, precisely because of his disavowal of the knowledge of virtue (the third claim in the trilemma given earlier). I now think this was a mistake, and offer what I take to be the appropriate correction to it herein. At any rate, however we take the connection exactly to be between virtue and happiness (and I will have more to say about this in later chapters of this book), it seems to be generally accepted that Socrates would not think that someone who lacked virtue could be happy.[10]

---

[6] See Vlastos 1991: 208, who claims this was the view of the Cynics and Stoics. I suspect such an attribution is controversial, however.

[7] See, for example, Annas 1994; Dimas 2002; Irwin 1977: 100, 1986: 91, 1995: 118–120; Reeve 1989: 136–144; Rudebusch 1999: chs 8 and 9; Russell 2005: ch. 1; Taylor 2000: 64; Vlastos 1978: 230–231, 1980: 318–323, 1991: 200–235.

[8] See Brickhouse and Smith 2010: 185–189; Reshotko 2006: ch. 7, 2013: 162–164. For more on the necessity and sufficiency theses, see Chapters 5 and 6 of this book.

[9] Brickhouse and Smith 1990 and Brickhouse and Smith 1994: ch. 4.

[10] So I continue to agree with Brickhouse and Smith 1994: ch. 4 (see esp. 135) on this point.

Plato, however, characterizes Socrates as an exemplar from this perspective as well.[11] In the *Apology* (36d9–10), Socrates has the audacity to tell his jurors that, unlike an Olympic victor, he does not just make people *think* they are happy; as he puts it, "I make you be happy." In the *Gorgias* he exhorts Callicles to "follow me to where I am, and when you've come here you'll be happy both during life and at its end" (*Gorgias* 527c4–6).[12] It seems that Socrates is also ready to extend such happiness even into the afterlife: in his third speech in the *Apology*, Socrates makes it clear that he would regard continuing to do there what he has done in this life as "an extraordinary happiness" (41c4).

This brief survey of the evidence of Plato's hagiography of Socrates is hardly exhaustive, but is enough, I hope, to show that denying the first of the claims in the trilemma is not a promising way out of our problem. It is tempting to say, indeed, that denying this claim would require a radical departure from most readings of Plato's works, and might now require some very new answer to why it was that Plato decided to feature Socrates as the main speaking character in so many of the dialogues.

1.3 Socratic Virtue Intellectualism

Aristotle's main (and oft-repeated) complaint against Socrates concerned the latter's virtue intellectualism:

> Socrates the senior thought that the end is to get to know virtue, and he pursued an inquiry into the nature of justice and courage and each of the divisions of virtue. And this was a reasonable procedure, since he thought that all the virtues are forms of knowledge, so that knowing justice and being just must go together, for as soon as we have learnt geometry and architecture, we are architects and geometricians; owing to which he used to inquire what virtue is, but not how and from what sources it is produced. (*Eudemian Ethics* A.5.1216b2–10; trans. Rackham)[13]

---

[11] See Vlastos 1991: 233–235. A dissenting view has recently been argued in Jones 2013a. For further debate, see Smith 2016 and Jones 2016.

[12] Diogenes Laertius tells a similar story about Socrates' first meeting with Xenophon: the philosopher blocks the younger man's way and asks him where people can go to become good and noble, and when Xenophon reacts with puzzlement, Socrates says, "Then follow me, and learn" (Diogenes Laertius 2.48; my translation).

[13] Similar Aristotelian criticisms of Socratic virtue intellectualism appear at *Nicomachean Ethics* Γ.8.1116b3–5, Z.13.1144b14–30, *Eudemian Ethics* Γ.1.1229a12–16, Γ.1.1230a7–10, *Magna Moralia* A.1.1182a15–23, A.1.1183b8–11, A.20.1190b27–29, and A.34.1198a10–13. For discussion, especially regarding what Aristotle's testimony may tell us about developmentalism and the historical Socrates, see Smith 2018.

The intellectualism about virtue that so bothered Aristotle is also abundantly on display in Plato's dialogues.[14] At the end of the *Protagoras*, for example, Socrates despairs at the way his argument with Protagoras has gone:

> It seems to me that our discussion has turned on us, and if it had a voice of its own, it would say, mockingly, "Socrates and Protagoras, how ridiculous you are, both of you. Socrates, you said earlier that virtue cannot be taught, but now you are arguing the very opposite and have attempted to show that everything is knowledge – justice, temperance, courage – in which case virtue would appear to be eminently teachable. On the other hand, if virtue is anything other than knowledge, as Protagoras has been trying to say, then it would clearly be unteachable. But if it turns out to be wholly knowledge, as you now urge, Socrates, it would be very surprising indeed if virtue could not be taught." (*Protagoras* 361a3–b7)[15]

Socratic virtue intellectualism has been a source of great controversy among scholars in recent years.[16] But their disagreements are mostly on details and not on whether or not Plato depicts Socrates as an intellectualist about virtue. On this point ancients and moderns are entirely in agreement. So the second of the three claims that create the trilemma that is my focus here does not seem likely to be mistaken.

1.4   The Socratic Disclaimer of Knowledge

Thus far, I have indicated that there are good reasons for accepting the first two of the claims that create the trilemma for Socratic hagiography. The third – Socrates' profession of ignorance – is the best attested of the three claims in the works of Plato.[17] An important sample is quoted in the

---

[14] This may be one reason why some scholars have claimed that whatever Aristotle thought about Socrates was simply gained from his reading of Plato's dialogues. But there are reasons for thinking that Aristotle was also aware of Xenophon's works, and the same attribution of an intellectualist position to Socrates can also be found in them. See, for example, *Memorabilia* 3.9.5, 4.6.1, and 4.6.11. For further discussion of this topic, see Smith 2018.

[15] Other texts indicating Socratic virtue intellectualism include *Euthydemus* 278e3–282a7, *Meno* 89a3–5, and *Laches* 199d4–e4.

[16] See Brickhouse and Smith 2010.

[17] Examples may be found at *Apology* 20c1–3, 21d2–7, 23b2–4; *Charmides* 165b4–c2, 166c7–d6; *Euthyphro* 5a7–c5, 15c12, 15e5–16a4; *Laches* 186b8–c5, 186d8–e3, 200e2–5; *Lysis* 212a4–7, 223b4–8; *Hippias Major* 286c8–e2, 304d4–e5; *Gorgias* 509a4–6; *Republic* I.337e4–5. Other ancient sources also provide support for the attribution of the profession of ignorance to Socrates: see Aristotle, *Sophistical Refutations* 183b6–8; Aeschines Socraticus *Alcibiades* 10C (Dittmar); Aelius Aristides *Oration* 45.21 (W. Dindorff II, p. 25); Antiochus of Ascalon *ap.* Cicero *Academica* 1.4.16; Arcesilaus *ap.* Cicero *Academica* 1.12.45; Plutarch *Against Colotes* 117D. The only place in

next section, but it is this familiar Socratic claim that scholars have most often called into question (perhaps as a way to avoid the trilemma).[18]

The problem with this way out of the trilemma, however, is obvious – and it is also no doubt why Vlastos himself later repudiated the view he had proposed in his first published work on Socrates:[19] it would require that Socrates is willing to deceive those to whom he makes his famous disavowals, which would include not only a great number of different interlocutors but also the jurors at his trial, in spite of his emphatic and repeated claims that he tells them only the truth (*Apology* 17b5–8, 18a5–6, 20d5–6, 24a4–6,[20] 28d5, 29e2, 31e1–2, 32a8–9, 33c1–2, 33c9, 34b5, 38a7–8, 39b5, 41c9). It is not surprising, accordingly, that most recent scholarship has taken the Socratic profession of ignorance to be sincere, even if scholars continue to debate its scope and meaning.[21]

1.5 A Way Out: It Is Not "All or Nothing"

My argument in this section is that the apparent inconsistency in Plato's portrait of Socrates is actually generated by an incorrect, all-or-nothing understanding of the main claims of the trilemma. To see how this is so, let us consider the first of the problematic claims: Socrates is an exemplar of virtue. In the very text in which Socrates is singled out as the "wisest of men," it is also quite explicit that his wisdom amounts to nothing in comparison with the wisdom of the god:

> What is probable gentlemen, is that in fact the god is wise and that his oracular response meant that human wisdom is worth little or nothing, and that when he says this man, Socrates, he is using my name as an example, as if he said, "This man among you, mortals, is wisest who, like Socrates, understands that his wisdom is worthless." (*Apology* 23a45–b4)

It is a peculiar feature of Socrates' self-assessment that he counts his wisdom as "worthless" in comparison to the wisdom of the god. But does that make him, as Vlastos (1971: 7) put it, "one of the damned"? To answer this question

---

Xenophon where Socrates expresses ignorance is limited to the subject of household management (at *Oeconomicus* I.ii.12–13). See note 2.

[18] See Gulley 1968: 69; Shero 1927: 109; Vlastos 1971. A recent and extensively argued expression of such doubts may be found in Senn 2013.

[19] See the quotation from Vlastos at the beginning of this chapter. Vlastos explicitly abandons his earlier view in Vlastos 1985.

[20] This passage also seems to rule out not just dishonesty but also any distortion of any kind: "That, gentlemen of the jury, is the truth for you. I have hidden or disguised nothing."

[21] An extensive discussion of the recent literature, and an important addition to that literature, may be found in McPartland 2013.

completely correctly, we need to contextualize it. The god, Socrates says, is the one who is *really* wise, and the wisest of human beings is nothing in comparison. But does that mean that all human beings are equally and utterly worthless when it comes to wisdom? *Sub specie aeternitatis*, it would seem that we are, but it is also, as we have seen, at the core of Plato's characterization of Socrates that he is even so exemplary *among human beings*. From the *human* perspective, Socrates is not only the wisest he is also famously engaged in a mission to persuade us "not to care for your body or your wealth in preference to or as strongly as for the best possible state of your soul" (*Apology* 30a5–b2). But what's the point? Does Socrates really think that by adjusting our core values and living as he does, we will ever achieve anything more than continuing to be "worthless"? Of course he does! Whatever we might thus achieve will actually still be "worthless" in comparison to the divine. Even so, a man like Socrates is very plainly *not* "worthless" in comparison to other human beings. From the god's-eye view, even the loftiest of human achievements, when it comes to wisdom, are nothing. Plato does not want us to forget that fact; but he also wants us to recognize that there is another perspective available to us – a human perspective – and from this vantage point there can be very significant differences between people, for better and for worse.

At the heart of scholars' puzzlements about Socrates' profession of ignorance is a conception of the knowledge that Socrates claims not to have that is so familiar to us from contemporary philosophical analyses as to be the starting point for scholarly interpretation. In this conception, knowledge is a cognitive state of a certain kind – what is called a "threshold" achievement: either one has achieved the cognitive condition of knowledge with respect to some specific bit of information or one has not, and it all depends on what we take the necessary conditions of knowledge to be, and whether some cognitive agent has met those conditions in some instance, or not. If we apply this conception of knowledge to Socrates, then when he claims not to have knowledge, he should be taken as saying that he has not met the conditions necessary to be in a cognitive state of knowledge about some subject under discussion.

Even if we take this to be the correct way to understand Socrates' profession of ignorance, it is worth noticing that Socrates could nonetheless think there were very significant differences among those who failed to have knowledge, depending on the extent and degree to which they failed to meet the necessary conditions of knowledge. For example, we might broadly conceive of knowledge as warranted (or justified) true belief.[22]

---

[22] For a discussion about why we might prefer one of these two formulations, see Evans and Smith 2012: chs 1, 4, 6.

Plainly, two people might share the same true belief on some subject, and both might fall short of knowledge, but one might have far more or better warrant (or justification) for the belief than the other. So even if we assume that Socrates conceived of knowledge as a threshold achievement, he could still hold that some human beings were a great deal further along in *approximating* that achievement than others, even if all of us actually ended up falling short. In this way of thinking, Socrates' being the "wisest of men" would amount to his having much better justification or warrant for his beliefs, even if neither he nor anyone else actually knew anything important.[23]

The problem with this way of explaining how Socrates is better than other human beings comes when we try to apply it to the second of the claims in the trilemma: virtue is a kind of knowledge. The problem is that even if we can credit Socrates as being much superior to other human beings in ways that do not amount to knowledge, these will avail him nothing when it comes to virtue. If virtue is a kind of knowledge, but knowledge is a threshold achievement and Socrates has not reached that threshold, then he has also not achieved virtue. It might still be true that Socrates could *approximate* virtue to the same degree as he approximates knowledge in his better-warranted or better-justified beliefs. But if knowledge is a threshold he has not reached, then it is still the case that Socrates cannot be wise, just, temperate, pious, or courageous.[24] If so, it makes no sense to characterize him as an exemplar of any of these virtues, since as a matter of fact he has achieved none of them.

Here, then, is the very heart of the problem. It is a problem, I contend, scholars themselves have created by applying an anachronistic conception of knowledge to our texts. If we go back and look at the very text in which Socrates explains the origins of his reputation for wisdom, we find a very different conception of knowledge in play. After hearing about the Delphic oracle to Chaerephon regarding his supposed wisdom and wondering at it,

---

[23] Scholarship on Socratic ignorance has struggled with the fact that Socrates both disclaims having knowledge and occasionally claims to have knowledge. See McPartland 2013 for a full review of these discussions. I now think the debates about this subject are mostly beside the point, since I think that the sense of knowledge engaged in such debates conceives it as a threshold achievement. In any case, no one seems to disagree that Socrates disclaims having the kind of knowledge that amounts to wisdom about "the most important things" (see *Apology* 22d7). Compare *Euthydemus* (293b7–8).

[24] I base this claim on Socrates' apparent endorsement of what has come to be known as the "unity of virtue" or the "unity of the virtues," for which, as with so many other Socratic views, a number of interpretations have been given. But this result would follow for any of the interpretations of the relevant unity that I am aware of. (For discussion of the interpretive alternatives, see Brickhouse and Smith 2010: section 6.2.)

Socrates seeks to examine the meaning of the oracle[25] by going to people reputed to be wise. He finds that politicians think they know something worthwhile, but actually don't (21d2–22a8). Poets, too, turn out to know nothing of significance, but suppose themselves to be very wise (22a8–c8). He then turns his attention to the skilled artisans.

> Finally I went to the artisans,[26] for I was conscious of knowing practically nothing, and I knew that I would find that they had knowledge of many fine things. In this I was not mistaken; they knew things I did not know, and to that extent they were wiser than I. But, gentlemen of the jury, the good artisans seemed to have the same fault as the poets: each of them, because of his success at his craft, thought himself very wise in other most important things,[27] and this error of theirs overshadowed the wisdom they had, so that I asked myself, on behalf of the oracle, whether I should prefer to be as I am, with neither their wisdom nor their ignorance, or to have both. The answer I gave myself and the oracle was that it was to my advantage to be as I am. (*Apology* 22c9–e6)

There are a couple of things to notice here:

(1)   As Socrates puts it at the end of this description, he finds that he actually is at an "advantage" relative to those he examined. In other words, the oracle turned out to be literally correct: none of those he examined turned out to be wiser than he is. Instead, he is wiser than they are. The way Socrates conceives of things does not simply make him less deficient than others, but actually advantaged. His point is not about a reduction of a deficit, but about his having achieved a positive condition, relative to theirs.[28] Moreover, Socrates also endorses what has come to be known as the "unity of virtue." The specific way in which we are to understand this view – that all of the

---

[25] Not "refute" the oracle, as many have proposed (and as the translation of *Apology* 21c1 in Cooper 1997 has it), along with an insinuation that this somehow indicates a certain degree of skepticism about customary religious beliefs. He does say that he sought to "examine the oracle" (21c1) but only after he insists that the god cannot lie (21b6–7).

[26] The translation in Cooper 1997 has "craftsmen," but Plato's actual term here is gender neutral: he calls them "*cheirotechnai*." I will throughout this book refer to craftspeople as "artisans" or simply as "skilled" to avoid this error.

[27] Translation modified here. The text does not include anything so specific as "pursuits," as the translation in Cooper 1997 has it. Rather, the Greek supplies only a neuter plural (22d7), which is probably best rendered in the way I have here. On the other hand, as my subsequent argument will show, I do not disagree that these "most important things" should not be supposed to be the contents of something like justified true beliefs, but rather concern activity and practical application.

[28] For a discussion of the significance of these different ways of describing the Socratic advantage, see Smith 2016 vs. Jones 2016. Both agree that Socrates is superior to others in virtue. However, Jones argues that this superiority in virtue is not enough to make Socrates happy; I argue the opposite: that Socrates' superiority in virtue affords him some degree of positive happiness.

virtues are in some sense the same – has been a matter of debate among scholars.[29] Taken in any of the ways that scholars have proposed, it would follow that insofar as Socrates is not wise, neither is he pious, just, temperate, or courageous. Insofar as he is wise, however, he is also all of the rest of these. It follows that we must understand Socrates' claim to be wiser than others – even if, again, only to a degree that is beneath notice from the divine point of view – as conclusive evidence that he is also more pious, just, temperate, and courageous. Accordingly, his claim of advantage in this text amounts to an explicit admission and explanation of what I am calling Plato's Socratic hagiography.

(2) Unlike the politicians and poets, Socrates finds that the artisans actually do know some things and this knowledge does constitute wisdom that they have. No doubt the artisans have cognitive states that we would call knowledge and that Socrates does not have, because he has not learned what the artisans have learned in learning their crafts. But Socrates is not talking about facts that they are justified in believing; instead, the artisans have their *crafts*, certain skills, abilities, or capacities to do those things associated with that craft. It is their *know-how*, in other words (and not some kind of knowing *that*) that Socrates compares to his own lack, and that gives the artisans an advantage over Socrates to that extent. But their knowledge(-how) and wisdom is not the kind that Socrates cares so much about – wisdom in what he here calls "other most important things" – and moreover the artisans seem to think they have that other wisdom when they do not have it. Because Socrates is aware that he does not have this other wisdom, he does not make the error made by the artisans. His not making this error more than makes up for the other advantages the artisans have, which is constituted by the wisdom that they have.

This focus on *craft*-knowledge, or what we often call "know-how," has come to be known as Socrates' "craft analogy." Socrates invariably compares being virtuous to having some (other) craft – between being a carpenter, for example, and being pious, or just, or courageous. The analogy is the result of Socrates being an intellectualist about virtue – that is, again, his view that virtue is a kind of knowledge. But it is a *kind of*

---

[29] See, for examples of different approaches, Vlastos 1981; Penner 1973, 1992b; Brickhouse and Smith 1997, 2010: 154–167.

knowledge that we should not confuse with fact-knowledge – with the cognitive state that we typically have in mind when we do contemporary theory of knowledge. It is, rather, skill or know-how.[30]

One very important consequence may immediately be drawn from this point: know-how is not an all-or-nothing affair, but rather a matter of degree, and one can become better at a certain kind of skill. For example, having attended dancing school when I was an adolescent, I know how to dance the cha-cha. Having not practiced dancing the cha-cha for many years now, I think it is most accurate to say that my knowledge of the cha-cha amounts to being able, rather clumsily, to do the basic step. For a professional ballroom dancer, my own skill would be so poor as probably not even to qualify as dancing the cha-cha (or perhaps not even as dancing *at all*). So the standards by which we measure some skill – for example, someone's knowing how to dance the cha-cha – are going to be highly contextual. At a professional ballroom dance competition, I would be immediately disqualified as hopelessly inept. Compared to someone who never learned the basic steps of the cha-cha, however, I qualify as (maybe even still just barely) knowing how to do the dance. But this is a very important difference from the cognitive state we tend to have in mind when someone talks about knowledge. Knowing how is not something that one either has or does not have; it is, rather, one that is *improvable* and achieved in degrees.[31]

This is not to say, however, that knowledge-that or fact-knowledge has nothing to do with the sort of knowledge that Socrates has in mind as a virtue intellectualist. A carpenter must know *that* this tool is a hammer

---

[30] I have claimed that this fact has gone mostly unnoticed by scholars, but there are indications in Senn 2013 that he sees at least some recognition of degrees of achievement in Socrates' views. See esp. Senn 2013: 87: "Socrates clearly he thinks he has a goodness (or *at least* some degree of it *relative* to what others have or do not have)." But Senn immediately seems to ignore the consequence of the relativity of Socrates' claim when he continues by claiming that Socrates' relative goodness "affords him a remarkable kind of protection against *any* injury (including injury from death, exile, disenfranchisement, as well – one assumes – as from imprisonment, torture, maiming) that an inferior may try to bring about for him." Had Senn also recognized the improvability in this consequence of Socrates' goodness, it seems we would be in agreement. I do agree with Senn when he claims that "*all that ultimately matters* to Socrates – as far as good and bad, benefit and harm is concerned – is something that he thinks he has *already* got (at least some of)" (Senn 2013: 87). We differ on just how much this "at least some of" counts, for Socrates. Senn concludes that the profession of ignorance is insincere. In my view, it is sincere because Socrates continues to regard himself as falling far short of his aspiration standards when it comes to knowledge. Elsewhere (in Senn 2005), Senn argues against the idea that Socrates thinks virtue is a craft, skill, or expertise.

[31] This does not mean that even the smallest share of know-how will count as an example of the relevant skill – what will count as at least enough to qualify as an example of real skill (even if incomplete or only partial) will generally be a matter of context and the standards applicable to that context.

and that one is a saw, and also know *that* the saw is used to cut wood, and so on. We should also remind ourselves that the Socrates we see at work in Plato's dialogues seeks definitional knowledge, and seems to think that those who actually have some virtue will be able to define it – and definitions, plainly, are propositional in form. But even this frequent feature of Plato's early dialogues – the Socratic "what is F-ness?" questions that he asks his interlocutors – has led to errors of interpretation.

1.6 Craft and Definitional Knowledge

Studies of Socratic epistemology have often focused on Socrates' commitment to the priority of definitional knowledge The standard way this is characterized is probably best given in the most influential work on this subject by Hugh H. Benson, who counts the following claim as a fundamental Socratic commitment:

> (PD) If A fails to know what F-ness is, then A fails to know anything about F-ness.[32]

This principle articulates the view that definitional knowledge is a requirement of any other sort of knowledge: one cannot know of some particular thing, X, that it is F; nor can one know of any other characteristic (G-ness) that it is F without knowing what F-ness is.[33] And what counts as knowing what F-ness is (whether it involves knowing a definition) is being able to answer one of Socrates' "what is F-ness?" questions – which, of course, no interlocutor in our texts ever manages to do. The reason no interlocutors manage to do this is that their answers always end up being refuted in conversation with Socrates. So from this point of view, if we ask whether anyone Socrates ever meets has the knowledge required for virtue, the answer is "no." This negative answer also famously applies to Socrates himself: Socrates became well known for professing his own ignorance and inability to answer the questions he asks others.[34] Given Socratic intellectualism about virtue, then, it would seem that Socrates is convinced that no one has the required knowledge and so no one is virtuous. The very question of whether he or anyone else might be virtuous *to a degree* does not appear to be apt when and if we understand the having of virtue as the having of definitional knowledge.

But even if we are to accept this characterization of what Socratic virtue intellectualism consists in, things are perhaps not quite as definite as the

---

[32] Benson 2013a: 137.   [33] Benson 2013a: 138.   [34] See note 17.

earlier characterization would have them be. First, from the fact that Socrates so often responds to someone's confidence about some virtue (such as, for example, Euthyphro's confidence about piety) by asking the "what is it?" question, it does not follow that Socrates takes the having of the relevant virtue to be nothing other than the having of the answer to that question.

An example will help here. In his discussion with Callicles in the *Gorgias*, Socrates indicates that he regards swimming as a kind of craft-knowledge:

SOCRATES: Do you think that a man ought to make sure that his life be as long as possible and that he practice those crafts that ever rescue us from dangers . . .
CALLICLES: Yes, and by Zeus, that's sound advice for you!
SOCRATES: Well, my excellent fellow, do you think that expertise in swimming is a grand thing?
CALLICLES: No, by Zeus, I don't.
SOCRATES: But it certainly does save people from death whenever they fall into the kind of situation that requires this expertise. (*Gorgias* 511b7–c9)

Socrates' point is obviously that the skill or knowledge required to preserve one's life is not always or obviously anything especially estimable. The example of a not particularly estimable skill that he uses to make this point is swimming. He goes on, in the lines immediately following this one, to categorize another such skill (helmsmanship/*kubernêtikê*) in more or less similar terms (*Gorgias* 511d1–e3). Helmsmanship may be a more demanding skill than swimming; but even so, the way Socrates describes it does not make it seem especially estimable, despite the fact that when done effectively it can save lives.

So does Socrates believe that the *epistêmê* (knowledge, expertise) or *technê* (craft, skill) of swimming consists in the ability to say what swimming is? Obviously not: one might know perfectly well what swimming is and not be able to swim. But perhaps we might suppose instead that Socrates at least thought that being a swimmer required one to be able to answer the question, "what is swimming?" But even this condition seems too strong: it is perfectly obvious that being able to swim is entirely independent from being even minimally articulate.

Now, one might object here that Socrates often seems to insist that having a skill includes the ability to teach that skill to others (see, for example, *Protagoras* 319a10–c8). And, no doubt, some kinds of teaching do involve a great deal of articulate verbal advice. But even if the teaching of swimming, for example, may involve the giving of verbal advice to the one learning to swim, it is obvious that such advice need not include the specific information that amounts to telling the novice (or, for that matter, getting the novice into a position where they can say) what swimming is.

So if being able to give an answer to Socrates' "what is F-ness?" questions is not an *essential* part of knowing or having a skill, why do we find Socrates putting so much emphasis on asking such questions and insisting on his interlocutors trying to answer them? Many years ago, my coauthor Thomas C. Brickhouse and I, noting that Socrates tended to ask such questions of interlocutors who presented themselves as *experts*, proposed that the point of such questions was to test whether the interlocutor was in a position to serve as a judge of the F-ness of F things, where such judgments would need to go beyond the levels of skill we expect of nonexperts.[35] Socrates does seem to think that an expert about F-ness should be able to explain what F-ness is, and also be able to teach others how to be F (if being F is the sort of thing that human beings can be).

To go back to the humble example of swimming: does Socrates believe that no one could have the craft of swimming unless they could teach others to become swimmers, too? He does seem to think that experts or masters of skills could also teach those skills; but does the same requirement hold for just having the skill at all? It is not obvious to me that Socrates would think such a requirement obtained.

In the passage quoted earlier about swimming, it seems as if all that would be needed for one to qualify as having the knowledge/expertise/craft of swimming would be that one could keep from drowning if one fell into the water. As much as we may admire the incredible achievements of swimmers such as Michael Phelps or Tracy Caulkins, it is also clear that their level of skill was vastly greater than what is needed for one simply to save one's own life when in the water. In the case of swimming, then, it seems that having the skill requires clearing a very low threshold of achievement. But more importantly, there is next to nothing about having this craft or skill that invites or requires the sort of condition that we study in philosophical epistemology courses. Scholars who have structured their understanding of Socratic epistemology in terms of anything like justified true belief, accordingly, have tended almost from the beginning to create misapprehension of our texts.

Socrates does seem to think that if someone really were a master of the craft of virtue, that person could explain what the virtue is and teach others how to attain it. We might plausibly suppose that this sort of know-how, too (knowing how to explain, knowing how to teach), will come in degrees, and thus also infer that Socrates must suppose that he can do a better job of this than can any of the interlocutors with whom he speaks in the

---

[35] Brickhouse and Smith 1994: 46–55.

dialogues.[36] So in saying that Socrates' virtue intellectualism has a kind of know-how as the sort of knowledge in which virtue consists, we should not suppose that there is nothing in our texts that rules out uses of epistemic terms that would be readily suited to the more familiar versions of contemporary epistemology. The distinction made herein is about which sort of knowledge is the essence of Socratic virtue intellectualism. Some knowledge-that may be symptomatic of knowing how, or even a necessary condition of it. Accordingly, we should not be surprised when Socrates seems to indicate that no one could be good or virtuous who fails to know (that) something or other is true.[37]

1.7 The Relative Importance of Different Skills

If we try to take my point about the improvability of craft-knowledge and virtue further, however, we encounter an interesting puzzle. Let us grant (what I hope has now been established) that Socrates intends to be comparing degrees of some improvable skill(s) in the *Apology* when he compares his own level of skill with what he finds in the artisans, and decides that he is more skilled than they. Now, what *they* are more skilled at is obvious: they are more skilled at their crafts than Socrates is skilled at those crafts. In what, then, is *Socrates* more skilled? It seems he is more skilled in the only other kind of wisdom that is mentioned in the passage, and only just mentioned: skill in "other most important things." He does not say what these other things are, or why they are "most important." But whatever they are, it is clear that Socrates not only thinks they are more important than whatever skills the artisans actually do have but also that the jury will at least understand that there are more important things that one might aspire to be wise about than the practices and products of the (other) crafts. But even so, we might pause to wonder what Socrates has in mind – and what he expects his jurors to have in mind – when he declares that what he has amounts to being wiser than what the artisans have, despite their obvious advantages.

The complaint against Socrates is that he has a reputation for wisdom, and it is this reputation that he seeks to explain in this passage (see *Apology*

---

[36] One account of how Socrates helps others to improve their skill in giving definitions may be found in May 1997. I explain my own view of how this works in Section 4.7 of this book.

[37] One example among many might be where Socrates says that he "knows that it is evil and disgraceful to do what's wrong and to disobey one's superior, whether god or man" at *Apology* 29b6–7. Such knowledge, we may suppose – or at least the relevant belief – would be required for anyone even to approximate virtue.

20d6–7). If wisdom is to be understood as a kind of know-how or skill, then what Socrates is explaining to the jurors is how and why he (rightly) has come to have a reputation for having more of this know-how or skill than others – indeed, if the oracle is right, there is no one who has it more than Socrates. But even though he has this reputation, and even though Socrates is convinced that he really is more skilled than others, the actual nature and content of that superior skill is not here specified. So what is it? I propose that the superior skill that Socrates has a reputation for having is what he and the jurors would count as *real* wisdom – the same kind(s) of skill he and they would count as *real* virtue, *aretê*.[38] The artisans have the virtue of their crafts, which is to say that they can be *good* or even *excellent* at what they do. Socrates is not good at what the artisans are good at. Instead, he is good in the way that *really* matters. That is what he has come to have a reputation for, and he is telling his jurors here that his reputation is actually correct, at least relative to other human beings. He is *better* than other human beings. Later on, he reassures the jurors who voted for him that the gods do not neglect good men (41d1–2). The point is obvious: he has not been harmed by what has happened, despite the result of the trial, because he is a good man and the gods look out for good men. So again, the entire effect of this passage is an emphatic endorsement of what I am herein calling Plato's hagiography of Socrates.

The way in which Socrates is so much better than other men is not an all-or-nothing matter, but a matter of skill and conduct. It is not that he has some specific cognitive state – some justified true belief(s) that others do not have. As something more like a skill – the most valuable of all skills – whatever Socrates has is something we can all improve in, and it is this message that he brings to the Athenians as if he were a "gift from the god" (*Apology* 30d8). We should care more about attaining this skill (29d7–30b4, 31b4–5, 38a1–7). Because this is what he has dedicated his life to doing, Socrates actually claims to make people happy (36d10). I will have a great deal more to say about this in subsequent chapters, but for now, it is enough to see that such a claim is a claim to have a very significant kind of expertise.

---

[38] Given the way Fine understands the knowledge that is constitutive of wisdom (see note 3), she concludes that the only "wisdom" Socrates has is "not genuine wisdom" (Fine 2008: 79). As I have been arguing, this leaves Socrates with no real advantage in wisdom over the artisans. Fine reads Socrates' claim he has "*sophian tina*" at *Apology* 20d7 as meaning not that he has a kind of wisdom, but rather that what he has is "something like wisdom" (2008: 79). Thus, in her view, "Socrates distinguishes wisdom from something that is like wisdom, but is not wisdom at all" (2008: 80). This, however, seems to destroy the very claim that Socrates is seeking to make here, which is that Socrates is superior *in wisdom* to the artisans, *in spite of the real wisdom they have in their crafts*.

1.8 Two Alternatives Considered

I have argued that the kind of knowledge that Socrates thought virtue consisted in is improvable. But accepting this does not all by itself get us out of the trilemma. As I indicated earlier, those who do not understand knowledge as improvable, for Socrates, might argue that although knowledge is not improvable, one's level of justification or warrant for a true belief could well be improvable. Accordingly, as I put it there, one might argue that Socrates took knowledge to be something that neither he nor any other mere human being had achieved, but still compare himself cognitively (and thus ethically, given his intellectualism) favorably to others. Following the way I characterized this view early in the previous section, let us call this the "approximation view," or AV for short. In this view, knowledge or wisdom might be taken as more of an aspirational standard, like perhaps the condition of the god who Socrates says is wise in the way that he, despite being the "wisest of human beings," is not (*Apology* 23a5–6). Whatever human beings could achieve, at best, might be improvable, but could never actually meet this standard.[39] But even so, it could well be that Socrates (and anyone else who made a genuine attempt to lead "the examined life") could be counted as approximating this aspirational ideal more than others, because his justification for what he believes might be better than others, and might still be improved further.

In AV, we should understand Socrates' own cognitive and ethical self-assessment as being that he has achieved a better approximation of virtue than the politicians, poets, and craftspeople. So could this (AV) perhaps be what Plato's hagiography of Socrates amounts to? I think not. If we go on to try to make our way out of the trilemma in AV, we encounter problems. The first of these might make its appearance when we try to adjust the second point of the trilemma in such a way as to allow Plato to make his case for Socrates. The problem is that Socrates plainly says that virtue is a kind of knowledge and (given the unity of virtue) all virtue is none other than wisdom. Now, suppose we attempt to understand the way that Socrates exhorts us to improve ourselves in the way that AV requires. For example, consider the way he puts this in the *Euthydemus*:

> [Socrates speaking] Then let us consider what follows: since we all wish to be happy, and since we appear to become so by using things and using them rightly, and since knowledge was the source of rightness and good fortune, it seems to be necessary that every man should prepare himself by every means to become as wise as possible. (*Euthydemus* 282a1–6)

---

[39] I take this to be the view presented in Fine 2008 (see note 38).

Taking "wise" here to mean the kind of infallible cognitive perfection of a god, we will see Socrates as urging us to "become as infallible as possible." The problem – and at the heart of AV – is that the kind of knowledge/wisdom that is the only one recognized in AV (an infallible kind) is not one that allows of degrees. If Socrates makes only three errors in roughly twenty attempts per day at some task, whereas I make fifteen errors in the same number of attempts per day, that does make Socrates less fallible than I am in that task, but it does not make him "more infallible." So similarly, if all fall short of knowledge or wisdom, then some (e.g. Socrates) may qualify as less ignorant than others, but none will qualify as more knowing or more wise, since none will actually achieve these ideal thresholds. If this were Socrates' view of things, it would not make sense for him to exhort us "to become as wise as possible," since becoming wise *at all* would not be an option for any of us. Moreover, it would not make sense for Socrates to claim to be wiser than anyone else (much less "the wisest," since he would not be wise at all). Plainly, this does not match what Socrates actually says about himself. My own view – that Socrates actually has achieved a level of what really does count as knowledge and wisdom (even if he still regards it as a very low level of each) – thus fits what Socrates actually says on this topic better than AV does.

This is not to say, however, that the notion of approximation has no place at all in Plato's hagiography of Socrates. Its place, I claim, is not in the supposition that the best any of us can do is to approximate virtue, but never really to achieve (at least some level of) it. Approximation to an ideal that we can never really hope to measure up to is not part of Plato's portrait. What is absolutely a part of it is that those of us who are prepared to dedicate ourselves to self-improvement can actually make every effort to approximate a very nonideal standard, one that, if we are dedicated and persistent, we might even manage to measure up to: the figure of Socrates himself. Plato portrays Socrates as someone who can readily be imitated (for example, at *Apology* 23c1–6), and he quite explicitly urges others to do that (for example, at *Apology* 41e1–42a2, and *Gorgias* 527c4–6). The oracle told Chaerephon that there was no one wiser than Socrates. Perhaps it is not even possible for a human being to be wiser than Socrates. But nothing in our texts prevents us from trying – and just possibly succeeding – in becoming as wise as Socrates was.

1.9 Summary and Conclusion

I began with what I characterized as a trilemma facing Plato's hagiography of Socrates – the result of a characterization of Socrates as an exemplar of virtue, as a virtue intellectualist, and as someone who disclaimed know-ledge and wisdom. I have focused on one particular expression of the Socratic profession of ignorance in Plato's *Apology* to show that it was never intended to amount to making Socrates "one of the damned," as Vlastos so colorfully put it (1971: 7). The way out of the trilemma, I have claimed, comes from recognizing the improvability of the kind of know-ledge and wisdom that Socrates exemplifies, the kind of knowledge and wisdom that virtue consists in, and thus the degree to which Socrates and others can be ignorant. Socrates qualifies as the wisest and the most virtuous of human beings, because in comparison with others, he works the hardest (and is at least to some degree reliably effective in his efforts) to improve in the most important of skills. Relative to a god, of course, he is "worthless," and relative to his own aspirational ideals, he is painfully aware that he has a long way to go. Even so, if we compare him to other (mere) human beings, he is an exemplar – and his modest disclaimers *never* amount to a denial of that fact. Indeed, as we can see, although he is careful to remind us that one's proper aspirational goals should always aim *much* higher than he has achieved himself, Socrates actually affirms his exemplary status, and also says that we would do well to emulate him. He is ignorant, and offers little hope for any of us to be less ignorant than he is. But such ignorance is a matter of our humanity, and is also a matter of degree. We would all do well to be like Socrates, always trying our best to remediate our human condition of ignorance. We may thus become happy – at least, as happy as a human being can be. In so doing, we may also become "god-like" (see *Theaetetus* 176a5–c3[40]): not *as* gods, but as *like* them as human beings can ever be.

---

[40] For discussion of this theme in Plato, see Sedley 1999, and more recently Giannopoulou 2011.

CHAPTER 2

Socrates as Apprentice at Virtue

2.1 Introduction

In the last chapter, I argued that the kind of knowledge Plato's Socrates mostly talks about – and the kind he strives always to attain – is a kind of craft-knowledge, where the craft in question amounts to expertise in living well. But as we also find in Plato's texts, Plato's Socrates routinely disclaims having this special expertise,[1] though as I argued in the last chapter, he also says a number of things that seem to indicate that he thinks he is *better* than others when it comes to how well he performs within the province of this craft. Given his disclaimers, however, it is startling to find Socrates claiming:

> I believe that I'm one of a few Athenians – so as not to say I'm the only one, but the only one among our contemporaries – to take up the true political craft and practice the true politics. This is because the speeches I make on each occasion do not aim at gratification but at what's best. They don't aim at what's most pleasant. (*Gorgias* 521d6–e1)

What Socrates says in this passage, I aver, is clear evidence of the general interpretation I am promoting in this book. But in order to establish my interpretation with respect to this passage, I will need to show that Socrates means precisely what he says here. I accept that the claim appears within a significantly charged dialectical context between Socrates and Callicles; but I do not think Socrates' claim needs to be understood as conditioned in any way by that context. Rather, in my interpretation, there is nothing that Socrates says in the claim that he does not literally mean, or that must be understood in terms of what is happening between the two discussants. In the interpretation I provide, Socrates' claim is a significant one that tells us a great deal about his assessment of his own ethical achievement. In what

---

[1] Examples may be found at *Apology* 20c1–3, 21d2–7, 23b2–4; *Charmides* 165b4–c2, 166c7–d6; *Euthyphro* 5a7–c5, 15c12, 15e5–16a4; *Laches* 186b8–c5, 186d8–e3, 200e2–5; *Lysis* 212a4–7, 223b4–8; *Hippias Major* 286c8–e2, 304d4–e5; *Gorgias* 509a4–6; *Republic* I.337e4–5.

follows, then, I will go step by step through Socrates' claim and compare what we find to other things he says elsewhere.

2.2   Is Socrates Not the First?

Let us begin by reviewing very carefully each of the specific elements of Socrates' claim. He begins by saying that:

> (1)   Only a few Athenians in the past have ever taken up the true political craft or practiced the true politics.

Given the ways in which the "true political craft" has been described earlier in the dialogue (for example, that it consists in two parts, legislation and justice – see 464c2–3), one might wonder whether Socrates really does believe that anyone has *ever* tried to practice this craft, and certainly when Socrates makes this claim, he has not anywhere earlier in the dialogue held anyone up as deserving such recognition. Rather, he has shown only a very critical attitude toward those who have been mentioned so far in the discussion.

Many scholars have claimed that Socrates was an ideological enemy of the Athenian democracy, aligned with the radical oligarchic faction in Athens. In some accounts, this was the real reason – or at least one important reason – why Socrates was put on trial, convicted, and put to death.[2] In fact, however, Socrates seems no less critical of famous members of the oligarchic faction than he is when he evaluates the political performances of those among the democrats.[3] It is true that he has hardly anything good to say about Pericles, for example – perhaps the most famous of the democrats from Athenian history.[4] Other famous democrats are also subjected to similar criticisms, often in the same passages.[5] But Socrates turns out to be completely even-handed in his scorn for famous politicians from the past. In many of the same passages in which he shows contempt for the political skills of democratic politicians, he also includes famous members of the oligarchy as exemplars of the same sorts of failings.[6]

---

[2] See especially Stone 1988. Although Stone's characterization is perhaps the most vehement, this "political" understanding of the trial shows up in most accounts of the motives for the trial and execution. The only dissenters to this understanding, to my knowledge, are Vlastos 1991, Brickhouse and Smith 1994, and McPherran 1996, who argue that the trial had a religious motivation.

[3] In what follows, I repeat a discussion given in more detail in Brickhouse and Smith 1994: section 5.3.

[4] See, for example, *Gorgias* 472a5–b3 (false witness); *Meno* 92d7–94e2 (bad father to his sons); *Gorgias* 514c4–517a6 (made Athenians wilder and less controlled).

[5] Nicias and Aristocrates: *Gorgias* 472a5–b3; Themistocles, Aristeides, and Thucydides (son of Melesias – not the historian): *Meno* 92d7–94e2; Themistocles: *Gorgias* 515c4–517a6.

[6] For example, Cimon and his father Miltiades: *Gorgias* 515c4–517a6; members of The Thirty: *Apology* 32c3–d4.

Given Socrates' mission of refutation in Athens, it is not surprising that those with whom he is associated in Plato's dialogues are revealed to lack the wisdom they are reputed to have (see *Apology* 21c3–e1). But in at least a couple of places, we actually find Socrates offering some praise of past politicians. Just a few Stephanus pages after the passage at 521d6–e1 that is my focus here, Socrates actually does single out one politician from Athenian history who stands out for having been just in spite of having had ample opportunity to be unjust: Aristeides, son of Lysimachus (*Gorgias* 526a3–5) – who is also known as "Aristeides the Just." We learn elsewhere (at *Meno* 92d7–94e2) that whatever virtue Aristeides had managed to achieve was not passed on to his son, who is elsewhere, too, characterized as having been undistinguished in spite of his father's much more note-worthy achievements (see *Laches* 179c2–d2). Accordingly, we can safely conclude that even if Aristeides was Socrates' precursor (the only one I have found in Plato's texts) in "taking up" the true craft of politics, we may reasonably doubt that he mastered that craft – since one of the things Socrates says about true artisans is that they are able to teach their craft to others (*Gorgias* 514a5–b3; *Laches* 185b1–4, e4–6; *Protagoras* 319b5–c8), by explaining to others the nature of that craft's objects and their causes (*Gorgias* 465a2–6, 500e4–501b1; *Laches* 189e3–190b1). Socrates notes that Cimon and Themistocles made the Athenians wilder and less controlled, and cites the fact that both were ostracized as evidence (516d6–8). Aristeides is not included in this list (which Socrates took from Callicles – see 503c1–3), but could have been: Aristeides, too, was ostracized in 482 BCE, though he was recalled within two years to command the Athenian victory at Salamis in 480 (see Nails 2002: 48). From the Socratic point of view, then, while distinguished, Aristeides' political and paternal achievements would have failed as exemplars of fully realized virtue. Even so, the praise Socrates eventually does give to Aristeides, at the close of the *Gorgias*, seems at least to moderate his earlier claim that "we don't know any man who has proved to be good at politics in this city" (516e9–517a2). Perhaps Socrates would have been ready to name others who had at least "taken up the true political craft" in Athens, but what he has to say about Aristeides may be enough to show that he really did think that there were at least some who had done so in earlier generations.

2.3   Only Socrates

Whatever may have happened in former generations, Socrates seems convinced that:

(2)   Socrates is the only one of the current generation who has "taken up the true political craft."

Socrates and Callicles seem prepared to agree that among the current generation, there are no *true* political artisans to be found. Socrates takes this one step further, moreover, in claiming to be the only one among his cohort even to have taken up the craft. But what can Socrates mean by this part of the claim? For some help in discerning Socrates' meaning, we might be inclined to look to Irwin's commentary in the *Clarendon Plato Series*:

> Socrates does not say that he *has* this craft, but that he "undertakes" (or "attempts," *epicheirein*) it, looking for its principles; and so this remark need not conflict with his previous disavowal of knowledge. Socrates is never clear about how this ideal of a moral and political craft is to be realized; for he offers no clear account of happiness showing how it requires justice; and without such a clear account of its goal, in "undisputed" terms (cf. 451d), the political craft cannot begin. (Irwin 1979: 240–241)

One might respond to Irwin's understanding with a certain puzzlement: how can one "undertake" or "attempt" something, but do so in a way that is so deficient that, as a matter of principle, the undertaking "cannot begin"? (Imagine trying to explain to your partner that you really did "attempt" to buy bread from the store, even though not only is there still no bread in the house, but moreover you had yet to make even a single step in the direction of the store!)

Perhaps lurking behind Irwin's puzzling analysis is an assumption often made by those who have written about Socratic virtue intellectualism. As I explained it in Chapter 1, "Socratic virtue intellectualism" is the view generally attributed to Socrates[7] that holds virtue to be a kind of knowledge. In contemporary epistemology, knowledge is generally treated as a cognitive state, with propositional (or at least propositionalizable) content, and functions as an "all-or-nothing" achievement: an epistemic agent either knows or does not know. If one satisfies the conditions for knowledge (however these are conceived in a given theory), then one knows; unless and until one satisfies those conditions, one does not know. In other words, in most contemporary treatments of knowledge, the achievement of knowledge is not *improvable*; it does not come in

---

[7] Even in ancient times – see, for example, Xenophon *Memorabilia* 3.9.4–5, 4.6.11; Aristotle, *Nicomachean Ethics* Γ.8.1116b3–5, Z.13.1144b14–21, 28–30; *Eudemian Ethics* A.5.1216b2–10, Γ.1.1229a12, 14–16, Γ.1.1230a7–10; *Magna Moralia* A.1.1182a15–23, A.1.1183b8–11, A.20.1190b27–29, A.34.1198a10–13.

degrees.[8] I suspect that because this is what might now be called "Epistemology 101," scholars considering Socratic virtue intellectualism apply our familiar conception of knowledge to the sort of knowledge that Socrates has in mind when he talks about virtue. But this is a serious mistake.

Scholars have also had a great deal to say about what is typically called "the craft analogy," according to which Socrates compares virtue to a technical skill, expertise, or craft.[9] According to the craft analogy, virtue is like one of the crafts. Elsewhere, I have argued that better attention to the craft analogy can resolve the kinds of puzzles scholars have encountered over what has come to be known as the "unity of virtue" doctrine – Socrates' claim in the *Protagoras* (349b6–c1) that virtue (and, indeed, all of the virtues) turns out to be just one thing. Were this the only text on the topic, there would not have been the volume of scholarship that has now been produced on it.[10] The problem that has energized so much scholarship comes when we find other texts in which Socrates makes clear that he also believes that the various virtues are (proper) parts of the whole of virtue (see *Laches* 190a1–199e7, *Meno* 78d7–e2) and another text where Socrates makes one of the virtues (piety) a proper part of another (justice – see *Euthyphro* 12d2).[11] I have claimed the craft analogy actually helps to resolve the problem, on the ground that the very same knowledge that grounds a craft (the example I initially used was the knowledge of triangulation, as it applies to both land surveying and navigation[12]) might be precisely the same in each instance, but different in its applications (so, no one would

---

[8] The view I am representing here has come to be known as "invariantism" among contemporary epistemologists, and has been opposed by certain theorists called "contextualists." (For discussion and explication of the varieties of views on this topic, see Evans and Smith 2012: ch. 3.) To my knowledge, all applications of contemporary epistemological assumptions to the Socratic view have been by invariantists; no one has attempted to characterize Socrates as a contextualist about knowledge. Though I will go on to insist that the sort of knowledge Socrates has in mind is improvable, I do not at all intend to characterize him as a contextualist about knowledge. Rather, I contend that the sort of knowledge Socrates has in mind has all along been regarded by epistemologists as improvable, and is, hence, not the sort of concept epistemologists generally work on in the theory of knowledge. A contemporary account of knowledge that is closer to the one I am attributing to Socrates may be found in Hetherington 2011.

[9] Important recent studies include Reeve 1989: 37–45; Woodruff 1990; Brickhouse and Smith 1994: 37–38; and Smith 1998. Senn 2005 dissents.

[10] For citations and review of at least many of the options that have been offered, see Brickhouse and Smith 1997 and 2010.

[11] Note that in the *Gorgias*, Socrates says that there is a single craft of care for the body that has two parts: gymnastics and medicine, which correspond to the two parts of the political craft, legislation and justice (*Gorgias* 464b–c). So there should be nothing surprising if it turns out that the general craft of virtue (or one of the virtue-crafts) has parts, as Socrates indicates.

[12] See Brickhouse and Smith 1997.

say that land surveying *just is* navigation or the other way around, even though the same knowledge of triangulation is used for both). In brief, then, I argued that the unity of virtue was in terms of the knowledge used commonly by all of them (moral knowledge; or, if you like, knowledge of good and bad) but applied differently in each (what Brickhouse and I called the "*ergon* condition" that would complete the definition of a given virtue).

But what never came up in this earlier debate about the unity of virtue is *another* aspect of the craft analogy, which I think will help us to figure out not only what Socrates has in mind in saying that he has taken up the true political craft, but also (I think) what has gone wrong in Irwin's puzzling response to that claim. Briefly, as I explained in Chapter 1, unlike the kind of knowledge that has mostly preoccupied modern epistemology, craft-knowledge is *not* a threshold achievement; instead, craft-knowledge is improvable – it comes in degrees. Even contemporary epistemologists count "know-how," which is a much better approximation of the sort of knowledge I claim Socrates has in mind, as improvable.[13] This feature of the craft model for knowledge helps considerably to explain what Socrates has in mind when he claims to have taken up the true political craft. My claim is that we should understand Socrates as having committed himself to becoming as adept at this craft as he possibly can. As Irwin proposed, when Socrates says that he has taken up the true craft of politics, he is not claiming to have mastered the craft, and given his continued disavowal of knowledge, we may also suppose that he does not think that he is yet even close to such a goal. But even so, for Socrates to claim even to have taken up the craft allows us to get a sense of what he might think about his own achievements.

First, it is important to recognize that Socrates' apprenticeship, as I call it in the title of this chapter, is one that is without benefit of the mentorship of a master at the craft of virtue. As a result, what Socrates is attempting to do is to bootstrap the craft of virtue on his own. That is obviously not the best way to try to gain a craft, but it is the only way that is open to Socrates: there are no masters of virtue for Socrates to study with – if there were, the oracle that claimed no one is wiser than Socrates (*Apology* 21a2–6) would turn out to be false. But we know that Socrates does believe one can learn a craft even without a master to teach it to one (see *Laches* 185e7–9, 186b1–5, 187a1), and so we may assume that this project is what Socrates has "taken up."

---

[13] See Ryle 1949: 59.

But secondly, and much more importantly, Socrates regards himself as in a position to ascertain[14] that the true craft of politics requires one to speak in ways that do not aim at gratification, but at what's best. Indeed, this consideration – this mandate – of the true craft of politics is so important to that craft that he can explain his having taken up the craft simply on the ground that he has taken it upon himself to act in accordance with this specific mandate. At least as he explains himself to Callicles, it is in virtue of his always acting in accordance with this mandate that he counts himself as having taken up the craft.

It is worth pausing to consider what the strength of Socrates' claim might be. Does he suppose that he always succeeds in achieving what's best when he speaks? If we focus, again, on his disavowals of knowledge, we might well assume that he cannot possibly mean to claim so much success. On the other hand, we can also find Socrates at least intimating that he regards himself as having been quite remarkably successful in achieving this aim of the political craft: at *Apology* 37a6–7, he claims that he has never wronged anyone willingly, which might be supposed to be no significant boast given the famous Socratic view that *no one* ever goes wrong willingly, except that he goes on, only a few lines later, to claim that "I am convinced that I wrong no one" (*Apology* 37b2–3), without the qualification.

He makes or implies the same claim several times in the *Gorgias* as well: at 511b4–5 it is at least implied; at 521b6, where Socrates says that anyone who prosecuted him would be a wicked man prosecuting a good one; at 521d2, where he describes himself as "one who is not a wrongdoer"; and at 522b9–c1, where he says that everything he says and does is in the interest of justice. But he goes on to characterize himself as someone very much to be admired, even though he acknowledges that he would not do well trying to win a trial before a jury of Athenians:

CALLICLES: Do you think, Socrates, that a man in such a position in his city, a man who's unable to protect himself, is to be admired?

SOCRATES: Yes, Callicles, as long as he has that one thing that you've often agreed he should have: as long as he has protected himself against having spoken or

---

[14] I purposely use a somewhat ambiguous term to describe Socrates' cognitive condition on this point – some may object that Socrates can't possibly *know* this (see, for example, Benson 2013a, who claims that without definitional knowledge of virtue, Socrates cannot know anything about virtue). I have argued elsewhere that Socrates can and does know at least some things of moral significance (Brickhouse and Smith 1994: ch. 2), and would note here that what Socrates "ascertains" is something to which he has devoted his life, so whatever we may wish to call it, Socrates' cognitive condition certainly satisfies a norm of assertion, but also the highest levels of norms of performance – he is plainly willing to "put his money where his mouth is." (On how we should understand the latter issues, in relation to Socrates' disavowals of knowledge, see McPartland 2013.)

> done anything unjust relating to either men or gods. For this is the self-protection that you and I have often have agreed avails the most. Now if someone were to refute me and prove that I am unable to provide *this* protection for myself or for anyone else, I would feel shame at being refuted, whether this happened in the presence of many or of a few, or just between the two of us; and if I were to be put to death for lack of this ability, I really would be upset. (*Gorgias* 522b4–d7)

It is difficult to see how Socrates could make such claims unless he thinks that he has actually had quite significant success in living up to what appears to be the main mandate of the true craft of politics.

Of course, it may be that Socrates has managed to do as well as he has mainly because he really has had a great deal of help along the way. At *Apology* 40a4–7, Socrates tells his jurors that his *daimonion* has frequently opposed him when he was about to do something wrong, and so the fact that he experienced no such opposition as he made his defense speech counts as powerful evidence (*mega tekmêrion* – 40c2) that he has done well in court. We may make two inferences here: (i) Socrates has not been so successful in achieving the aim of the craft of politics because his judgment of what he should and shouldn't do has become even nearly flawless – were that the case, his *daimonion* would not have needed to be so active over the years. Accordingly, the high levels of activity of the *daimonion* underscore how far Socrates has yet to go in his mastery of the true craft of politics. But (ii) even if the *daimonion* cannot be strictly relied upon to keep Socrates from making any errors *ever*, its high levels of activity that extend to even fairly trivial affairs (see *smikrois* at 40a7) show it to be at least highly reliable. We may assume that between Socrates' own resources and those provided by the *daimonion* we have enough to explain adequately how Socrates can claim to be convinced he has wronged no one.

On the "inside" of Socrates' apprenticeship in virtue, accordingly, we may confidently suppose that Socrates regarded his own achievements as being quite modest, which is why he continues to make his disavowals of knowledge and also why his *daimonion* has needed to be so active. At the level of practice (the "outside," if you will, of Socrates' apprenticeship), we have reason to think that he has actually done remarkably well. In his attempts to follow the main mandate of the true craft of politics, then, Socrates is actually not aware of any specific failures. It may well be that he would strongly qualify our observing this on his behalf, by insisting that he could do so much better if only he could significantly improve his inner condition (and thus rely less on what would accordingly become a much less active *daimonion*). After all, although the *daimonion*'s opposition is a clear enough signal that he was about to do something *wrong*, Socrates cannot rely on his sign to show him what is the *best* thing to do in any given circumstance. So he may both reasonably suppose that he has not wronged anyone and suspect that he has often fallen far short of "what's best," which is how he characterizes the ultimate aim of the political craft. This conclusion thus supports Socrates' claim to have taken up the political craft, without further indicating that he supposes that he is yet anything like a master of the craft. But even if we limit Socrates' actual achievements in this way, we may nonetheless confidently reject Irwin's assessment that Socrates cannot even have *begun* in artisanship.

2.4   Being an Artisan and Performing the Functions of a Craft

In the previous section, I made a distinction between the "inside" and the "outside" of Socrates' taking up the craft of politics. Another way to put this distinction is to think of it in terms of having the actual skill involved in the craft, as opposed to engaging in the practices and producing the products of that craft. These two – the skill and the actual practices and achievements – are very closely linked, in Socrates' view.

> [Socrates speaking] In working and using wood there is surely nothing else that brings about the right use except the knowledge of carpentry, is there?
>
> [Cleinias speaking] Certainly not.
>
> And, again, I suppose that in making utensils, it is knowledge that produces the right method.
>
> He agreed.
>
> And also, I said, with regard to using the goods we mentioned first – wealth and health and beauty – was it knowledge that ruled and directed our conduct in relation to the right use of all such things as these, or some other thing?
>
> It was knowledge.
>
> The knowledge seems to provide men not only with success but also with well-doing, in every case of possession or action.
>
> He agreed.
>
> Then in heaven's name, I said, is there any advantage in other possessions without good sense or wisdom? (*Euthydemus* 281a1–b6[15])

---

[15] Translation slightly modified. The Greek term translated here as "success" is often translated as "good luck" or "good fortune," but the examples Socrates actually uses to demonstrate what he has in mind are all clear cases of what we would characterize as success in some endeavor. This translation is one of those recognized as a possibility in Liddell, Scott, Jones, and McKenzie 1940 (s.v. εὐτύχεια). For further discussion, see Brickhouse and Smith 2010: 168–172.

But Socrates' *daimonion* seems to open up another alternative here, or at least requires a nuance. The covariance of knowledge/wisdom with the right practices can still be maintained if we (reasonably, I think) understand the *daimonion* to be a manifestation of knowledge/wisdom that Socrates does not have himself – *inside*, that is. Instead, when Socrates acts on the basis of a daimonic alarm, he receives divine guidance that allows him to avoid the errors he would otherwise have made. Socrates' discussion with Cleinias in the *Euthydemus* is presumably restricted to what we can expect from individuals insofar as the entire control over whatever they do comes from whatever they can muster from the inside.

Even so, we might wonder which of the two aspects really carries the most weight, for Socrates – inside or outside. Indications of an answer are not difficult to find. The discussion in the *Euthydemus* within which we find the exchange just quoted begins with the assertion, taken by all parties as being simply obvious, that everyone wishes to do well (*eu prattein*; 278e3). During the course of the rest of the argument, "doing well" is treated as being equivalent to "being happy" (see *eudaimonein kai eu prattein* at 280b6). The argument then turns to the question of how to do well, and considers that it is perhaps through having good things (279a2–3). After considering what such good things might be, Socrates gets Cleinias to see that, in fact, the only good thing that anyone really needs is wisdom, since wisdom is what makes people succeed (280a6–8). But Socrates then goes on to say that it is not anyway the actual *possession* of good things that matters, since there would be no advantage to simply possessing good things without using them (280b8–d7). So "doing well" and "being happy," according to Socrates, comes not just from the possession of something of value, but from *doing* what actually possessing that valuable thing allows the agent *to do*.[16]

This emphasis on activity, then, allows us to recalibrate upwards our assessment of just how well Socrates takes himself to have done in his apprenticeship in virtue. He remains steadfastly modest about what he has on the *inside* with respect to the virtue, but has positive things to say about what he manages on the *outside* – that is, with respect to how well he has actually done in the activities associated with the operation of the craft. Since the latter – the outer activities rather than the inner condition – are what bring real advantage, we are now in a position to regard Socrates as doing rather well, as opposed to someone who has, as Irwin put it, not even *begun*. That is not to say, again, that he could not wish – or even long – for better,

---

[16] I will discuss this feature of the argument in greater detail in Chapter 5.

both on the inside and the outside. But neither should we suppose that the best Socrates could say for himself, by way of "doing well" or "being happy," is that he remains, as Russell Jones has put it, "short of minimally happy" (2013a: 83), unless, of course, we think that someone who actually manages never to wrong anyone continues to fall short of "doing minimally well."[17]

But at this point, we should perhaps remind ourselves that Socrates also believes that people who are too deficient on the inside should by all means avoid even trying to accomplish anything on the outside.

> [Socrates speaking] Would a man with no sense profit more if he possessed and did much or if he possessed and did little? Look at it this way: if he did less, would he not make fewer mistakes; and if he made fewer mistakes, would he not do less badly, and if he did less badly would he not be less miserable? (*Euthydemus* 281b6–c3)

We might be tempted to take this passage together with Socrates' own epistemic modesty to show that he regards himself as doing well only insofar as he attempts to do as little as he possibly can and would actually assess his own achievements as amounting at best to his being less miserable than he would otherwise have been. This conclusion, however, would be an error, and again, the improvability of virtue as a craft allows us to understand better that Socrates is here talking about an extreme that seems to be a theoretical possibility only. Learning crafts takes practice, and when we find Socrates actually exhorting those with whom he speaks, his actual advice is inevitably the same as he gives to Cleinias: "every man should prepare himself by every means to become as wise as possible" (*Euthydemus* 282a5–6; see also *Apology* 39d8). We should all of us, always, seek to practice virtue, so that we might become more adept at it. The kind of case Socrates seems to have in mind, where someone would be better off not even attempting to practice virtue, does not ever seem actually to apply to any of the interlocutors with whom Socrates speaks in Plato's dialogues. Not even Callicles, who seems to be about as far from virtue as any of them,[18] is told that he would do better not even to *try* to act virtuously.

2.5 How Socrates Performs the Craft of Politics

It might now occur to us to ask how or in what ways Socrates thinks he performs as an apprentice political craftsman. Recall that he has already

---

[17] I discuss my disagreement with Jones on this point in greater detail in Chapter 6.
[18] Another who seems at very great risk would no doubt be Thrasymachus. But I have elsewhere argued that Socrates' interactions with this interlocutor also invite optimism – see Hoesly and Smith 2013.

described the political craft as having two distinct parts, which he terms legislation and justice. The legislative part corresponds to gymnastics, a subcraft of body-care, inasmuch as both of these subcrafts aim at creating the best "health" of their objects, soul and body, respectively. Both body-care and soul-care also have a subcraft that aims at correction – medicine for the body and justice for the soul. Note that even if Socrates only manages to engage in one of the two parts of soul-care, he will at least to that extent qualify as having taken up the true political craft. But I think we can see that in fact Socrates has taken up both of the subcrafts of politics.

On the legislation side, we immediately confront a problem: in the *Apology*, Socrates proclaims that he has actually avoided engaging in politics in the way we would ordinarily expect from someone seeking to improve his political skill (*Apology* 23b7–c1, 31d4–32a3; see also 32e–33a4, quoted later). But there is, even so, a way to understand his avoidance of the normal kinds of political engagement that is consistent with his making a serious effort to work hard as an apprentice at the political craft. After all, he understands his *daimonion* to have opposed any attempt to engage in normal political activity, on the ground, as he puts it, that "a man who really fights for justice must lead a private, not a public life, if he is to survive for even a short time" (*Apology* 32a1–3). It follows that Socrates believes that normal political activity actually provides a very poor environment in which to practice the true craft of politics, which, in aiming at what is best, would certainly require a serious apprentice always to "fight for justice." So, Socrates' abstention from normal political activity, at least as he understands what that involves, is not at all in conflict with his apprenticeship in the true political craft.

Legislation seems to be the part of the political craft in which one seeks to exhort, guide, and support others in the pursuit of what is best. Although it seems he does not do this sort of thing in the customary political venues, we do find Socrates characterizing his own activities in a way that seems to indicate that he does make regular efforts to promote what is best. In the *Apology*, for example, he claims to his jurors that "I was always concerned with you, approaching each one of you like a father or an elder brother to persuade you to care for virtue" (31b3–5). And even if it is true that Socrates has avoided most political activity of the ordinary sort, he did serve when his name was selected by lot among other members of his tribe to serve on the Boule, and actually did "fight for justice" when people were demanding a mass trial of the Arginusae generals, which Socrates opposed as illegal. As he recalls the event, he was the only one on the presiding committee who held out against the illegal procedure, running a great risk by doing so (*Apology* 32b1–c2). The fact that Socrates was the only one who stood for justice on that day lends at least some small support for his claim to Callicles that he is the *only* one among his contemporaries who has taken up the true political craft. At least on that day, he was alone in doing what the political craft would prescribe. He also recalls disobeying The Thirty when they ordered him to bring in Leon of Salamis for execution – an affair he describes as indicative of The Thirty's habit of trying to "implicate as many as possible in their guilt" (*Apology* 32c3–8). Although he presumably had no hope of preventing such an offense against justice, Socrates did act in such a way as not to allow himself to become implicated in it. In these events, accordingly, and in a number of other places in which he indicates how he has lived his life and what has mattered most to him, we do seem to find Socrates aligned well with what he takes the true craft of politics to require:

> Do you think I would have survived all these years if I were engaged in public affairs and, acting as a good man must, came to the aid of justice and considered this the most important thing? Far from it, gentlemen of the jury, nor would any other man. Throughout my life, in any public activity I may have engaged in, I am the same man as I am in private life. I have never come to an agreement with anyone to act unjustly. (*Apology* 32e2–33a4)

Socrates' activities in the part of politics he calls "justice" – where correction is the aim – are easier to see, since they appear on virtually every page of Plato's early dialogues. Here is not the place to mount a full interpretation of the Socratic *elenchos*, but it will be worthwhile at least to make a small attempt to counter one understanding of the so-called Socratic method that would make it only a fairly thin and poor example of the true craft of politics. Scholars interested in the *elenchos* have generally divided into two distinct camps. "Constructivists" have argued that Socrates supposes he actually does some positive philosophical work through elenctic argumentation, and thinks he can make progress in trying to figure out the topics in which he engages his interlocutors. "Anticonstructivists," on the contrary, have argued that all Socrates ever sought to accomplish with his elenctic arguments was to refute his interlocutors, revealing their pretense to wisdom.[19] The literature on this topic has focused almost entirely on the logical and epistemic features of Socratic argumentation – that is, on which inferences can and cannot be made from its premises or conclusions and on what sorts of evidential weight such

[19] For a full review of the recent literature on the topic of the "Socratic method," see Wolfsdorf 2013.

arguments can generate or sustain. Certainly, Socrates is not uninterested in such matters, but we would do well to notice that it is not primarily in logical or epistemic terms that he describes his own activities. He does, of course, acknowledge that when he finds someone who thinks he is wise, but is not, Socrates will "come to the assistance of the god and show him that he is not wise" (*Apology* 23b6–7). We should pause to consider why Socrates would think the god has any investment in such a practice. Is it just that the god is offended, for example, by *non sequitur*? Why, in other words, is the god so concerned with human epistemic fallibility? I think Socrates reveals his own view of the matter when he more broadly characterizes what he does:

> For I go around doing nothing but persuading both young and old among you not to care for your body or your wealth in preference to or as strongly as for the best possible state of your soul. (*Apology* 30a7–b2)

The god is concerned with human epistemic failure because the god understands that the kinds of failure Socrates can call our attention to are the kinds that tend to make us care for and dedicate ourselves to the wrong sorts of things, rather than the right sorts of things. This, then, is why Socrates says:

> I was attached to this city by the god – though it seems a ridiculous thing to say – as upon a great and noble horse which was somewhat sluggish because of its size and needed to be stirred up by a kind of gadfly. It is to fulfill some such function that I believe the god has placed me in the city. I never cease to rouse each and every one of you, to persuade and reproach you all day long and everywhere I find myself in your company. (*Apology* 30e2–31a2)

For Socrates, it seems the most important aspect of what he does with his fellow Athenians – while it may have logical and epistemic aspects – is to "persuade and reproach," and thus to engage in both parts of the true craft of politics.

2.6   Summary and Conclusion

In this chapter, I have argued that when Socrates described himself as having taken up the true craft of politics, we should believe him. I have tried to give several indications that the claims he makes in this announcement to Callicles are entirely consonant with other things we can find out about Socrates in the ways he is portrayed and in the things he does and says in Plato's (other) early dialogues. For Socrates, taking up the true craft of politics is the same thing as attempting to become as wise as possible. It is not clear just how wise Socrates thinks mere human beings can ever become. His own case is one of devotion to that effort, and yet he seems to regard himself as still falling far short, at least relative to the god, who he says is "really wise" (*Apology* 23a5–6). But he is one who has taken up the true political craft, and he is also one who thinks the rest of us can and should do the same. Even if we never outgrow apprenticeship, it seems there is a great deal we can accomplish, in terms of doing well, if we put in the effort. Socrates had help from his *daimonion*, but lest those of us who are not so blessed give way to despair, we might also remember that "the affairs [of a good man] are not neglected by the gods" (*Apology* 41d2–3). It is plain that Socrates regards himself as such a man, but by telling the jurors who voted in his favor that they "too should be of good hope as regards death" (41c7–8), he seems ready to include others in that category. In brief: were anyone among us to join Socrates in taking up the true craft of politics, by seeking to "become as wise as possible," we may also hope to become good, even if we can never surmount apprenticeship in the craft of virtue. That may not be as good as it gets; but it is, perhaps, good enough for us to be at least minimally happy. The case for that conclusion, however, will require a closer look at what Socrates has to say about the connections between knowledge, virtue, and happiness. In the following chapters, I hope to complete the case for claiming that Socrates thinks that self-improvement can actually bring positive happiness.

CHAPTER 3

Socratic Motivational Intellectualism

3.1 Introduction

In the previous two chapters, I have discussed a few puzzles concerning Socrates' epistemology, which, I have claimed, takes the most important kind of knowledge to be more like craft, skill, or expertise. But, as I will try to show in this chapter, Socratic epistemology is not entirely distinct and separable from his views in the area of ethics and moral psychology, because the way in which Socrates thinks about these subjects is what scholars call an "intellectualist" conception. "Socratic intellectualism" is actually a term applied to Socrates' conception of virtue, and it is this intellectualist conception of virtue I have been discussing in the previous two chapters. Socrates is said to have been a "virtue intellectualist" because he believed that virtue is in some sense constituted by knowledge. Accordingly, Socratic epistemology and virtue theory must be understood together. But it turns out that the same kind of deep connection may be found between Socrates' epistemology and his views about ethics and motivation. Socrates is a "motivational intellectualist" because he is convinced that all human actions reflect what agents *believe* is best for them, among the available options recognized by the agents at the time of acting. Accordingly, it follows that, as Terry Penner has put it, "for Socrates, when people act badly or viciously or even just out of moral weakness, that will be merely a result of intellectual mistake."[1] The reason this conception of motivation is inextricably linked to Socratic epistemology is thus obvious: the motivation for S to do X requires that S *believes* that doing X will be the best thing for S to do, among the options that are available and salient to S at the time of action. In order to appreciate and understand Socratic ethics and epistemology – the main focus of this book – we must be clear

---

[1] Penner 2000: 165.

about how Socrates thinks that cognition and motivation are connected. This, then, will be my focus in this chapter.

I will be going into many details of Socrates' views about motivation in this chapter, and it may not always be obvious how each piece of this fairly complicated puzzle fits with my main focus in this book, which is about how the Socratic views of knowledge, virtue, and happiness are all improvable. That aspect of my thesis, however, is really just the foundation of what I am claiming is actually at the core of Socrates' project, which is for all of us to devote ourselves to "becoming as wise as possible," as I have quoted him[2] as insisting (*Euthydemus* 282a6). I have called attention to the fact that this project entails that we have the ability to improve not just our epistemic conditions but thereby also our *ethical* conditions. But how are we supposed to do this? The beginning of an answer to this question will be to attend closely to the ways in which epistemology and ethics are interconnected, but beyond that, we can begin to understand the project of self-improvement even better by coming to recognize and learning how better to control the effects of the psychological elements within us that impede our progress. I will try to make this explicit as I go along, but I also ask for some assistance from my readers: when we find Socrates telling us something about human psychology, the importance of this issue for the focus of this book will be how our psychologies are both cognitively and conatively *improvable*.

3.2 Socratic Pragmatism

In a revealing passage of Plato's *Gorgias*, we may see one of Socrates' central ethical theses:

SOCRATES: Now didn't we agree that we want, not those things that we do for the sake of something, but that thing for the sake of which we do them?
POLUS: Yes, very much so.
SOCRATES: Hence, we don't simply want to slaughter people, or exile them from their cities and confiscate their property as such; we want to do these things if they are beneficial, but if they are harmful we don't. For we want the things that are good, as you agree, and we don't want those that are neither good nor bad, nor those that are bad. (*Gorgias* 468b8–c7)

It is plain in the context that Socrates and Polus have in mind a quite narrow conception of what will count as the right kind of benefit – it is benefit to the *agent* they claim we all want. Polus, certainly, would never

---

[2] In Sections 1.6 and 2.4.

agree that we want only benefit to *someone* to be achieved, even if it is at the price of self-sacrifice. I call this view "pragmatism," because it makes clear that Socrates and Polus do not see any distinction between what is good and what is in the interest of the agent – the real interest, that is, and not merely some subjective sense of interest the agent may have (and which, as we will see, Socrates thinks may often be mistaken). Accordingly, we can attribute to Socrates (and for that matter, most of his interlocutors in Plato's dialogues) the following principle:

> X is good = X is conducive to securing or sustaining what is in the agent's real interest.

Such a principle seems to fit rather poorly with any theory of ethics that takes doing good to involve at least some occasional degree of self-sacrifice. But the apparent gap between pragmatism and what we might regard as ethically appropriate will close, at least to a degree, if we attend to other basic aspects of the Socratic view.

3.3   Eudaimonism

So what does Socrates regard as being in our interest? In what does our interest consist? Central to the ethics we find in Plato's early dialogues is a commitment to what is generally called "eudaimonism." Briefly, eudaimonism is the view that ethics is the study of how best to live, where the measure of success is "*eudaimonia*," which is most often but potentially misleadingly translated as "happiness." The main problem with translating "*eudaimonia*" as "happiness" is that we tend to regard the latter term to refer to a certain kind of subjective condition. It was much more common for the Greeks, and for Plato's Socrates specifically, to regard *eudaimonia* as referring to an objective condition (which, however, would presumably entail or at least typically be associated with some positive subjective condition as well). The scholarly world has generally united in counting "human flourishing" as a more exact translation, but "happiness" will do just as well as long as we bear in mind that we do not mean the term to be taken in the primarily subjective way. Someone who has everything they desire and is giddy with their "success," but whose desires are ultimately unhealthy or self-defeating, would not count, accordingly, as *eudaimôn* (the adjective).

In his conversations in Plato's dialogues, Socrates and his interlocutors all seem ready to agree that whatever *eudaimonia* might be, it may be assumed that to be *eudaimôn* is the same thing as to "do well" (*eu prattein*).

Some of Socrates' interlocutors seem to be committed to some version of hedonism, such that *eudaimonia* and *eu prattein* are to be understood in terms of the achievement, frequency, or sustenance of pleasure. In some dialogues, Socrates seems ready to accept this position himself, at least for the sake of his arguments (e.g. the *Protagoras*); in others (e.g. the *Gorgias*), Socrates argues against at least some version of hedonism. So it is perhaps best for now not to put too fine of an interpretation on what Socrates himself might have supposed *eudaimonia* to consist in. But whatever it is, one who achieved such a condition would thus have achieved at least some relative level of *success* in one's life.

On the other hand, Socrates is at least clear in saying that he did not believe that true life success could be measured in terms of wealth, political power, or social standing (so see *Apology* 29d7–e2). Rather, Socrates generally seems to argue for or from a eudaimonist position that has both a psychological and an ethical basis. A passage in Plato's *Euthydemus* gives the psychological aspect:

> [Socrates speaking] "Do all human beings wish to do well? . . . I suppose it is stupid even to raise such a question, since there could hardly be anyone who did not wish to do well."
> "No, there is no such person," said Cleinias. (*Euthydemus* 278e2–279a1[3])

Here, then, is a universal psychological fact about all human beings: we all wish to do well, to be happy.[4] Ethics, then, is the intellectual project of trying to figure out and to achieve this sort of success in our lives – to do well and be happy. Accordingly, we may attribute to Socrates what I have elsewhere[5] termed the "principle of eudaimonism":

> X is good = X is conducive to *eudaimonia*.[6]

It follows (by substitution) that "*eudaimonia*" is a name for our real interest and what all human action intends to pursue or achieve. Because, moreover, "what is in our real interest" and "*eudaimonia*" both refer to some *objective* condition, it will be a matter of objective fact that some

---

[3] Translation slightly modified, substituting "human beings" for "men" since the Greek word does not require a gender identification. I also spell the name "Cleinias" since the Greek name contains an epsilon.

[4] This explains why Socrates also holds that everyone actually desires the good. Since whatever is good is whatever conduces to happiness and we all desire happiness, we all desire the good.

[5] In Brickhouse and Smith 1994; the exact wording of the principle is slightly modified here.

[6] It might be supposed that this poses a problem for the claim that *eudaimonia* is good. But obviously, *eudaimonia* is conducive to itself (trivially), and so it follows from this definition that *eudaimonia* itself is obviously good.

actions are really good, really in our interest, while others are not – independently of what the agent may *suppose* is good or in their interest. Ethics, then, is the pursuit of whatever may be in our real interest. So in terms of what I have called the core of Socrates' philosophical project, improving ourselves, becoming *better* means that we become more skilled in doing and achieving what is really in our interest.

3.4   Egoism?

Socratic eudaimonism is sometimes criticized as being "egoistic," and is by some regarded as ethically flawed as a result.[7] Others have defended the Socratic view by claiming that Socrates really wasn't a eudaimonist after all.[8] I find these debates misplaced here. If, as we usually suppose, egoism is opposed to altruism, then it is as mistaken to call Socrates an egoist as it would be to call him an altruist, since he plainly does believe that we always seek to pursue what is beneficial to us, but he clearly both engages in and recommends that others engage in other-regarding behavior. Indeed, his recommendations that tie our most profound self-interest with other-regarding behavior are among the most striking of Socrates' ethical views.

At the heart of Socrates' prescriptions involving other-regarding behavior is the way he understands what it means actually to harm another person:

> [Socrates speaking] Do horses become better or worse when they are harmed?
> [Polemarchus] Worse.
> With respect to the virtue that makes dogs good or the one that makes horses good?
> The one that makes horses good.
> And when dogs are harmed, they become worse in the virtue that makes dogs good, not horses?
> Necessarily.
> Then won't we say the same about human beings, too, that when they are harmed they become worse in human virtue?
> Indeed.
> And isn't justice human virtue?
> Certainly. . . .

---

[7] "Here desire for happiness is strictly self-referential: it is the agent's desire for his own happiness and that of no one else. This is so deep-seated an assumption that it is simply taken for granted: no argument is ever given for it in the Platonic corpus" (Vlastos 1991: 203, n. 14).

[8] Recent versions of such a denial may be found in Ahbel-Rappe 2010; Morrison 2003; and White 2002.

[C]an those who are good make people bad through virtue?
They cannot.
... And a just person is good?
Indeed.
Then, Polemarchus, it isn't the function of a just person to harm a friend or anyone else, rather it is the function of his opposite, an unjust person?
In my view, that's completely true, Socrates. (*Republic* I.335b6–e1)

Socrates' view, then, is that it is the proper function of a just person to benefit others and never to harm them, which means to make them worse *as human beings*. But we might wonder if there might not be circumstances in which a self-interested agent might rightly suppose that it was in the agent's interest to harm another person – that is, to act unjustly. Socrates has an answer to this question, too.

[Socrates speaking] Come now, do you accuse me here of corrupting the young and making them worse deliberately or involuntarily?
[Meletus] Deliberately.
What follows, Meletus? Are you so much wiser at your age than I am at mine that you understand that wicked people always do some harm to their closest neighbors while good people do them good, but I have reached such a pitch of ignorance that I do not recognize this, namely, that if I make one of my associates wicked I run the risk of being harmed by him so that I do such a great evil voluntarily, as you say? I do not believe you, Meletus, and I do not think anyone else will. (*Apology* 25d6–e6[9])

It is plain that Socrates thinks that agents have a distinct *pragmatic* interest in not harming but only benefiting those around them. If one harms another, one can reasonably expect to be harmed by them in return; if one benefits another, one can reasonably expect to be benefited in return.

But it is not just this argument from probability that Socrates has to offer to those who might contemplate harming others, as if doing so might in some cases be profitable. He also thinks that doing wrong – quite apart from its effect on the victim of the wrongdoing – also has the effect of damaging (and again, according to Socratic pragmatism, thus *wronging*) the agent themselves, and in the worst possible way:

SOCRATES: Come now, if we ruin that which is improved by health and corrupted by disease by not following the opinions of those who know, is life worth living for us when that is ruined? And that is the body, is it not?
CRITO: Yes.

---

[9] Translation slightly modified: "voluntarily" is substituted for "willingly."

SOCRATES: And is life worth living with a body that is corrupted and in bad
    condition?
CRITO: In no way.
SOCRATES: And is life worth living for us with that part of us corrupted that unjust
    action harms and just action benefits? Or do we think that part of us,
    whatever it is, that is concerned with justice and injustice, is inferior to
    the body?
CRITO: Not at all.
SOCRATES: Is it more valuable?
CRITO: Much more. (*Crito* 47d8–48a4)

It is precisely because Socrates believes that wrongdoing damages the
very core of who we are – damages our *soul* – that he famously advises Polus
that if he or anyone else he cares about is acting unjustly, "he should go to
the judge as if he were going to a doctor, anxious that the disease of
injustice shouldn't be protracted and cause his soul to fester incurably"
(*Gorgias* 480a6–b2). And this same reason explains why he tells Callicles,
later in the same work, that "injustice is the worst thing there is for the
person committing it" (*Gorgias* 509b1–3).

Socrates' combination of pragmatism and regard for the welfare of
others is obviously coherent, as long as he also believed, as Socrates very
obviously did, that acting in ways that are harmful to others is not in an
agent's interest, and acting in ways that are beneficial to others is in the
agent's interest. Anyone who has ever had a friend or a loved family
member plainly already knows this much! But as we have seen, Socrates
also extends his prohibition against harming others and his prescription to
benefit them much more broadly – indeed, he universalizes both mandates.
Accordingly, it is misleading, at best, to brand Socratic ethics as either
"egoist" or "altruist." Acting out of interest for others, in the Socratic view,
is also acting in a way that promotes our own self-interest, properly
conceived.

3.5 Making Motivational Intellectualism Explicit

Socrates' expressions of motivational intellectualism are not frequent, but
when he does get onto the subject in various dialogues, the view is explicitly
endorsed.[10] One example of such an endorsement comes in the *Gorgias*,

---

[10] Even so, some scholars refuse to attribute the view to Socrates. One recent example of such a refusal
appears to derive from the (correct) observation that Plato was *not* an intellectualist about motivation (the divided soul of the *Republic* and several other later dialogues makes this clear), and so
concludes that when Plato has Socrates seem to affirm the view, the mode of affirmation is merely

where Socrates clearly distinguishes between doing what one thinks is best and doing what one wants:

SOCRATES: Since we're in agreement about that then, if a person who's a tyrant or an orator puts someone to death or exiles him or confiscates his property because he supposes that doing so is better for himself when actually it's worse, this person, I take it, is doing what he sees fit, isn't he?

POLUS: Yes.

SOCRATES: And is he also doing what he wants, if these things are actually bad? Why don't you answer?

POLUS: All right, I don't think he's doing what he wants. (*Gorgias* 468d1–7)

Socrates' point is that everyone *always* does what they think is best for them; but even so, it doesn't follow that they always do what they *want*, since what they want is not what *seems* best, but what really *is* best for them.[11] This intellectualist view of motivation is why Socrates famously (or notoriously) denied the possibility of synchronic belief *akrasia*[12] – the view that at least sometimes people will act in ways that they *do not* believe is best for them, even at the time the action takes place (see *Gorgias* 509e5–7 and *Protagoras* 345d6–e6). Let us turn to this subject now, then.

3.6   The Denial of *Akrasia*

Most people think not only that the phenomenon of *akrasia* is possible; they also think that it is actually quite common. Ancient intuitions about this were no different. Here is what Aristotle had to say about the Socratic views:

Some say that if he has knowledge of how to act rightly, he cannot be akratic; for, as Socrates thought, it would be strange for a man to have knowledge and yet allow something else to rule him and drag him about

hypothetical (see Kamtekar 2017 for a presentation of this view). (Plato's) Socrates may be willing to change his beliefs, should they prove to be faulty, but that is no reason to think he remains neutral about the things he asserts and argues for. Moreover, it seems to me that Aristotle (for example, at *Nicomachean Ethics* VII.2.1145b21–34) seems entirely willing to attribute to Socrates the sort of motivational intellectualism I explore in this chapter. Those who wish to reject this attribution need to offer some plausible argument for why Plato's best student was persuaded of it. Kamtekar offers no such argument.

[11]   Some have supposed that Socrates offers a different view from this at *Meno* 77d7–78b2 – see Santas 1979: 188. I am persuaded, however, by the counterargument given in Penner and Rowe 1994, and so take the *Meno* to express the same view as Socrates gives here in the *Gorgias*.

[12]   This denial does not extend to diachronic belief *akrasia* – Socrates is aware that people can change their minds about what is best for them, and thus regret things they have done. See Penner 1990: 47. In the same article, Penner also shows that Socrates denied both synchronic and diachronic knowledge *akrasia*.

like a slave. For Socrates was entirely opposed to this view and held that there is no such thing as akrasia; for he thought that no one with the right belief does what is contrary to the best, but if a man does so, it is through ignorance. Now this argument obviously disagrees with what appears to be the case; and if a man acting by passion does so through ignorance, we should look into the manner in which this ignorance arises. For it is evident that an akratic man, before getting into a state of passion, does not think that he should do what he does when in passion. (Aristotle, *Nicomachean Ethics* VII.3.1145b22–31; trans. Apostle and Gerson 1991, modified)

We shall see that Aristotle is right to insist that blaming the putative akratic behavior on ignorance requires us to ask from whence such ignorance came. It is to this question that I now turn, in exploring the Socratic view.

3.7   Nonrational Desires

Until relatively recently, scholars have tended to portray Socratic motivational intellectualism as simply denying that nonrational factors[13] play any role at all in the explanation of human behavior. So, for example, we find Terence Irwin claiming that Socrates' conception of motivation "requires all desires to be rational and good-dependent; if A wants x, he wants it for its contribution to some good y, and ultimately to the final good, and if he ceases to believe that x contributes to the final good, he will cease to want x" (Irwin 1977: 78). Only in Plato's later works, we are told, are nonrational factors recognized as having some influence on human behavior. According to this view, only in later dialogues does Plato have Socrates recognize a role in motivation for nonrational desires.[14]

This view, however, does not do a good job of explaining the ways in which the kinds of psychological states that are allegedly ignored appear quite often in the texts – if they play no role in explaining human behavior, why does Socrates talk about them so often? Here are just a few examples.[15]

---

[13] By "nonrational factor," I mean to refer to any psychological process that does not have its origin in reason or reasoning, and may not be entirely responsive to persuasion by a rational process. In the literature on this topic, the kinds of processes that Socrates usually identifies as appetitive are "nonrational" in this sense. Scholarly debates about this issue concern whether such processes play any role in how human beings behave, or if they do, how that role is to be understood.

[14] Irwin counts the *Gorgias* as transitional between early and middle periods and finds the first appearance of nonrational desires in that dialogue (Irwin 1977: 128; see also Irwin 1995: 75–76). See also Cooper 1999; Frede 1992: xxix–xxx; Kahn 1996: 227; McTighe 1984; Nehamas 1999: 27–58; Reeve 1988: 134–135; Rowe 2003, 2006, 2007; Santas 1979: 183–194; Taylor 2000: 62–63; and Wolfsdorf 2008: 33–59.

[15] Many of the following are also given in Brickhouse and Smith 2013; I list here other specific discussions of the relevant passages.

3.7.1 Anger

- *Apology* 21b1–23e3: the anger people have felt when he refutes them has led some of Socrates' "victims" to make various accusations against him.[16]
- *Apology* 34b6–d1: Socrates pleads with his jurors not to cast their votes in anger.[17]

3.7.2 Fear

- *Apology* 21e3: Socrates feels fear when he recognizes that he has become unpopular because of his "mission."
- *Apology* 29e3–30a2: Socrates will not desist from his philosophical "mission" out of a fear of death.[18]
- *Apology* 32b1–d4: Socrates has never done anything unjust out of fear.[19]
- *Crito* 46c5: the many would like to frighten Socrates and Crito with all kinds of threats.
- *Crito* 47b5 and 47d1–3: one should fear the blame of an expert, but not the many.

3.7.3 Shame

- *Apology* 29b7: Socrates strikingly claims to *know* that it is evil and shameful to disobey one's superiors.
- *Apology* 29d9: Socrates thinks his fellow Athenians should be ashamed to value other things more than virtue.
- *Apology* 31b8: the accusations against him are shameless.
- *Apology* 35a8: those who play to the emotions of jurors bring shame to Athens.

3.7.4 Erôs *and Appetitive Desires*

- *Charmides* 155d4, where Socrates describes himself as struggling for self-control as he suddenly burns with desire for the youthful Charmides.[20]

---

[16] Brickhouse and Smith 2010: 53–57.   [17] Brickhouse and Smith 2010: 60–61.
[18] Brickhouse and Smith 2010: 57–59; see also Sanderman 2004 and Woodruff 2000.
[19] Brickhouse and Smith 2010: 59–60.   [20] Brickhouse and Smith 2010: 52.

- *Charmides* 167e1–5, where Socrates draws a distinction between appetite (*epithumia*), which he says aims at pleasure, wish (*boulêsis*), which he says aims at what is good, and love (*erôs*), which he says aims at beauty.[21]
- *Lysis* 220e6–221b8, where Socrates explicitly argues that the appetites, such as hunger and thirst, and also *erôs*, can be both good or bad, but the experiences of these do not depend for their existence on both good and bad existing.[22]

3.7.5   Pleasures and Pains

- *Laches* 191e4–7, where Socrates says that pleasures, pains, appetites, and fears all provide opportunities for people to display courage.[23]
- *Protagoras* 352b3–c7, where Socrates claims that knowledge would prevent one from being "overcome" by anger, fear, or pleasure, because knowledge "conquers pleasure and everything else" (357c1–4).[24]

Irwin and others are, of course, right to notice that such phenomena are often mentioned in the *Gorgias*, as well – especially with respect to the effects of appetite for pleasure and aversion to pain (for example, at 491d10–e1, 493a3–4, 500d8–10, 505a6–10, 507b4–8, 521d8–e1, 525b1–c6). But if, as so many have supposed, Socrates recognizes no role at all in motivation for anything other than rational desires, why does he seem so often to refer to such factors in explaining how people act in the ways they do?

More recent work on the Socratic theory of motivation has at least recognized that Socrates does acknowledge at least the *existence* of nonrational factors. Even so, in several such accounts appetites and passions still do not play any active role in motivation. Here is a particularly good example of such a view:

> According to this theory, all desires to do something are rational desires, in that they always automatically adjust to the agent's beliefs about what is the best means to their ultimate end. If in the particular circumstances I come to believe that eating this pastry is the best means to my happiness in the circumstances, then in plugging this belief into the desire for *whatever is best in these circumstances*, my (rational) desire for whatever is best becomes the desire to eat this pastry. On the other hand, if I come to believe that it would be better to abstain, then once again my desire for what is best will become

---

[21] Devereux 1995: 400.   [22] Brickhouse and Smith 2010: 52.   [23] Devereux 1995: 388.
[24] Devereux 1995: 388.

the desire to abstain. Rational desires adjust to the agent's beliefs. In fact, on this view the *only* way to influence my conduct is to change my opinion as to what is best. (Penner 1992a: 128; Penner's italics)

Socrates can thus allow for the existence of such things as appetites and passions in Penner's understanding. Penner elsewhere claims that Socrates would countenance the existence of "mere hankerings, itches, or drives [that] cannot automatically result in action when put together with a belief" (Penner 1991: 201, n. 45; see also Penner 1990: 59–60 and Penner 1997: 124). In this interpretation, nonrational experiences count simply as sources of information.

> In my view, an appetite never plays a role that is more instrumental than any other piece of information that the intellect has used in order to determine what is best to do as motivated by the desire for the good. I hold that appetites are like sense impressions: they are phenomena that help us form judgments, but they do not interact with judgments that have already been formed. (Reshotko 2006: 86)

I have elsewhere compared this view of the appetites to a thought experiment about a disorder in which having an experience as of wearing a hat – when one is not actually wearing a hat – could lead one to realize that one was having a health crisis.[25] The point of the example is that there is nothing *conative* in having an experience as of wearing a hat. This is not the case with having experiences of appetites, aversions, or passions. The question thus becomes this: how could Socrates have recognized the conative force of appetites and passions, while still maintaining an intellectualist view about motivation?

3.8   Emotions and Appetites

Socrates treats the emotions differently from the way he conceives of more basic urges and aversions – what are generally called the appetites in the literature.

> A passage in the *Charmides* (167e1–5) seems to indicate that human beings experience different kinds of desire, which target different sorts of goals. These include appetite (*epithumia*), which aims at pleasure, wish (*boulêsis*), which aims at what is good, and love (*erôs*), which aims at what is beautiful. Each of these seems to have an aversive alternative, as well: we avoid pains, what is bad, and what is ugly. Our natural attractions and aversions, we

---

[25] Brickhouse and Smith 2012.

contend, are the grounds for a variety of non-rational beliefs: Insofar as
something seems or promises to be pleasurable, beneficial, or beautiful, the
agent will be naturally inclined to believe it to be something good; and
insofar as something seems to be painful, detrimental, or ugly, the agent will
be naturally inclined to believe it to be something bad. Unless the natural
inclination to believe in such cases is mitigated or defeated by some other
(for example, rational) belief-forming process, one will form beliefs about
goods and evils accordingly. The beliefs created by these natural attractions
and aversions, because they derive from non-rational processes, are veridically unreliable, but are also to some degree (by their nature as non-rational)
resistant to rational persuasion and other belief-forming processes.
(Brickhouse and Smith 2015: 14–15)

This view of how the appetites have both conative force, while also
serving as an etiological source of belief, was actually first argued by Daniel
T. Devereux (1995), who characterized the appetites as having the natural
power to incline us to believe that their objects are valuable. Devereux
concluded that this is why Socrates thought that knowledge of what is
called the "measuring craft" in the *Protagoras* would be our salvation in life
(356d7–e1): it is because mere opinions *can* but knowledge *cannot* be
"dragged about like a slave" (*Protagoras* 352c1–2).

According to this view, knowledge can always be relied upon to guarantee the correct action in the situation. True or correct belief, on the other
hand, is unstable – vulnerable to temporary displacement or suppression
owing to the proximity of pleasure, pain, or fear. (Devereux 1995:
393–394)

Socrates certainly does make knowledge invulnerable to the ways in
which nonrational impulses can otherwise influence our cognitive processes, but the earlier characterization of the Socratic view seems to leave
Socrates and anyone else who lacked the knowledge of the "measuring
craft" forever at risk of error from the cognitive effects of appetitive urges.
Evidence from the *Gorgias*, however, points to a way in which even those
without knowledge might hope for some immunization against cognitive
failure due to appetite.

So this is how I set down the matter and say that it is true. And if it is true,
then a person who wants to be happy must evidently pursue and practice
self-control. Each of us must flee away from lack of correction (*akolasian*) as
quickly as his feet will carry him, and must above all make sure that he has
no need of being corrected, but if he does have that need, either he himself
or anyone in his house, either a private citizen or a whole city, he must pay
his due and be corrected (*dikên epiteon kai kolasteon*), if he is to be happy ...

he must not allow his appetites (*epithumiai*) to be uncorrected or to undertake to fill them up. (*Gorgias* 507c8–e3[26])

Having one's appetites under control is thus a necessary precondition to being virtuous at all. The idea seems to be that the more appetites are indulged without constraint by more reliable ways of discerning how we should behave, the more they tend to take control over us. The way in which appetites generate beliefs about what is best for us is defeasible: those of us who do not allow our appetites to become unruly and out of control will be able to judge (again, using more reliable, rational methods of deciding) when an appetite is inclining us to do what we would be better off not doing. By taking care not to indulge our appetites beyond our basic needs, and by continuing to exercise our more reliable belief-forming processes in ways that allow us to continue to recognize their greater reliability as guides for what we should and shouldn't do, we keep our appetites in a controlled condition.

With this kind of self-monitoring in mind, Socrates could well suppose that finding the way to keep the appetites in a controlled condition would be a good first step on the path to acquiring the "craft of measurement." In other words, one who was in a position to manage one's appetites would already be better off, with respect to measurement, than one who lacked the capacity for such management, or didn't bother even attempting it. So here, too, one finds reason to suppose that Socrates recognized some degree of improvability in the acquisition of expertise. The better we become at managing our nonrational impulses (what contemporary psychologists call "impulse control"), the better we will be at pursuing what is really in our best interest. This one improvement in self-knowledge will promote improvements in achieving what we really want in life.

3.9 Persuasion

Different accounts of Socratic motivational intellectualism have also, not surprisingly, offered different pictures of how persuasion actually works. Most interpreters have, as I said earlier, required the entire process to be rational.

> There is in Plato's early dialogues . . . a certain "intellectualism" that is quite foreign to the middle and later dialogues . . . . Indeed, that intellectualism,

---

[26] Translation slightly modified: "corrected" and "correction" replace "disciplined" and "discipline," since the sense of the Greek here refers to corrective punishment.

with its implication that *only philosophical dialogue* can improve one's fellow citizens, is decisively rejected by Plato in the parts of the soul doctrine on the *Republic*. . . . For Socrates, when people act badly or viciously or even just out of moral weakness, that will be merely a result of intellectual mistake. (Penner 2000: 164–165; his emphasis)[27]

As an intellectualist, Socrates is plainly committed to the view that the only way to get someone to change their behavior is to change what they believe about what is best for them when they might behave in the relevant way. For those who regard Socratic moral psychology as entirely rational, it follows that the only way to persuade someone to change their ways is through "philosophical dialogue." But if there is a cognitive process – that is, a belief-producing process – that has its etiological origins in a nonrational process, then we should be able to find evidence that Socrates thinks that acting on an agent in a way that disturbs or interferes with that nonrational process might affect the way in which the agent comes to have the beliefs on the basis of which they act in the relevant way. In fact, there is such evidence.

3.10 Punishment

In Chapter 2, I discussed how Socrates compares the political craft, which he conceives as the craft of care for the soul, to the craft of care for the body (464b3–8). Both, Socrates says, are composed of two analogous subcrafts: for the body, there are gymnastics, which attends to putting the body in the best possible condition, and medicine, which corrects things in the body when they have gone wrong; for the soul, there are legislation, which attempts to instill the good condition of the soul, and justice, the analog to medicine, which corrects things that have gone wrong in the soul (*Gorgias* 464b3–c2). In both cases – body and soul – the aim is to have "organization (*taxis*) and order (*kosmos*)" (*Gorgias* 504b2–d3). Gymnastics and legislation serve to create and sustain that order in body and soul, respectively; medicine and justice attempt to restore such organization and order when it has been damaged or lost. Punishment, accordingly, is an instrument of justice. This is why, despite Polus' incredulity, Socrates insists that the only good use of oratory would be to get some wrongdoer as quickly as possible to

> go of his own freewill where he may soonest pay the penalty, to the judge as if to his doctor, with the earnest intent that the disease of his injustice shall

---

[27] See also Rowe 2006: 166 and Taylor 2000: 63 for other explicit affirmations of this approach.

not become chronic and cause a deep incurable ulcer in his soul . . . . If his crimes have deserved a flogging, he must submit to the rod; if fetters, to their grip; if a fine, to its payment; if banishment, to be banished; or if death, to die. (*Gorgias* 480a6–d3: trans. Lamb 1925)

Plato's Socrates, it seems, thinks that punishments of these familiar kinds can have the effects of restoring justice to a soul that has lost it, or at least to improving the condition of a soul that has been damaged by wrongdoing. What is not yet clear, however, is just how such things as whipping or imprisonment are supposed to do this.

Some scholars, indeed, have insisted that Plato's Socrates should not be supposed to believe any of this, and instead supposed that the customary forms of punishment could play no role at all in the correction of wrongdoers.[28] The ground always given for such doubts is that Plato's Socrates is a motivational intellectualist – he supposed that one's actions always follow from what one believe is best for one at the time of action. Recall Penner's claim that "on this view the *only* way to influence my conduct is to change my opinion as to what is best" (Penner 1992a: 128; Penner's italics). Punishment, however, seems poorly equipped to do this. How could punishment induce the appropriate cognitive change that is required by Socratic motivational intellectualism? To get a better picture of how this might work, however, we will do well to survey a few more pertinent passages in Plato.

One such passage appears in the *Apology*, where Socrates scolds Meletus in a way that does not seem to square with what he says about wrongdoing elsewhere:

> If I corrupt them [sc. the youth] involuntarily (*akôn*), the law does not require you to bring people to court for such involuntary wrongdoings, but to get hold of them privately to instruct them and exhort them. For clearly, if I learn better, I shall cease to do what I am doing involuntarily. You, however, have avoided my company and were unwilling to instruct me, but you bring me here, where the law requires one to bring those who are in need of punishment, not of instruction. (*Apology* 26a2–8[29])

---

[28] Christopher Rowe, for example, claims that "'punishment,' or *kolazein*, for Socrates, is not a matter for the courts but for *philosophical dialectic*" (Rowe 2007: 34). Rowe does notice that Socrates contrasts "*nouthetein*" (admonishment) with "*kolazein*" (punishment) at *Apology* 26a1–8 (Rowe 2007: 32), but even so insists that Socrates identifies these in the *Gorgias*. "My conclusion is that the Socrates of the *Gorgias* does not endorse flogging, imprisonment, or any other vulgar kind of punishment" (Rowe 2007: 36). Socrates does not really mean what he says to Polus and Callicles about punishment, but rather, "Socrates mounts his argument in the terms he does . . . because they are the terms his opponents, or interlocutors, can readily understand" (Rowe 2007: 34). Another example of this view may be found in Penner 2018.

[29] Translation modified. The Grube translation in Cooper 1997 has "unwilling" where I have "involuntary."

Socrates' words here are puzzling because it is clear that he elsewhere argues that all wrongdoing is involuntary.[30] If so, then it would appear to be his actual view that the role of punishment that he says belongs to the legal system is entirely pointless.[31] But a distinction might be in order here: we can (and I believe Socrates did) make a distinction between the involuntariness of doing things that are ultimately contrary to one's own interest, on the one hand, and the ways in which people might voluntarily intend and enact harm to others, on the other. By doing the latter (voluntarily harming others), one will also harm oneself. In that way, the wrongdoing will be involuntary in the self-interested sense, but also voluntary in other-regarding terms.[32]

But even if we understand the passage in this way, it is still unclear just how punishment (presumably applied appropriately when someone voluntarily wrongs another) will have the appropriate cognitive effects – changing the beliefs (or at least motivating such change) in wrongdoers with respect to how they should behave. To begin to see how this might work, we should go back to the *Gorgias*. In the closing myth, Socrates talks about what happens to souls in the afterlife. Of particular interest here is what he says about punishment there:

> It is appropriate for everyone who is subject to punishment rightly inflicted by another either to become better and profit from it, or else to be made an example for others, so that when they see him suffering whatever it is he suffers, they may be afraid and become better. Those who are benefited, who are made to pay their due by gods and men, are the ones whose errors are curable; even so their benefit comes to them, both here and in Hades, by way of pain and suffering, for there is no other possible way to get rid of injustice. From among those who have committed the ultimate wrongs and who because of such crimes have become incurable come the ones who are made examples of. These persons themselves no longer derive any profit from their punishment, because they're incurable. Others, however, do profit from it when they see them undergoing for all time the most grievous, intensely painful and frightening sufferings for their errors, simply strung up there in the prison in Hades as examples, visible warnings to the unjust who are ever arriving. (*Gorgias* 525b1–c8)

---

[30] See *Gorgias* 468b8–c7, where Socrates argues that wrongdoers do not do what they want; *Meno* 77d7–e4, where he argues that no one wants what is bad; and *Protagoras* 345d6–e4, where Socrates (implausibly) attributes his own view of the matter to Simonides: "anyone who does anything wrong or bad does so involuntarily" (345e3–4). For discussions, see Segvic 2000; Brickhouse and Smith 2010: ch. 2.

[31] See note 28.

[32] For a detailed defense of this understanding of the passage, see Brickhouse and Smith 2018. See also Kamtekar 2017: 72.

There is a lot going on here. First, in this picture, not even the gods can correct some damaged souls – the ones that Socrates calls the incurables. Their suffering can only serve to benefit others. But the benefit the others will receive derives from the "fearful sufferings" that are patently the "greatest" and "sharpest." Bearing witness to such sufferings, Socrates says, is a process that makes them "in fear amend themselves."

So let us start here. How does making someone afraid help them to become better? Many scholars, seeing these lines, have concluded that by the time he wrote this part of the *Gorgias*, Plato had already given up on the motivational intellectualism that he had (allegedly earlier) associated with Socrates.[33] But there is at least one good reason to reject this reaction.[34] In two other dialogues, Socrates indicates that he is a cognitivist about fear: at *Protagoras* 358d6–7 and at *Laches* 198b8–9 Socrates characterizes fear as the expectation (*prosdokian*) of something bad. But if fear is this cognitive condition, as Socrates seems to hold, then the witnessing of the great sufferings of the incurables in Hades actually does produce a belief that could induce a change of behavior: the fearful witnesses, instead of perhaps thinking that wrongdoing will promote their own welfare, will now induce in them the expectation of something to which they are strongly averse. They will thus change their belief about what is in their best interest in the way required by Socratic motivational intellectualism.

But even this explanation is not yet enough, for it doesn't even begin to explain how Socrates could both believe that all actions reflect the agent's belief about what is best for the agent at the time of action and maintain that "there is no other possible way to get rid of injustice" than through "pain and suffering." On the contrary, the former (intellectualist) view seems to have it that the way to be rid of injustice is not through pain and suffering but through changes of belief. So the question that still needs answering is how and why pain and suffering cause a change of belief in a wrongdoer's soul.

In regard to this question, there are (at least) three interpretive approaches. One of these, mentioned earlier, is that Socrates really doesn't believe this, and that this view is a Platonic view being presented as if it were Socratic. The obvious problem with that view is that it doesn't seem to be supported by the many texts in which Socrates recognizes and seems

---

[33] For example, see Cornford 1933: 306–307; Irwin 1979: note on 507b, 222, and Irwin 1977: 123–124; Cooper 1999: 29–75.

[34] Several other reasons for rejecting this approach are offered in Brickhouse and Smith 1994: 97–101 and 2010: 248–258.

to accept that (conventional) punishments can play effective roles in changing behavior.[35]

More promising, accordingly, are interpretations that recognize some connection between pain and suffering, on the one hand, and cognition, on the other. One such view, already mentioned earlier, is that "all desires to do something are rational desires, in that they always automatically adjust to the agent's belief about what is the best means to their ultimate end" (Penner 1992a: 128). Here, at least, there is some connection between conative and cognitive processing. One problem, however, is that this view seems very implausible as a matter of phenomenal psychology: from the fact that I know my coming trip to the dentist will be in my best interest, it doesn't seem to follow that all of my aversion to the pain that I anticipate disappears. The same may be said for our attractions to things that we are fully committed to avoiding: (too many) foods continue to appeal to me even though I am adamant about not violating my diet by eating them. My desires to avoid pain and enjoy pleasure do not simply adjust to what I think is in my best interest. Socrates does seem to hold that our actions always follow what we believe about our best interests at the time of action. But I see no reason to attribute to him the extremely implausible view that desires always accord with belief.

Another problem here is that what Socrates says about the beneficial effects of "pain and suffering" seems to require the connection between the conative and cognitive aspects of motivation to go in the opposite direction: instead of the noncognitive psychological element following the cognitive element, the order seems to be that the noncognitive element can have an effect on the cognitive. If the only way to change behavior, in Socratic motivational intellectualism, is to change belief, and the only way to cure injustice is through pain and suffering, then it seems that pain and suffering must be able to change belief. Only an account that accommodates that direction of cause and effect can make what Socrates says about punishment cohere with his intellectualism about motivation.

Partly on the basis of considerations like these, several scholars[36] now have proposed a somewhat different picture of the relationship between

---

[35] The most obvious of these is *Apology* 26a2–8 (quoted earlier), where Socrates mentions those who "require punishment." Conventional forms of punishment are also mentioned in several other texts, with no indication that such treatments are never appropriate, as this interpretation requires: see *Crito* 51b5; *Hippias Major* 292b4–11; and all of the forms of punishment that Socrates rejects as appropriate for him at *Apology* 37b7–e2. Socrates argues there only that he regards such punishments as clearly worse (for him) than the death penalty sought in the indictment. Because he steadfastly maintains his innocence, no punishment (including the fine he ultimately offers to pay) is really appropriate in his case.

[36] I cite Devereux 1995 later, but Brickhouse and I have also argued at length for this view in our 2010, 2012, and 2015.

conation and cognition. Here is how Daniel T. Devereux expressed the view:

> [W]hen we perceive something pleasant near at hand, our desire is aroused and begins to undermine our better judgment; desire only "gets its way" by first getting us to judge that the immediate pleasure is what we ought to choose. The desire thus explains the fact that the pleasure appears greater than it is, and not the other way around. (Devereux 1995: 395)

The same process, we may assume, would work in the case of aversive desires: the desire to avoid pain gets us to judge that we should avoid it. Once we form that belief – as long as no other belief-forming process intervenes or trumps this one – an agent will act in such a way as to avoid the pain. This explains both why I dread going to the dentist and continue to do so even as I force myself to go, because I am convinced that going is really in my best interest. Were it not for that other belief-forming process (the one that persuades me that going to the dentist is what I should do), I would quite naturally judge that avoiding the dentist and her painful treatments was in my best interest.

By applying this account to what the unjust soul witnesses in the treatment of incurables in Hades, the following would be an explanation: seeing the pain suffered by the incurable, and connecting that experience to the injustice done by the incurable, the curably unjust soul anticipates some (perhaps similar) painful experience if it continues to engage in injustice. Having (as we all do) a strong natural aversion to pain, the soul comes to believe that acting in ways that would lead to suffering as the incurable soul does is not in one's best interest. That does not mean that such a soul would no longer feel any attraction to acting unjustly; but it would explain why the witness to the incurable's punishment arouses an "expectation of something bad." The "something bad" is the idea that the curably unjust soul might become incurably unjust, and then have to endure what the witness observes fearfully in Hades.

This seems to get the belief-forming process in the right order – with a change of belief a result of the curably unjust soul's aversion to what he witnesses. So this is a case of cognition following conation, and not the other way around. What remains to be explained, however, is why Socrates would think that "there is no other possible way to get rid of injustice" than through "pain and suffering." This explanation, too, can be found in the *Gorgias*.

This process of belief-formation explains why we are naturally inclined to believe that the things to which we are attracted are good for us and the things to which we are averse are bad for us. This process, however, can be somewhat unreliable: at times, things to which we are attracted are not really good for us and should be avoided, and things to which we are averse really are good for us and should be pursued. In order to avoid errors, accordingly, we will need some other belief-forming process to present our real interests to us more accurately. In an ideal case, we might find some way to attain what Socrates calls the "craft of measurement" that "can make the appearances lose their power by showing us the truth" (*Protagoras* 356d7–e1). But while the attainment of such a craft seems like a good aspirational ideal, it also seems to be one that none of us can really hope to master: Socrates is the wisest of men, not because he has mastered such a craft, but because he understands that he does not have such mastery. The good news about the belief-forming process that goes from natural attractions and aversions to beliefs about what is best for us, despite its unreliability, is that the process is defeasible: the craft of measurement would defeat it every time that the beliefs such a process incline us to accept are wrong. But we don't need to have the craft of measurement to see that sometimes we need to shun what we are attracted to and pursue what we are averse to. For that, all we need to be is open to other belief-forming processes that are available to us, such as memory, sense perception, testimony, and ratiocination. As we all know, Socrates heavily privileges the last of these, famously saying that "the unexamined life is not worth living for a human being" (*Apology* 38a5–6).

The problems come, then, not because we do not have a number of processes that can compete with and defeat the inclinations to believe that result from our natural attractions and aversions, but because none of these are infallible. Socrates seems to think that philosophizing is the most reliable of these processes, but even this process can go wrong and leave uncertainty.[37] Such uncertainty would seem to be part of what Socrates regards as the human condition. But even if we cannot hope to master the measuring craft, he also seems to think that we can do things that will make our condition significantly deteriorate when it comes to making good decisions about what is and is not in our best interest.

---

[37] Perhaps the best example of this result is depicted at the end of the *Hippias Minor*, where Socrates and Hippias seem to reach a conclusion that neither finds satisfactory. I believe the same can be said for any Socratic discussion that ends in *aporia*. What Socrates invariably concludes when this happens is not that we simply "go with our gut," as the (foolish) saying goes, but that we continue to inquire in the hope that we might make progress.

SOCRATES: And so the satisfaction of one's desires – if one is hungry, eating as much as one likes, or if thirsty, drinking – is generally allowed by doctors when one is in health; but they practically never allow one in sickness to take one's fill of things that one desires: do you agree with me in this?

CALLICLES: I do.

SOCRATES: And does not the same rule, my excellent friend, apply to the soul? So long as it is in a bad state – thoughtless, licentious, unjust and unholy – we must restrain its desires and not permit it to do anything except what will help it to be better: do you grant this, or not?

CALLICLES: I do.

SOCRATES: For thus, I take it, the soul itself is better off?

CALLICLES: To be sure.

SOCRATES: And is restraining a person from what he desires correcting him?

CALLICLES: Yes.

SOCRATES: Then correction is better for the soul than uncorrected license, as you were thinking just now.

CALLICLES: I have no notion what you are referring to, Socrates; do ask someone else. (*Gorgias* 505a6–c2)

3.11 The Gadfly's Sting

As soon as Callicles balks, in the passage at the end of the previous section, Socrates says something quite striking about what he, Socrates, is trying to do in his discussion with Callicles:

> Here is a fellow who cannot endure a kindness done him, or the experience in himself of what our talk is about – a correction (*kolazomenos*)! (*Gorgias* 505c3–4[38])

Xenophon, too, offers the same assessment of what happens during Socratic examinations:

> If any believe, as some write and say on the basis of mere conjecture, that Socrates was extremely influential in exhorting people to virtue yet power-less to lead them to it,[39] they should examine not only the punishment (*kolastêriou*) he dealt out in cross-examining (*élegchen*) those who thought they knew everything, but also the conversations in which he passed the

---

[38] Trans. Lamb 1925. The very popular Zeyl translation in Cooper 1997 translates "*kolazomenos*" as "disciplined," which could have the same sense, but could also mean being put into a more well-organized regimen. As I will explain in this section, Plato's Socrates plainly thinks that appropriate *kolasis* induces such a regimen in the soul, but the process by which it does this is "disciplining" in the sense of correction or punishment.

[39] One finds this criticism voiced by Cleitophon in (Ps.-)Plato's dialogue of that name at 410b3–c6.

time of day with his friends. (*Memorabilia* 1.4.1; trans. Benjamin, slightly modified)

Scholarly discussions of Socratic philosophizing have focused exclusively on its logical and epistemological features. In a recent (2013) literature review on the subject, David C. Wolfsdorf provides careful and accurate accounts of twenty scholarly works on the ways in which Socrates engages his interlocutors, starting with Vlastos' influential 1983 article, "The Socratic Elenchus." Not one of those articles pays any attention to the ways in which both Plato and Xenophon characterize what Socrates took himself to be doing in his philosophical conversations.[40] It is presumably this same aspect of what Socrates did that he had in mind when he describes himself as Athens' "gadfly" in Plato's *Apology* (at 30e5), a nasty insect whose bite normally causes pain, burning, itching, and swelling. Anyone witnessing a horse beset by a gadfly can clearly see that the horse suffers. It is to this kind of suffering that Plato has Socrates compare his own effects on his fellow Athenians as a result of his "rousing and persuading and reproaching" (*Apology* 30e7). It seems, then, that Socratic persuasion was understood by both Xenophon and Plato as having more than just logical and epistemological features.

Only once does Plato have Socrates explicitly claim to be engaging in corrective punishment with his cross-examining, and that is in the passage from the *Gorgias* I quoted earlier, where Socrates claims to be punishing Callicles as a form of correction. And even here, we might think that the sense of "correction" is not appropriately compared to punishment. Socrates isn't really talking about *punishing* Callicles, but, rather, only about trying to change his opinion from the wrong to the right one. Plainly, we would not best understand this exchange entirely in terms of punishment: Socrates and Callicles aren't agreeing that it is best to keep the soul in a *punished* condition. But the contest makes clear that it is precisely this condition – what Socrates and Callicles are calling the "corrected condition" of the soul – that both have in mind as the effect of appropriate *punishment*. This is evident just a couple of Stephanus pages later when Socrates insists that one "must contrive, if possible, to need no correction; but if he have need of it, either himself or anyone belonging to him, either an individual or a city, then right must be applied and they must be corrected" (*Gorgias* 507d3–5).

---

[40] The same lack of attention may be found in the one book wholly dedicated to "the Socratic Method": Scott 2002.

How, then, does Plato's Socrates understand the process of punishment as correction? Again, if the *Gorgias* is to be consistent on this matter, it must be that the effects of correction are cognitive: since one will always do what one takes to be in one's best interest, for injustice to be cured, it will have to be that the belief(s) involved in voluntarily harming others will be replaced by some other belief(s) that leads one not to behave in such ways. This process, Socrates claims, must involve a certain degree of pain. Socrates seems to suppose that the very processes that lead one to voluntarily harm others are driven by a belief-forming process that inclines one to believe that acting in such a way as to pursue pleasure is good for one, whereas acting in ways that cause pain is bad for one. If acting in a way that one expects to create pleasure brings pain, instead, then one's inclination to believe that way of behaving is good for one will be obstructed. By creating conditions in which the unreliability of appetitive belief-forming processes becomes manifest to one, punishment diminishes the power of this belief-forming process to dominate one's deliberation and decision-making. In a single instance, such an intervention cannot count as a complete cure. But it is at least a first step toward correction, because the more unjust one becomes, the more automatic one's reliance on an unreliable cognitive process becomes. By interfering in such habituation, punishment compels greater thoughtfulness about what is and is not in one's best interest. In brief, punishment provides a very natural and basic disincentive for behaving in the ways that lead one to get punished. In the Socratic account, the disincentive is cognitive, even if the belief-forming etiology involved has its origins in a conative psychological process.

This, then, is my account of "the gadfly's sting." Socratic examination may simply call one's attention to inconsistencies in one's life-shaping beliefs. But it also recognizes that not all belief-forming processes are rational ones. Accordingly, I cannot agree, for example, with the claim that "*only philosophical dialogue* can improve one's fellow citizens" (Penner 2000: 164). Other, much more conventional, ways of making wrongdoers uncomfortable with the decisions they have made – and thus with the way they have made decisions – can also be effective. But I do agree that philosophical dialogue can also be effective in the same way and *for the same reasons*. In brief, it is not just that Socrates' superior rationality can (sometimes) be persuasive; it is also that his elenctic examinations of others can cause a kind of pain that can help to correct his most intractable interlocutors by inducing in them at least enough doubt to reconsider the ways in which they make the decisions that shape their lives.

3.12 The Pain of Shame

Several scholars in recent years have noticed that there is more to Socratic conversation than calm ratiocination. One of the ways in which Socrates characterizes his philosophizing emphasizes the way in which he shames others.

> Then, if one of you disputes this and says he does care [above wisdom, truth, and the care of the soul], I shall not let him go at once and leave him, but I shall question him, examine him and test him, and if I do not think he has attained the goodness that he says he has, I shall reproach him because he attaches little importance to the most important things and greater importance to inferior things. (*Apology* 29e3–30a3)

One might well wonder if Socrates' use of shame[41] can be explained in the kinds of solely rational ways most scholars have understood Socratic motivational intellectualism.

> Shame is a painful emotion one feels at the thought of being exposed in weakness, foolishness, nakedness, or perhaps even wickedness, to the view of a community whose laughter would scald. Shame is closely related to fear of exclusion from one's group, since derision generally marks the exposed person as an outsider. (Woodruff 2000: 133)

Other scholars have taken this insight even further. For example, it certainly seems at times that Socrates goes so far as to *mock*[42] his interlocutors and purposely humiliate them.[43] Socrates goes out of his way to praise interlocutors for their wisdom (an especially vivid example of this may be found in the *Euthyphro* – see esp. 5a3–c5). Such praise makes the interlocutor's subsequent failures even more painful, as he experiences the full reality that he is no longer gaining the honor Socrates seemed to have initiated.[44]

Some scholars have argued that shame is not merely an occasional or unusual Socratic tactic:

> The *Gorgias* shows that appeals to a person's feelings of shame and admiration may be able to succeed, when rational arguments have failed, in bringing him to see that a harmful pleasure is to be avoided, or that a beneficial pain is to be pursued. (Moss 2005: 140).

---

[41] See Woodruff 2000; McKim 1988; Kahn 1983: 106–107.   [42] See Sanderman 2004.

[43] Perhaps the best example of this is in *Republic* I, where Socrates reduces Thrasymachus to sweating and blushing (350c12–d3).

[44] Moss (2005: 150) notices a similar case in the *Gorgias*, where Socrates begins by praising Callicles for his manliness or courage (494d4), only later to compare him to scratching catamite (494e3–5).

In this view, the special role of shame in Socratic discussions is featured in the way he compares what he does with what doctors do for the body:

> This analogy between Socrates and the doctor is far from innocuous. Looking at the dialogue's characterization of medicine, we will see that it serves two major purposes. First, it allows Plato to present Socrates' practice, and indeed philosophy in general, as beneficial – as a valuable and vital art that looks to the wellbeing of the soul. Second, it provides an account of why Socrates is often unsuccessful in his efforts to persuade people to value justice and philosophy. For there are many people who find what Socrates does *unpleasant*, and these people will refuse to submit to his arguments, just as some people refuse to submit to the doctor's painful cures. (Moss 2007: 231)

Socrates' use of shame may be directly connected to his perception that nonrational impulses have sometimes led interlocutors to make bad judgments of value:

> On the account I have offered, Polus initially thought injustice good because he was attracted by its pleasures. Now, Socrates hopes, he will realize that injustice is bad because he is repelled by its shamefulness. Responses to the pleasant and the painful on the one hand, and the *kalon* and the *aischron* on the other, are two bases for non-rational, quasi-perceptual value judgments. What one takes pleasure in strikes one as good; what one feels shame at strikes one as bad. In proceeding as he does with Polus, Socrates is emphasizing that these two types of response tend to conflict: many *kalon* things are painful, while many pleasant things are *aischron*, and thus our value-judgments are pulled in different directions. Moreover, Socrates is making the point that pleasure pulls us in the wrong direction, toward false value-judgments, while shame pulls us in the right direction, toward the truth. (Moss 2005: 146)

Socrates' use of shame thus seems, as I have been arguing, to point to a different etiology of belief-formation than what most scholars who have discussed Socratic motivational intellectualism recognize. Some scholars have seen evidence of a contradiction in Socratic philosophy. This would be the result if we agree that Socrates "allows only knowledge-based procedures to count as rational and raises the standards for knowledge so high that no one – not even Socrates – is found to satisfy them."[45] If so, any examples of human success in the moral domain cannot be explained in terms of cognitive success, since there is essentially none of that to be

---

[45] Woodruff 2000: 131.

found. Instead, any such success must be accounted for by appeals to "factors outside of what counts as rational,"[46] including fear of shame.

Given my argument thus far in this book, I am obviously not prepared to accept the claim that not even Socrates can satisfy the standards that he sets for rational endeavor. If Socrates is using a craft model of knowledge, as I have claimed, then it is at least open to him to regard not just mastery of craft but also a much lower level of achievement in it to count as rational. In other words, Socrates could regard rationality as improvable in the same way that I have claimed he regards knowledge, virtue, and happiness.

The account of moral psychology that I have sketched so far in this chapter also provides Socrates with a way to be innocent of the charge that by relying on shame, he violates his own intellectualist conception of motivation. For that to be true, shame would have to be a motivating factor that is distinct from, and does not require, specifically cognitive content. There are two ways to block this conclusion, however. The first would account for shame as one of the many nonrational factors that could cause changes in one's beliefs about what is best for one.[47] In this view, appetites and passions function in more or less the same way: either an appetite or a passion (such as shame) could cause one to believe that they should do something other than what they might normally think is the right thing to do. On that account, shame would not itself be cognitive – just as we continue to think that, for example, thirst is not cognitive. But what shame (and thirst) can do, on this account, is to be a (defeasible) cause of an evaluative belief: the experience of shame could lead us to believe that what causes us shame is bad for us and should be avoided. Such a process is defeasible insofar as there are other belief-forming processes (including others with nonrational sources, but also ones with rational sources) that can incline us to believe something other than what shame might incline us to believe. As an etiological source of belief, those who feel shame and come to believe what shame inclines them to believe will also always function in the way Socratic motivational intellectualism requires.

There is also another way to reconcile shame with Socratic intellectualism. As I mentioned earlier, there is at least some plausible evidence for thinking that Socrates was a cognitivist about emotions;[48] that is, he supposed that emotions *just are* beliefs. If Socrates' views about shame

---

[46] Woodruff 2000: 131.

[47] This is how Brickhouse and I accounted for the role of shame in belief-formation in our 2010.

[48] Brickhouse and I changed our view about the emotions to this position in our 2015. The evidence for this conclusion may be found at *Protagoras* 358d6–7, where Socrates says "fear (*phobos*) or dread (*deos*) is an expectation (*prosdokian*) of something bad" (see also *Laches* 198b8–9). Socratic

follow this pattern, then shame would be an example of a belief that resulted from the nonrational belief-forming processes that had their origins in our most basic attractions and aversions – what Socrates usually calls appetites. In this view, negative emotions (such as shame) would not be the etiological origins of value beliefs, but would instead just *be* the beliefs that were caused by some aversive reaction. Shame would be how one reacts to one's basic instincts to avoid the "scalding" effects of social rejection, and would consist in the beliefs that would arise in response to the perception that such rejection might be the result of acting in some way.

The texts seem to lend some support to the view that Socrates was a cognitivist about fear. I do not think that the specific etiology of belief-formation involved in shame is made sufficiently clear in Plato's dialogues to understand it in the same way as fear. But it is enough for my purposes herein to note that if either of the accounts just described is how Socrates viewed the way shame works, the motivational effects of shame will be entirely consistent with Socratic motivational intellectualism. Whether shame is a nonrational cause of evaluative beliefs, or is itself an evaluative belief that is caused by nonrational factors, acting in response to shame will always be describable as the agent acting on the basis of what they believe is in their best interest, from among the options salient to them at the time of acting. I thus reject the view that Socrates' inclusion of shame as a resource in persuasion creates dissonance from his view that motivation is always a reflection of an agent's evaluative beliefs.

3.13 The Damage That Is Done by Wrongdoing

I have already noted that Socrates believed that all wrongdoing was at least in some sense involuntary. He recognized, of course, that people could and sometimes did seek to wrong or harm others and succeed in doing so. In that sense, they can voluntarily do wrong.[49] But even so, what they do is also involuntary in another sense. This is because wrongdoing always damages the soul of the agent, and even as they wrong *others* voluntarily, they wrong themselves *involuntarily*.

SOCRATES: Come then: If we ruin what becomes better by health and destroyed by disease when we're persuaded by the opinion of those who lack expertise, is our life worth living when this has been corrupted? This is, surely, the body, isn't it?

---

cognitivism about fear also seems to be evident at *Apology* 28a5–7, where Socrates says that the fear of death is nothing but ignorance.

[49] See Section 3.10 and especially note 35.

CRITO: Yes.

SOCRATES: Therefore, is our life worth living with a body in bad condition and corrupted?

CRITO: Certainly not.

SOCRATES: But is our life worth living with this thing being corrupted that injustice mutilates and justice improves? Or, do we believe that what justice and injustice concern – whatever it is of the things that make us up – is inferior to the body?

CRITO: Certainly not.

SOCRATES: It is, rather, to be respected more?

CRITO: Much more. (*Crito* 47d8–48a4; see also *Gorgias* 478c3–e5, 511c9–512b2; *Republic* I.353d3–354a7)

Readers of Plato are perhaps familiar with the reasons Plato gives for this result in the *Republic*, where we are told that justice consists in harmonizing and balancing the different parts of the soul, in which case injustice would result in a kind of psychic conflict and destabilization (IV.444b1–4).

> [Glaucon speaking] But Socrates, this inquiry looks ridiculous to me now that justice and injustice have been shown to be as we have described. Even now, if one has every kind of food and drink, lots of money, and every sort of power to rule, life is thought to be not worth living when one's body's nature is ruined. So even if someone can do whatever he wishes, except what will free him from vice and injustice and make him acquire justice and virtue, how can it be worth living when his soul – the very thing by which he lives – is ruined and in turmoil? (*Republic* IV.445a5–b4)

In the *Gorgias*, too, Plato has Socrates refer to "that in the soul in which we have appetites" (at 493a2–3 and b1). His insistence on keeping the soul in an orderly condition (504b4–505b12, 506d5–507a3, 507e6–508a4) may also suggest that he regards the soul to be composed of parts. The appearance of soul-parts in the *Gorgias* might thus encourage us to suppose that Plato wished to depict Socrates as accepting some kind of partition of the soul all along. But even if we did come to accept such a view (without any explicit additional evidence from the other early dialogues, except for the fact that they, too, seem to recognize some roles for appetites and passions, as I have noted in this chapter), we would still have to confront the fact that the moral psychology of the tripartite soul in the *Republic* explicitly undergirds a *nonintellectualist* view of motivation. Psychic injustice, in the *Republic*, recall, involves the suborning of the rational part by one of the lower parts of the soul: the rational part of the soul may believe that the agent should do X, but another part of the soul could end up leading the agent to do not-X. Plato gives a case that seems to be a clear example of this:[50]

> Leontius, son of Aglaion, was coming up from the Piraeus outside the North Wall when he saw some dead bodies lying by the public executioner. At the same time, he had an appetite to look and was also disgusted with himself and made himself turn away. For a while, he struggled and covered his face, but at length, overpowered by the appetite, he opened his eyes wide, ran towards the corpses, and exclaimed, "Look, you wretches! Fill yourselves with the beautiful sight!" (*Republic* IV.439e7–440a3; see also IV.440a8–b7)

In Socratic motivational intellectualism, on the contrary, an agent's actions always follow the agent's current belief as to what is in the agent's best interest, among the salient available options, at the time of action. The Socrates who spoke in the *Crito* cannot have this kind of explanation in mind for how wrongdoing damages the soul. Instead, whatever explanation Socrates had to offer that was compatible with his motivational intellectualism would have to be a different one.

Given the intellectualism of the Socratic view, it would appear that the damage to an agent's soul from wrongdoing would have to be explicable in *cognitive* terms. Harming others must either somehow produce or else increase one's vulnerability to false belief. Given the constraints of Socratic motivational intellectualism, one might think that "harming another in the belief that we will benefit by doing so predisposes us to have many ill-conceived notions about how the world works" (Reshotko 2006: 72). But it is difficult to see why this must be the case. Why wouldn't especially a habitual wrongdoer already have all of the relevant "ill-conceived notions about how the world works," which would explain why the wrongdoer continues to do wrong? Such "ill-conceived notions" might well explain the cognitive failure required by an intellectualist account of wrongdoing, but it does not seem adequate to support the view that wrongdoing might *continue* to damage the soul of one who is already ignorant and suffering from false beliefs. "The damage to the soul cannot be the cognitive failure that is *antecedently* required in order for the agent to do wrong; it must, therefore, be some *further* negative consequence, in addition to the original cognitive failure" (Brickhouse and Smith 2013: 205).

---

[50] Carone 2001 argues against the interpretation of this passage that I provide here (and which is generally accepted among scholars). See Brickhouse and Smith 2010: 206–209 for a reply to her argument.

I claim that the required explanation can be provided by the etiological role in belief-formation played by nonrational factors. Recall the way Socrates insists that we must keep these nonrational factors in a controlled condition:

> And about the soul, oh best one, isn't it the same thing? As long as it is bad, being foolish and out of control and unjust and impious, it ought to be kept from its appetites and not turn to anything other than what will be better for it. Do you agree or not? – I do. – For isn't it the case that the soul becomes better in this way? – Of course. – Keeping it from its appetites is correcting it? – Yes. (*Gorgias* 505b1–10)

Socrates' view seems to be that wrongdoing damages the soul by making one's appetites become *less controlled*. Some initial wrongdoing might be done because the agent had simply been misinformed about how to behave. But the wrongdoing would also satisfy some appetite the agent might have felt – thus in a way confirming the impression that appetite had made to the agent's soul that behaving in this way would be a good thing to do. When given the opportunity to act in similar circumstances in the future, the agent might feel less need to consider alternative belief-forming processes (such as taking into account the sorts of considerations that might count against acting in such a way). In Socrates' view, acting in accordance with an appetite *strengthens* that appetite, whereas refraining from acting in accordance with the appetite *weakens* it. By weakening the appetites, one makes oneself better able to consider evidence and deliberate more effectively – with greater influence from veridically more reliable cognitive processes. Strengthening one's appetites has the opposite effect. The more habitual wrongdoing becomes, accordingly, the more its effects on the soul will be of this kind. And at the bitter end of this process, one can actually manage not just to have a damaged soul, but a *ruined* one. As he reports this in the great myth of the afterlife in the Gorgias, souls in this condition cannot even be cured by the great judges (or gods) who rule in the afterlife.

In the two previous chapters of this book, I discussed how Socrates' conceptions of knowledge, virtue, and happiness should be seen as *improvable*, since his model of knowledge was a skill model. We might now reasonably add to this picture that even before one's cognitive skill reached some level that would begin to approach the expertise required to count as knowledge, some more basic form of that skill might also be achieved, and in different degrees. A brief characterization of the damage to the soul that would result from wrongdoing can thus be given: wrongdoing damages the soul by making the soul less able to function in veridically reliable ways. One is less able to make good decisions, as an agent, because one acts in a way that makes one less skilled – even if one was already relatively unskilled – in the craft of living. And the reason that one becomes less skilled in such a way is that one strengthens the veridically unreliable processes by which human beings come to generate and hold beliefs, while also weakening one's ability to employ the more veridically reliable belief-forming processes. Unless and until one desists from such self-destructive behavior, one will have no hope at all of even taking up the craft of living well. As we continue, then, to consider the ways in which Socrates promotes better life-practices, we can now bear in mind the close connections between his intellectualist moral psychology and the ethics and epistemology that inform his philosophical mission. But perhaps at least this much is now clear: if we are to have any hope of improving our conditions, in knowledge, in virtue, and in happiness, we must do whatever we can to resist the kinds of belief-forming processes that are the least likely to give us the best guidance, and the most likely to mislead us into wrongdoing. It is not just that wrongdoing is contrary to what we really want for ourselves; rather, each time we go wrong, we actually make it more likely that we will go wrong even more often, and perhaps even more egregiously, in the future.

CHAPTER 4

Socratic Ignorance

4.1 Introduction

In Chapters 1 and 2 of this book, I have argued that the main epistemological interest of Plato's Socrates in the early dialogues was one that understood the most important kind of knowledge to be a kind of craft-knowledge, know-how, skill, or expertise. I described the kind of knowledge that he seeks and the kind that he so often claims to lack in these terms, and have cited texts that seem to me to make this characterization clear. I then turned to the moral psychology presented in Plato's early dialogues, and focused especially on what is called Socratic motivational intellectualism, according to which the way in which agents act is explicable in cognitive terms. Most importantly, I argued that Socrates recognized a belief-forming process that had its etiological origins in the appetites, and so found that there was not only a motivational role for nonrational psychological factors, but also a role for them in Socratic ethics. In this chapter, I intend to look more closely into the Socratic conception of ignorance – with particular emphasis now on what it means for himself and the rest of humanity to be as cognitively defective as we are in the relevant skill.

We should first and foremost continue to remind ourselves that the kind of skill or expertise that Socrates has in mind is the kind that would afford its possessor the ability to accomplish everything humanly possible in our mission to do well, to be happy. It is simply not enough that we have the resources to survive:

SOCRATES: Well, my excellent fellow, do you think that expertise in swimming is a grand thing?
CALLICLES: No, by Zeus, I don't.
SOCRATES: But it certainly does save people from death whenever they fall into the kind of situation that requires this expertise. But if you think this expertise is a trivial one, I'll give you one more important than it, that of piloting a ship, which saves not only souls, but also bodies and valuables from the utmost dangers . . . . The one who possesses the craft and who has accomplished

these feats, disembarks and goes for a stroll along the seaside and beside his ship with a modest air. For he's enough of an expert, I suppose, to conclude that it isn't clear which ones of his fellow voyagers he has benefited by not letting them drown in the deep, and which ones he has harmed, knowing that they were no better in either body or soul when he set them ashore than they were when they embarked. So he concludes that if a person afflicted with serious incurable diseases did not drown, this person is miserable for not dying and has gotten no benefit from the pilot. But if someone has incurable diseases in what is more valuable than his body, his soul, life for that person is not worth living, then it won't be any favor to rescue that person from the sea or from prison or from anywhere else. The pilot knows that for a corrupt person it's better not to be alive, for he necessarily lives badly. (*Gorgias* 511c4–512b2[1])

In the chapters to come, I will be looking much more closely at how Socrates thinks that improvement in our epistemic condition would also yield improvements in our lives. This – the question of how we should live – for Socrates is *the* question that we should dedicate ourselves to answering as well as we possibly can.

But (as I discussed in Chapter 1) in spite of being an exemplar of a man who leads the best sort of life, Socrates is also famous for his epistemic modesty – he declares his ignorance of "the most important things" even as he reveals, as we saw in the last chapter, that he is still far better off (epistemically and ethically) than the other human beings he has encountered. Even so, Socrates continues to regard his actual level of epistemic achievement as not one that is especially enviable or as anything very successful, from the point of view of the aspirations we should all have and pursue in our lives. So one question we must explore is what Socrates does – and what he does not – intend to disclaim in his profession of ignorance. In this chapter, I will argue that Socrates recognizes not just different degrees of epistemic failure but also different *kinds* of epistemic failure, and I will try to explicate what Socrates thinks we can do to avoid or at least remediate these. The result is that this chapter will focus on what Socrates has to say about the nature and causes of ignorance and also about the ways and degrees to which we might remove it from our lives.

4.2 Types of Ignorance

Socrates' focus on craft-knowledge does not mean that he cannot or does not recognize the kind of fact-knowledge that is the focus of most

---

[1] Translation revised from the one in Cooper 1997.

contemporary epistemology. In the Preface, I cited several passages in which Socrates actually makes claims of knowledge. So when Socrates proclaims his own ignorance, or finds it in others, he is not arguing for anything like global skepticism.

So what, then, should we think about the kind of ignorance Socrates finds in himself and others? If we go back to the important passage from Plato's *Apology* (quoted in Section 1.5) in which Socrates compares his own epistemic condition with those of the politicians, poets, and craftsmen, we can see that Socrates' own ignorance is simply a lack of the sort of craft-knowledge he wishes he could have. The politicians, poets, and craftsmen, however, suffer from compound ignorance, for they not only suffer from the same lack that Socrates notes in himself; they are also unaware of the fact that they have this lack. They are fact-ignorant of their skill-ignorance.

But being fact-ignorant that one is skill-ignorant does not simply compound one's epistemic failure: it threatens to have that failure also be the basis of a life-failure. If one supposes wrongly that one actually is an expert in living well, then one will fail in the very aims and practices that one takes oneself to know well. The first step in remediating such skill-ignorance is becoming aware of that ignorance, as Socrates has done. If I am right in the main argument of this book – that the kind of knowledge Socrates seeks and also finds so lacking in himself and others is skill-knowledge, or know-how – then the improvability of such knowledge offers each of us the hope that we might do better in the way we actually shape our own lives. The first step in this process does not take any special skill, but it does take a kind of integrity: we must begin self-improvement by the recognition that we *need* such improvement. We accomplish that first step by sharing Socrates' awareness of his own ignorance.

The way in which Socrates investigates others for knowledge and wisdom, however, clearly indicates that he regards some kinds of fact-ignorance to be at least symptomatic of the more important kind of ignorance, which, as I have been arguing, is skill-ignorance. Socrates investigates those who have a reputation for wisdom, and finds out, for example, that they are not able to offer explanations or fully adequate definitions of what they are reputed to know and in which they are reputed to be wise. Such explanations – if they were forthcoming – would be expressible in declarative sentences and would thus be examples of what I am calling fact-knowledge. So before we go on to consider how Socrates thinks he can remediate ignorance, let us look a little closer at what Socrates has to say about the indications and symptoms of ignorance.

4.3 How to Tell That Someone Is Ignorant

As any reader of Plato's early dialogues soon finds out, Socrates is extremely good at revealing others' ignorance. There is one specific example of this I want to pay special attention to, since it reveals a feature of Socrates' understanding of ignorance that is highly significant – and if I am right, it is one that anticipates some contemporary discussions in epistemology while also qualifying as an important contribution to the theory of knowledge. The specific example is expressed well in Plato's *Apology* where, as Socrates explains to the jury how he came to have a reputation for wisdom, he explains how and why he was able to judge that a certain group of others lacked such wisdom. The episode begins when Socrates recounts the visit his friend, Chaerephon, made to Delphi to consult the oracle there. Chaerephon asked if anyone was wiser than Socrates, and the oracle answered "no" (*Apology* 21a2–7). When Socrates heard about this answer, he assumed the oracle had pronounced one of its famous riddles, since Socrates says he is "aware that I have no wisdom great or small," but even so, "it is not within the god's nature to lie" (*Apology* 21b4–7[2]). So he hopes to reveal the true meaning of the oracle by examining others who are reputed to be wise, and he begins his search with famous politicians, and discovers that despite their reputations for wisdom, they actually have none. He does not tell his jurors precisely how he did this, but we can safely assume that they were not able to withstand his elenctic questioning. It is the next group that he went to who provide the more interesting case for my purposes here. His next group of those reputed to be wise were the poets:

> After the politicians, I went to the poets, the writers of tragedies and dithyrambs and the others, intending in their case to catch myself being more ignorant than they. So I took up those poems with which they seemed to have taken most trouble and asked them what they meant, in order that I might at the same time learn something from them. I am ashamed to tell you the truth, gentlemen, but I must. Almost all the bystanders might have explained the poems better than their authors could. I soon realized that poets do not compose their poems with knowledge, but by some inborn talent and by inspiration, like seers and prophets who also say many fine things without any understanding of what they say. The poets seem to have a similar experience. (*Apology* 22a8–b4)

---

[2] My own translation.

What is different here is that Socrates grants that the poets "say many fine things," and that is what has apparently earned them the reputation for wisdom. But when Socrates asks them to explain these "many fine things," he finds that "almost all of the bystanders might have explained the poems better than their authors could." Of all people, poets would be the ones we would most expect to be able to explain the things they say, since what they do is done with words. And yet Socrates finds the opposite is the case: as articulate and magnificent as their poetry may be, poets are inarticulate and incompetent when it comes to explaining any of it. So here, for my purposes, is the important insight: those who really have knowledge can explain the "fine things" they say; those who do not really have knowledge cannot. Again, even if we assume that the kind of knowledge Socrates is seeking in others is craft-knowledge, it seems that he thinks someone with that sort of knowledge will be able to explain the fine things that having such a craft allows them to say or do. The poets (and diviners) cannot explain the "fine things" they say, because what allowed them to say such things was not knowledge, but divine inspiration.

We find the same view of how poets and diviners manage in Plato's *Ion*:

> That's why the god takes their intellect away from them when he uses them as his servants, as he does prophets and godly diviners, so that we who hear should know that *they* are not the ones who speak those verses that are of such high value, for their intellect is not in them: the god himself is the one who speaks, and he gives voice through them to us. (*Ion* 534c7–d4)

There is good reason to regard Socrates' denial of knowledge to the poets and diviners as an example of what is called "the opacity objection" in contemporary epistemology.[3] The contemporary versions of this objection have been aimed at various versions of externalist accounts of knowledge. The gist of the objection is expressed well by one of its best-known framers, Keith Lehrer:

> There is . . . a general objection to all externalist theories that is as simple to state as it is fundamental: the external relationship might be opaque to the subject, who has no idea that her beliefs are produced, caused, or causally sustained by a reliable belief-forming process or properly functioning

---

[3] See Randall and Smith 2019. The following discussion relies heavily on our presentation there. Epistemologists have given different versions of this objection, but it was named as "the opacity objection" first by Keith Lehrer (in Lehrer 2000). We will not be discussing herein debates about whether there is a problem that knowledge itself might be left opaque to the knower in some theories. In most externalist theories a true belief generated by a reliable process (for example) is still knowledge, but the knower in question may not *know* that they know. For a discussion of this version of an opacity objection, see Pritchard 2001.

cognitive faculty. The person might fail to know because of the opacity to her of the external relationship and her ignorance of it. (Lehrer 2000: 185)

The version of this objection given by Socrates in Plato's early dialogues was importantly different from the modern versions – even though, as a matter of fact, it would also qualify as an objection to most contemporary externalist accounts of knowledge. In brief, what seems to be missing in those in the category of "saying many fine things" but knowing none of them was that the poets, diviners, and (as we learn in the *Ion*) rhapsodes do not *understand* what they say, and their inability – their lack of the craft or skill in which such understanding would consist – to explain the "many fine things" is due to this lack of understanding. Evidence that this is what Socrates thought was missing appears in the *Ion*, where Socrates (apparently ironically) explains why he has so much admiration for what the rhapsodes can do:

> You have to learn his thought, not just his verses! Now that is something to envy! I mean, no one would ever get to be a good rhapsode if he didn't understand what is meant by the poet. A rhapsode must come to present the poet's thought to his audience; and he can't do that beautifully without knowing what the poet means. (*Ion* 530b10–c5)

We soon discover that Ion has no such understanding or knowledge. So it turns out that what Ion is able to do is something divine, but done without knowledge (*Ion* 542a1–b4). The problem isn't that Ion's beliefs about what Homer says are false, and given their divine cause and source, neither should we suppose that the way Ion comes to have those beliefs is unreliable. Even so, Ion does not know any of it, because he cannot *explain* any of it. And he cannot explain it because he doesn't actually *understand* it.

It might be supposed that Socrates' famous searches for definitions indicate that he regards such understanding to consist in definitional knowledge. Some scholars have gone so far as to make definitional knowledge both necessary and sufficient for any other sort of knowledge.[4] It is at least true that Socrates inevitably takes an interlocutor's inability to produce a successful definition as at least strong evidence that the interlocutor lacks the very knowledge the interlocutor had taken themself to have.

I do not think, however, that the kind of understanding Socrates finds lacking in poets, diviners, and rhapsodes consists entirely in definitional knowledge – at least without there being a good deal more to say about what other conditions must be met for such knowledge. One could seem to

---

[4] See, for example, Benson 2013a.

have justified (or reliably produced) true belief about some definition but still fail to know, on the ground that the person might still not be able to explain the definition or why it is true. After all, one could be justified in thinking that it is true on the basis of recognizing that the source of the definition was divine, for example – which would also show that the belief in the definition has a reliable causal source.[5] Even so, one who had been supplied with such a definition but could not explain it because they did not understand it would not qualify, in Socrates' view, as knowing it. So it seems that Socrates would make understanding a condition of definitional *knowledge*. And again, what seems to be missing is not to be explicable simply in terms of what information one has, but in terms of one's ability to *do things* with such information. In earlier work on this issue, my coauthor (R. Wolfe Randall) and I concluded our analysis by presenting what a case that would give us a sense of a contemporary version of the Socratic opacity objection might look like. We imagine a man (Frank) who says to someone else that the building they are in is on fire, but who then gives no indication of any response that we normally think would be appropriate in such circumstances. Perhaps Frank can even explain what fire is and what it can do to people and buildings. Even so, he gives no reason for an observer to conclude that he really *understands* the danger he is in. We say of such a case,

> What is also needed is understanding of what the information means *at a practical level*, which (given Socratic motivational intellectualism) requires a very specific kind of information: Frank would have to know that fire has the capacity to damage him and others. It would not be enough for him to know that fire burns buildings (or even people), for example, because there is nothing *motivating* in that information, as such (unless and until Frank also recognizes that being burned is to be damaged). That is, the kind of understanding Socrates requires will involve the agent's readiness and ability to operationalize in practice all that the information should motivate. Frank will do a lot better in the way of giving us reason to think he *knows* that the building is on fire, if, after saying that, he gets up and runs for the exit, than if he shows us that he can state lots of facts, when challenged – again, even if what he can say includes extremely accurate definitions of "fire," "burn," "building," and so on. What Frank seems to lack is not knowledge-that or even definitional knowledge-that; what he seems to lack is an understanding of what it *means* to be in a building that is on fire. And so, we propose, Socrates would be right to say that in spite of being able to show that he has lots of pertinent information, Frank does not really know that the building

---

[5] Randall and Smith 2019.

is on fire. He doesn't *know*, because he doesn't *understand*. (Randall and Smith 2019: 21)

Socrates sometimes refers to what we lack as a kind of *craft* (*technê*), but in other places he simply calls such things "knowledge" or perhaps "science" (*epistêmê*), as we saw in the long passage from the *Gorgias* quoted at the beginning of this chapter. For now, it seems that even the version of the opacity objection that explains why he denies knowledge to poets, diviners, and rhapsodes brings in what I have been claiming is the more basic conception of knowledge as involving some kind of skill or expertise. To have fact-knowledge, for Socrates, requires that one understand what one knows; and understanding what one knows means that one has the relevant skill or expertise to apply what one knows to relevant practices. In the case of ethical knowledge, understanding, and wisdom, the expertise consists in knowing how to live well. Such expertise obviously requires certain kinds of fact-knowledge, but does not simply consist in such fact-knowledge. Expertise puts fact-knowledge to work, as it were.

4.4   The Sources of Ignorance

Given the kind of knowledge Socrates is interested in, we can see why the lack of such knowledge is not simply an epistemic fault but also will damage our quality of life. Because of this threat, Socrates thinks our first and most important aim in life should be the elimination of such ignorance, if such a thing is possible for human beings, and if not, at least we should seek in every way to ameliorate such ignorance. In order to do this, however, we must become more clearly aware of the ways in which we fall into ignorance, or what factors make us tend to remain in that condition.

Most scholarship on Socratic epistemology has simply assumed that Socrates recognizes only the kinds of cognitive processes we currently recognize:[6] our cognitions come from such things as sense perception, memory, testimony, and reasoning, to name a few examples. Of these, testimony, for Socrates, is obviously one of the most unreliable, and he regularly warns his interlocutors of the risks of accepting testimony from others who lack expertise in the area in which they express their views (see,

---

[6] An excellent review of recent scholarship on Socratic epistemology may be found in McPartland 2013. I note that all of the cognitive processes noted in McPartland's discussion, however, are familiar ones. The important additional one I discussed in the last chapter and again later in this chapter is not mentioned there.

for example, *Crito* 44d6–10, *Protagoras* 312b8–c4, and *Gorgias* 471e2–472a2).

The problems with testimony are especially acute when it comes to the formation and maintenance of ethical cognitions. Perception and memory can obviously also mislead us about value – we might appear to perceive success in life where, in fact, the appearance of success is deceiving. For example, we might recall Polus' unqualified admiration for tyrants, which Socrates interrogates in the *Gorgias*. Economic wealth and political power might appear as reliable indicators of success in life, but, as Socrates argues against Polus, these indicators are unreliable ones. Reasoning, too, if it is faulty, can lead us astray. Later on in this chapter, I will have more to say about the unreliable etiology for evaluative beliefs that I introduced in Chapter 3, and I will try to show that the ways in which Socrates seeks to respond to this other etiology is well designed for that purpose. But for now, let us ask simply about the more ordinary forms of false belief: how can we indemnify ourselves against the unreliabilities of our belief-sources?

4.5   The Socratic *Elenchos*

The ways in which Socrates goes about refuting interlocutors in Plato's early dialogues have been a lively source of scholarly discussion.[7] Virtually all of this literature has been devoted to the logical and evidentiary features of the Socratic *elenchos*: what inferences can Socrates (or his interlocutor) make from, and what degree of justification is conferred on, the consequence of an elenctic refutation, or even a series of such refutations?

This focus on the logic and justificatory features of elenctic argument was explored in an early and very influential paper by Gregory Vlastos (1994). Vlastos characterized typical Socratic argumentation as follows: (1) The interlocutor asserts a thesis that Socrates considers false and targets for refutation. (2) Socrates secures agreement to further premises, say q and r (each of which may stand for a conjunct of propositions). The agreement is ad hoc: Socrates argues from q and r, but not to them. (3) Socrates then argues, and the interlocutor agrees, that q and r entail *not-p*. (4) Thereupon Socrates claims that *not-p* has been proved true, and p false (Vlastos 1994: 11). "The problem of the elenchus," as Vlastos named it, is that (4) logically follows only if the truths of q and r can be regarded as established, but in

---

[7] For an admirably thorough review of much of the scholarly literature, see Wolfsdorf 2013.

most cases the premises in Socratic arguments are not themselves argued for, but only secured via the agreement of the interlocutor. So at the end of this sort of elenctic argument, at best, is $\sim(p \,\&\, q \,\&\, r)$. Vlastos asks, "how can Socrates claim ... to have proved that the refutand is false when all he has established is its inconsistency with premises whose truth he has not tried to establish in that argument?" (Vlastos 1994: 3).

Vlastos' account of "the Socratic method" and his attempt to solve "the problem of the *elenchus*" have not managed to persuade a consensus of scholars. Some scholars have gone so far as to doubt the entire project. Did Socrates actually conceive of what he did as involving a "method" by which he could prove the truth or falsehood of specific moral doctrines or definitions of ethical terms, or was he only ever interested in revealing the ignorance of his interlocutors? "Constructivist" accounts see Socrates as at least tentatively arguing for at least some of the conclusions reached in his arguments. "Anti-constructivist" accounts, by contrast, see Socrates as only engaged in revealing ignorance.[8]

Interpreters of either sort at least agree that the *elenchos* does in fact expose the interlocutors' confusions in such a way as to show that they are not experts in how to live. Experts on a subject will be able to express and display their expertise in ways that will be at least consistent: if subjected to elenctic examination, they will not find themselves saying contradictory things about their area of expertise.

In the *Apology*, Socrates famously tells his jurors that "the unexamined life is not worth living for a human being."[9] Socrates here seems to be advocating a life of dedication to philosophical examination as a *way* of life, and so we might suppose that it was this way of life – and not individual arguments – that Socrates really supposed would be valuable to us. Individual arguments might both expose an interlocutor's ignorance and encourage the interlocutor to reconsider their commitments and practices. Constructivists suppose that, at least for the most part, the interlocutor's revisions of their commitments and practices will lead to better ones. But such positive progress surely cannot be guaranteed. Socrates might suppose that those who led unexamined lives would be more likely to fall prey to the kinds of ignorance that lead people astray, especially for those who imagine that they are wise when they are not.

[8] A comprehensive review of all of the variations in such approaches in the recent literature is provided, again, in Wolfsdorf 2013.
[9] The translation given in Cooper 1997 has "man" instead of "human being," but the Greek term is not gendered.

4.6 *Elenchos* and the Rational Remediation of Ignorance

In Chapters 1 and 2, I discussed several passages in which Socrates seems to acknowledge that our epistemic condition is one that can realize different degrees of success, and in both chapters quoted his claim at *Euthydemus* 282a6 that we should all strive "to become as wise as possible." But how can he or anyone else undertake such a project? It seems the only answer Socrates ever gives to this question is what he says about "the unexamined life," and it also seems that the only way we ever see Socrates promoting these goals is in his elenctic examinations of others.

Socrates does not take his discussions with others simply as a service that he provides to them – as if Socratic questioning might potentially benefit only his interlocutors. In the *Charmides*, Socrates claims that there is benefit to anyone who engages in such conversations – including even those who merely stand by and observe them.

> [Socrates speaking] How could you possibly think that even if I were trying to refute everything you say, I would be doing it for any other reasons than the one I would give for a thorough investigation of my own statements – the fear of unconsciously thinking I know something when I do not. And that is what I claim to be doing now, examining the argument for my own sake primarily, but perhaps also for the sake of my friends. Or don't you believe it to be for the common good, or for that of most human beings,[10] that the state of each existing thing should become clear? (*Charmides* 166c7–d6; see also *Gorgias* 505e3–5)

This passage seems to lend support to a constructivist understanding of Socratic argumentation, since it seems to indicate that Socrates takes his conversations to promote the goal that "the state of each existing thing should become clear." Anti-constructivists, it seems, would have to argue that, as much as Socrates might value such a goal, there is no reason to think that elenctic refutation can actually contribute to its achievement.

I have claimed that Socrates regards the kind of knowledge that he pursues as *improvable*, and thus we might reasonably distinguish two very different questions:

(1) Does Socrates think his elenctic arguments can by themselves *produce* the kind of epistemic improvement he seeks? An even more forceful way to put this question (which is the way it is framed in much of the scholarly literature) would be: does Socrates think that individual (or

---

[10] Translation revised from the Sprague in Cooper 1997, which has "men" instead of "human beings." The Greek word is not gendered.

multiple) elenctic arguments can produce knowledge of their conclusions?

Or,

(2) Does Socrates think his elenctic arguments can make some progress toward such improvement – that is, does Socrates think that elenctic argument can produce some improvement in our epistemic condition, relative to the subject-matter of the argument(s)?

Without access to the improvability of our epistemic success, scholars have been forced to focus entirely on the first of these questions, and I believe it is this focus that has led anti-constructivists to reach their negative conclusions about the products of Socratic philosophizing. It is my argument herein, however, that Socrates is actually much more interested in the second of these questions, and the positive things he has to say about himself, relative to others, indicate that he would give an affirmative answer to *this* question, even if he were inclined (as per anti-constructivism) to answer the first of these two questions negatively.[11]

4.7 Definitional Knowledge and the Improvability of Epistemic Success

Many Socratic examinations pursue what have come to be known as "what is F-ness?" questions: "what is justice?", "what is piety?", "what is temperance?", and so on. In virtue of his search for answers to these, scholars have noted that Socrates seems to give some priority to *definitional* knowledge.[12] If we apply the first of these questions to Socrates' "what is F-ness?" questions, we will be asking if Socrates thinks he can use elenctic argument to attain the definitional knowledge of some ethical term. Socrates does provide some examples that he represents as being the kinds of definitions that he is after, but only for nonethical terms (so see *Laches* 192a9–b3 on quickness; *Meno* 76a4–7 on shape). But even if we take these examples to

---

[11] I do not mean to concede here even that a negative answer to the first question is the correct one. In Brickhouse and Smith 1994: 38–45, we argued for a somewhat positive answer to this question, contending that repeated elenctic arguments would improve one's warrant for believing certain things, which we claimed could count as a kind of nonexpert knowledge of those things. I now think that the improvement should not simply be regarded as applying to warrant; my claim herein is that one's cognitive condition itself is improved, and not just the warrant one has for true (or false) beliefs that one may accept. One gains, as one leads the examined life, greater expertise in the areas of examination.

[12] See Brickhouse and Smith 1994: 45–60 and Benson 2013a for discussion and analysis of the interpretive options (with different conclusions about Socrates' view of definitional knowledge).

indicate that Socrates believes that some instances of definitional knowledge are possible, nowhere in the dialogues do we get what is represented
as a fully adequate definition of any ethical concept. So anti-constructivists
might rightly doubt that Socrates thinks that elenctic argumentation could
ever produce a fully satisfactory definition. But if we consider the second
question posed, the evidence of our texts gives strong support to
constructivism.

Consider, for example, what happens in Plato's *Euthyphro*, where
Socrates asks Euthyphro to say what piety is, and Euthyphro first responds
simply by listing a number of examples of pious things (5d8–6a6). Socrates
obviously thinks this is no way to give the sort of definition that he has
asked for, and he clarifies that he wants a definition, not a list (6d9–e7). So,
it seems that Socrates does not even count this as an inadequate definition;
rather, it is no definition at all. Euthyphro then claims that piety is what is
dear to the gods (6e11–7a1). This counts, perhaps, as an improvement, but
it is not yet a successful definition, since Socrates points out that
Euthyphro believes the gods quarrel and disagree, in which case what is
loved by one god may be hated by another (7a7–8b6). Euthyphro then
revises his attempt, and now says that piety is what all the gods love (9e1–3).

In Euthyphro's first attempted definition, there were some things that
would be pious (loved by some god) that would also be impious (hated by
some other god). In the remainder of the dialogue, Socrates never once
suggests that there will be pious things that are not loved by all the gods, or
things loved by all the gods that are not pious. In other words, the revised
definition Euthyphro has now given suffers from no "scope inconsistency"
between the definiens and definiendum.[13] At least in that sense, accordingly, Euthyphro has provided an improvement on his first attempt,
though as the subsequent argument indicates, the definition he now
provides is also still faulty, but now for a different reason.

Socrates points out that this revised definition has the problem that it
seems to get the "arrow of explanation" backwards: the gods all love what is
pious *because it is pious*; it is not the case that what is pious is pious *because it
is loved by all the gods* (9e1–11b5). So Euthyphro's revised definition has also
failed. Euthyphro is now at a loss (called *aporia* in our texts), and seems not
to know how to proceed (11b6–8), and after an interlude, Socrates takes the
lead in the discussion and begins to work toward yet another attempt to
define piety – this time, as a part of justice (11e4–12d4). So now, Socrates

---

[13] I am using the terminology given in May 1997, and much of my argument is derived from the
analysis she provides.

indicates, all that is left for them to do is to say what part of justice piety is, and they will be done. Euthyphro, after struggling a bit to understand Socrates' proposal about parts and wholes, suggests that perhaps piety is that part of justice that is concerned with care of the gods, whereas the rest of justice concerns care of human beings (12e1–5). Now Socrates responds, "You seem to put that very well, but I still need a bit of information" (12e10–13a1).

The additional information has to do with how Euthyphro conceives of the "care" we are supposed to provide for the gods. Euthyphro suggests that it is not the kind of care that produces some benefit that makes the gods better (13c6–10), but rather a kind of service (13d5–7). But as a service, it must be aimed at some goal or product (*ergon*; 13e5–9). At this point, Euthyphro dithers. Challenged to indicate what the "excellent aim" of our pious service to the god might be, Euthyphro falls back on the notion that our aim is to do whatever is pleasing to the gods (15b2–4). When Socrates points out that this only returns them to the point of the earlier failed definition and so they must try again, Euthyphro hastily leaves the conversation (15e3–4), leaving the search for a definition of piety unfinished.

If we think about what happens in this dialogue, accordingly, we can see that the *elenchos* Socrates works on Euthyphro does not produce an adequate definition of piety, and thus definitional knowledge of piety is not achieved. But even so, it seems obvious that the search for such a definition had made significant progress – to the point where it seems like the only thing left to do would be to specify the "excellent aim" of piety. Euthyphro's progress in the dialogue thus gives an excellent example of how Socratic examination can allow those who engage in it to become more skilled in knowing how to provide a definition of piety (even granting that their skills never reach the point of mastery) and also to have a better sense of what an adequate definition of piety might look like.

This kind of improvement in one's definitional skill indicates improvement in one's conceptualization of the object of the inquiry – in this case, piety. Such improved conceptualization has important practical consequences.

> Socrates: Instruct me then about what this very characteristic is in order that by looking at it and using it as a standard, I can say what either you or someone else might do is the sort of thing that is pious and that what is not of this sort I can say it is not pious. (*Euthyphro* 6e4–7)

Were one able to provide a fully successful definition of some virtue-term (and also, to be clear, *understand* it), then one could be an inerrant judge of whatever applies to that virtue. At the other extreme, one who has no conception of some virtue – one who was completely ignorant of it – would not be able to offer any definition of it at all. But between these two extremes would be many levels of achievement with respect to comprehending that virtue. For someone like Socrates – someone who has taken up the true craft of politics, and has made at least some progress in his attempt to master that craft – we may suppose that he will not be as susceptible to the kind of errors that would typically be made by those who suppose they are wise but are not. The one who earnestly takes up a craft will be better able to give at least some approximation of an adequate definition of the subject-matter appropriate to that craft. Using this approximation, they could then stand as a better judge of whatever belongs to that subject than those who had not (yet) taken up the craft. In this way, then, Socrates can reasonably suppose that those who engage in philosophical examinations can improve their mastery of the ethical crafts. It may be that no human being could ever completely master the craft of virtue: as Socrates tells his jurors in the *Apology*, it is the god who is really wise (23a5–6). Try as we might to improve, it seems likely that we will never become wise in the same complete way.

4.8   *Elenchos* and the Nonrational Sources of Ignorance

In the last chapter, I explored Socratic motivational intellectualism, and the roles that our natural attractions and aversions, as well as our emotions, can play in why we come to believe we should do what we do. I also explained how Socrates often used shame as a way to persuade others. It is time to return to that issue, this time from a more epistemic perspective: just how does Socratic refutation respond to the nonrational aspects of cognitive processing?

Several fine examples of how this works may be found in the *Gorgias*. In a way, Callicles is on to the very issue at stake here: Callicles claims that Gorgias ended up agreeing to something that Socrates had said because he was ashamed to admit to what he really believed, and that is how Socrates ended up catching the Sophist in a contradiction (*Gorgias* 482c7–d4). Callicles goes on to say that Socrates played the same shame game with Polus, and then generalizes his accusation by saying that

> [I]f a person is ashamed and doesn't dare to say what he thinks, he's forced to contradict himself. This is in fact the clever trick you've thought of, with which you work mischief in your discussions. (*Gorgias* 482e5–483a3)

Now, I do not agree with Callicles that Socrates' uses of shaming tactics amount to a "clever trick" in his discussions.[14] But I do agree that our texts give us plenty of evidence that Socrates not only appeals to shame in his philosophical conversations; he also does things that seem like obvious attempts to make his interlocutors feel what Paul Woodruff has called the "scalding" emotion of shame.[15] And even if Socrates never completely admits to using shame in his refutations of Gorgias and Polus, it seems clear enough that it is precisely *shaming* that Socrates intends when he compares Callicles himself to a "torrent-bird" (a bird reputed to excrete as fast as it eats, which might account for its name[16]), to one who spends his life delighting in the pleasures of itching and scratching himself (494c6–8), and finally, to a *kinaidos* (a pathic homosexual) – all the while repeatedly (and obviously sarcastically) reminding Callicles that *aidôs* (shame) should not affect their conversation!

In the last chapter, I explained how shame might be regarded as one of the many nonrational impulses that Socrates thinks can affect what we believe, or, as I noted about fear, it could be that Socrates is a cognitivist about shame – supposing that shame itself is a kind of cognition. If the latter is Socrates' view of shame, I argued, its connection to nonrational sources of belief would be as a product of such sources (rather than itself being one of them). Either way, however, Callicles' accusation that Socrates gets people to say what they don't really believe because they are too ashamed to admit it has already become somewhat problematized. After all, if emotions *just are* cognitions, as cognitivism holds, then one can hardly accuse Socrates, as a cognitivist about emotion, of using motivational tactics involving some emotion(s) that thereby ignore or leave behind what the agent actually *believes*. Rather, what Socrates would be doing, in appealing to an interlocutor's emotions, would be revealing to the interlocutor some belief the interlocutor had that might be seen as being in conflict with something else the interlocutor might believe, or suppose they believed, and thus revealed as at least at risk of being guilty of contradiction. But being shown to accept or at least to say contradictory things does not, it seems to me, go outside the bounds of what Socrates

---

[14] I find it interesting that Callicles characterizes the use of shame in such a negative way, while also noting that he attempts to use this same "clever trick" against Socrates when he describes the sorts of things the latter does as "crowd-pleasing vulgarities" (482e3–4) of a sort that deserve a flogging (485d2), as themselves shameful (486a5), and as "silly nonsense" (486c7). Presumably, hypocrisy is permitted in what Callicles regards as the manly speech of a good rhetorician.

[15] Woodruff 2000: 133. An admirable discussion of Socrates' use of mocking and humiliation may be found in Sanderman 2004.

[16] See Irwin 1979: 197, note on 494b; see also Dodds 1959 on the same passage.

regards as a rational standard. Rather, it seems more like a failure to meet even a minimal standard of rationality – one that, as I argued earlier, would seem to indicate a rather significant lack of skill in the relevant area. Even if Socrates is not a cognitivist about shame, however, and regards it as a more basic desiderative impulse, Callicles' idea that Socrates uses it in such a way as to induce akratic behavior must also be rejected: at worst, Socrates could be regarded as using shame to change what people believe, but never to act in a way that is contrary to what they believe, at least at the time they act.

For Socrates, not all beliefs are equally worthy of our acceptance – and thus, as an intellectualist about motivation, it will also be true that not all beliefs are equally worthy of guiding our actions. Recalling the cognitive processes involving nonrational origins that I discussed in the previous chapter, we may remind ourselves that Socrates recognizes different etiologies for the production of belief – some more veridically reliable than others. The *least* veridically reliable of these processes had their origins in the nonrational processes involving our most basic attractions and aversions.

As I said in the last chapter (in Section 3.11), one finds evidence in both Xenophon and Plato for thinking that Socrates did not just hope to improve his interlocutor's logic or even challenge the justifications for their beliefs. He also used his elenctic questioning to help correct the ways in which they go about their cognitive business, by subjecting them to shaming and humiliation when they have allowed themselves to accept less reliable belief-forming processes, when more reliable ones are available. Recall Plato's Socrates confronting Callicles, who had been extolling the benefits of living one's life in ways that maximize the satiation of appetites. Socrates entirely rejects this view, and says instead that the soul of one who is "foolish, uncontrolled, unjust and impious . . . should be kept away from its appetites and not permitted to do anything other than what will make it better" (*Gorgias* 505b2–4). When Callicles feigns incomprehension, Socrates shows his hand clearly: "This fellow won't put up with being benefited and with his undergoing the very thing the discussion's about, with being corrected" (*kolazomenos*; *Gorgias* 505c3–4).

Indeed, if the analysis I have given is right, Socrates sees the nonrational and emotional processes that he engages as importantly epistemic ones, since they involve a process of belief-formation that may be the *only* recourse for improvement, for those who have already allowed themselves to fall into injustice. Once an agent may come to have the correct beliefs, via this process, only then may they go on to develop better epistemic habits, relying on more veridically reliable cognitive processes. The upshot is still a version of motivational intellectualism: agents will still in every case only act in the ways they believe are best for them, from the options available to them at the time of action of which they are aware.

In this view, it follows that one important source of ignorance is that one allows a veridically unreliable cognitive process to produce one's beliefs – and this kind of process is not only unreliable; it also tends to lead the epistemic (and ethical) agent to resist other, more reliable cognitive processes. Recognizing this additional possibility, I contend, gives us better insight not only into Socrates' understanding of ignorance, but also into Socrates' famous philosophical practice, the *elenchos*.

To bring this aspect of Socratic philosophizing into focus, I have relied heavily on what Plato has Socrates say in the *Gorgias*. But as I showed in the last chapter, that is not the only place where we find Socrates indicating a keen interest in engaging with the nonrational elements of human psychology. When he talks to his jurors in the *Apology* about what he does, recall, we find him making liberal mention of *shaming* and *reproaching* those who suppose they are wise when they are not (so see *Apology* 29d9–30a1, 30e7, 41e6), whose philosophical examinations make him like a gadfly who *stings* his victims (30e2–5) and troubles them (41e3). These kinds of passages – and the ways in which Socrates' interlocutors often show emotional responses – clearly indicate that Socrates does not think that his way of talking with them is aimed only at *rational* remediation of their ignorance. Instead, Socrates understands that refutation – especially *public* refutation – can have effects on the nonrational cognitive processes that can not only lead to false beliefs but also make one increasingly immune to reason. The way this works, presumably, is something he explains when he talks about how we need to keep our appetites in a controlled condition (*Gorgias* 505a6–b5), by not allowing them to get too much of what they crave. Once they become too strong, however, damage is done to the soul, and once that damage is done, Socrates says, the only remediation possible is through a certain degree of pain and suffering (*Gorgias* 525b1–c6). While certain kinds of punishment must be left to the agency of the state, in its legal system (so see *Apology* 26a2–8), Socrates seems to think that it is an appropriate part of his philosophical mission to play the role of one who can "correct" his interlocutors in ways that go beyond simple logic and the rational presentation of epistemic evidence, and thus we see him attempting to remediate ignorance in nonrational as well as in rational ways, using his *elenchos*.

4.9   Deliberation in Ignorance

Ignorance, in Socrates' view, prevents us from doing what we really want to do and from achieving what we really want to achieve. And since none of us is truly wise, none of us a master at the craft of virtue, all of us suffer to a considerable degree from ignorance. Quite obviously, if knowledge and ignorance were all or nothing, then Socrates' own disavowals of knowledge and wisdom would, from a practical point of view, ensure that his situation was hopeless. But that is not what we found in Chapters 1 and 2. Instead, what we found was that, even though he was very aware of the degree of his own ignorance, he nonetheless qualified (at least for Plato) as an exemplary human being, and as someone who was in a position to regard himself as having managed to take up "the true craft of politics." In this chapter, I have focused on how the Socratic *elenchos* functions as a practice that is well designed to help remedy human ignorance, while certainly not something that can ever hope to eliminate it altogether. But in Chapter 2, I also reviewed several texts that seemed to suggest that Socrates regarded himself as having managed to avoid doing injustice, but also to benefit others. One might be inclined to think that the Socratic *elenchos* is the only way in which Socrates supposed that he could practice the true craft of politics. In the following sections, however, I want to discuss the evidence we might have for thinking that Socrates can also engage successfully in positive action. Is finding flaws in others' (or his own) thinking about how to live the only way that Socrates can do well, despite his ignorance? Or can Socrates also engage with some hope of success in the business of positive practical deliberation? To put the question in a somewhat different way, I have emphasized that the craft model of knowledge requires anyone who hopes for self-improvement to *practice* at the craft of virtue. The question now becomes: is the only way to practice at virtue engaging in elenctic arguments? Or is there another way to practice at virtue?

4.10   Rational Preference

In an unusual moment of indelicacy, Gregory Vlastos raises what he regards as a fatal objection for what has come to be known as the "identify thesis" regarding the relation of virtue and happiness, according to which virtue *just is* happiness. Vlastos' famous objection goes as follows:

> Imagine that in a strange house where I must spend the night I have the choice of two beds. One is freshly made and the sheets are clean. The other was slept in the night before by someone in a drunken stupor who vomited

on the bed: the sheets are still soggy from the remains. Since my virtue would be unimpaired if, clenching my teeth and holding my nose, I were to crawl in between those filthy sheets for a bad night's sleep, why should not my happiness be similarly unimpaired? (Vlastos 1991: 215)

Vlastos' point is obvious: if all there were to happiness were one's condition of virtue, one would be left entirely without any ground for making any number of practical decisions (whose value to the agent, moreover, can be – as in Vlastos' case – abundantly evident). If the "identity thesis" really were Socrates' position about the relationship between virtue and happiness, then anyone of sense would reject the Socratic position out of hand.

Vlastos seems to think that it is simply obvious that Socrates would have a preference for the clean bed, rather than a dirty one. For my part, I tend to suspect that Socrates' preferences might be somewhat more difficult to discern, but that is not my topic here. Rather, I want to ask a somewhat different question; namely, on the basis of *what* would Socrates have believed that some person's preferences or the decisions based on them were rational or defensible, rather than simply arbitrary?

Vlastos' own answer to what grounds a preference for a clean place to sleep is that such preferences are indirectly related to virtue. In Vlastos' words,

> [L]et us allow happiness a multitude of lesser constituents in addition to virtue. Everything on Socrates' list of non-moral goods (cf. *Eud.* 279A–B) would come in under this head. *In disjunction from virtue each would be worthless.* But when conjoined with virtue (i.e. when used virtuously) they would enhance happiness in some small way. Variations in happiness which, on the Identity Thesis, would be a function of a single variable, on this alternative model would be a function of many variables: all of those non-moral mini-components of happiness would be incremental in some small way if conjoined with virtue; each would make a mini-difference, greater in the case of some than of others. (Vlastos 1991: 216)

Other scholars have characterized the relationship between Vlastos' "non-moral goods" and happiness in somewhat different ways, but everyone seems to agree that whatever it is that makes such things *preferable* to alternatives has to be in some way related to virtue, which Socrates unfailingly assigns the most important place, as a goal for humans to strive for.[17]

---

[17] For examples of this, see Socrates' famous prescriptions at *Apology* 30a7–b4; *Crito* 47e7–48b5, 49a4–b5.

But if some connection to virtue is *all* that can ground such preferences, for Socrates, we may find that examples such as Vlastos' vomit-soaked bed are actually not able to do the work they were supposed to do. So – just to use Vlastos' own example – the preference not to sleep in a vomit-soaked bed would *only* be rational, for someone like Socrates, if the better sleep one achieved in the clean bed were to be used virtuously. Now, we can understand well enough how Socrates might suppose that someone who would use the "advantage" of a good night's sleep for the extra sharpness it would provide in the pursuit of their vicious plans for wrongdoing on the following day would actually benefit more from a sleepless night in a vomit-soaked bed. After all, Socrates famously believes that wrongdoing damages the soul and so one who is disabled in some way from engaging in wrong-doing would actually be benefited, relative to the alternative.[18] Moreover, Socrates also believes that we all desire what is *really* best for us.[19] Hence, for a vicious person's desire with respect to a place to sleep to be truly rational, it would have to be for the vomit-soaked bed, rather than the clean one. So it doesn't look likely that any complete account of Socrates' conception of moral psychology will render it completely in accord with what one might think of as our usual intuitions on the subject.

The case of Socrates himself, however, is surely not that of a vicious man. But, much as we might like to think of Socrates as a virtuous person, his own disclaimers of wisdom,[20] together with his adherence to the unity of virtue,[21] pose a serious problem. If virtue is (or all of the virtues are) one, then anyone who lacked one of the virtues lacks all of them. It follows that if Socrates lacks wisdom, he is also not pious, or just, or temperate, or courageous. My arguments in Chapters 1 and 2 sought to show, however, that virtue (or any of the virtues) is improvable, so that one could have it (or them) to some degree. So, despite his avowed ignorance, we do not find Socrates describing himself as foolish, impious, unjust, intemperate, or cowardly.[22] If so, then insofar as his preferences could be defended in terms of his reasonable attempts to be as

---

[18] For discussion of this doctrine and what might ground it, see Brickhouse and Smith 2010: 89–131.

[19] On which see Penner and Rowe 1994.

[20] See, for example, *Apology* 20c1–3, 21d2–7, 23b2–4; *Charmides* 165b4–c2, 166c7–d6; *Euthyphro* 5a7–c5, 15c12, 15e5–16a4; *Laches* 186b8–c5, 186d8–e3, 200e2–5; *Lysis* 212a4–7, 223b4–8; *Hippias Major* 286c8–e2, 304d4–e5; *Gorgias* 509a4–6; *Meno* 71a1–7, 80d1–4; *Republic* I.337e4–5.

[21] His precise commitment here is a matter of scholarly controversy. For a sense of the spectrum of options, see Brickhouse and Smith 1994: 60–72 and 2010: 154–167; Devereux 1993; Ferejohn 1982 and 1983–4; Kraut 1984: 258–362; Penner 1973 and 1992b; Vlastos 1981: 418–423; Woodruff 1976.

[22] Indeed, Socrates characterizes himself far more positively than this at *Apology* 37a3–b3, 41d1–2, and is characterized by others, too, in much more favorable terms, with respect to the various virtues. See, for example, Xenophon *Memorabilia* 4.8.11, *Apology* 14–15.

virtuous as he could be, then they would qualify as rational. If we follow this line of reasoning, then, we could defend the rationality of a Socratic preference for a clean place to sleep on the ground that a good sleep would benefit Socrates in his pursuit of virtue. The same sort of case, we might expect, could be made for all the rest of Socrates' ordinary preferences in life, on the basis of which all – or at least most – of his activities could be regarded as rational.

Moreover, it seems plausible to suppose that one who simply lacked all such preferences, or who could not find a way to formulate them in such a way as to seem to that person to be reasonably preferred, would be all but incapable of life itself. From a psychological point of view, a lack of preferences on the basis of which to act would seem to threaten even the possibility of taking any of the many actions we must in order to get through the day. We must choose whether to eat, what to eat, and when, what clothes to wear, and which direction to take and what speed, if we are even to take a first step in the morning, and so on. If these are to be voluntary and deliberate acts, then they must reflect actual preferences and judgments we are making every step of the way. The very idea that Socrates or anyone else might lack such preferences, then, seems to be psychologically impossible, or at least deeply implausible. Socrates may at times strike us as weird. But he wasn't *that* weird.

4.11 The Threat of Skepticism (and Practical Paralysis)

As I indicated in the last section, however, it is one thing to grant that Socrates actually had preferences for practical deliberation, and quite another to be able to figure out how and why Socrates would actually be able to regard those he or anyone else had as rationally justified. Again, they *would* be rationally justified just in case they lent support to a life of the pursuit of virtue. But on the basis of *what* would Socrates be justified in thinking that one or more of his or someone else's specific plans for a specific day actually was an example of the pursuit of virtue? On the basis of what would Socrates suppose that any given decision about how to act would be an example of practicing at virtue, in order to improve in it? What, in other words, would Socrates think justified any one of his own or someone else's (moral or nonmoral) preferences, or the deliberations they guided, given that he (sincerely, I believe[23]) conceived of himself and the others he encountered as not knowing what virtue was? Not knowing this, shouldn't he also suppose that no-one (but the wise, if such there be) was in

---

[23] Not all scholars have agreed: see, for example, Gulley 1968. For a response, see Brickhouse and Smith 1989: 37–47, 100–108, 133–137.

any position to judge one course of action as more virtuous (or more conducive to virtue) than any other? If someone does not know what virtue is, how can they know what they should prefer, with respect to the actual pursuit of it in any given instance? It is not enough, it seems, for someone to have a preference simply on the basis of feelings of disgust, or because one option promises more creature comfort than some other option, for neither these nor any other of the more typical grounds for some practical preference – which most people regard as adequate – satisfy Socrates' more exacting standards. Again, we might expect that a vicious ignoramus might have the same preference as Socrates would have, in the case of Vlastos' choice of beds. But that ignoramus' preference and choice would not be rational ones, for they would actually promote the ignoramus' harm, rather than benefit. Each preference can only qualify as justified, for Socrates, if the agent can make a plausible case for why this preference or this action is likely to conduce to the good. But that is precisely the problem, for Socrates, and because he turns out to be the "wisest of men," for all the rest of us, too. Since all of us are ignorant in *at least* the way Socrates counted himself as being, on the basis of *what* can we have any confidence or justification that our preferences and deliberations *ever* qualify as justified or rational? With respect to *any choice we make*, we may ask: what reason do we have to think that *this* is what we should do, rather than something else, or even the opposite of what seems best to us? We all have preferences, of course, and so did Socrates. But can there be some ground for Socrates and others who recognize their own ignorance that could serve as adequate to justify some preference one might have, and the deliberations and decisions that might flow from that preference? If not, the Socratic view of rational preference is one we might also find unacceptable: all who are ignorant would be in no position to make judgments about or formulate preferences in regard even to the most critical decisions we are called upon to make. The result is that all decision-making would be unwarranted, and so all decisions would turn out to be equal in value – including, when such is possible, the decision *not to make any decision*. If ignorance is a categorical defeater for rational action, then even the most immoral and egregious decisions would be no less justified than those that appear to most of us to be morally mandated. If this, then, really is the Socratic view, then the Socratic view amounts to the most comprehensive and profound skepticism with respect to practical deliberation. It would obviously follow from this that Socrates would be a *moral* skeptic, as well, insofar as moral reasoning is a species of practical reasoning. In earlier chapters, I have tried to show that this conclusion cannot possibly be right.

I now want to try to explain what other resources we might have to practice at the craft of virtue, even when we are only novices.

Famously, Socrates claimed to Crito, in the dialogue of that name, that "I am not just now but in fact I have always been the sort of person who is persuaded (*peithesthai*) by nothing but the reason (*tô logô*) that appears to me to be best (*beltistos phainetai*) when I've reasoned (*logizomenô*) about it" (*Crito* 46b4–6; my translation). So one way of putting the problem might be this: does Socrates think there can be good reasons that do not derive from knowledge, and if so, what might be the sources of these good reasons, and on the basis of what (other than knowledge, *ex hypothesi*) do these reasons qualify to Socrates as good enough to ground preferences and practical deliberations? To put it back in terms of craft: when one does not have a craft, and does not have a master craftsman to teach it to one, how might one proceed in such a way as to try to take up the craft, as Socrates says he has done with the craft of politics?

4.12 Reining in the Problem of Ignorance

Should we believe that Socrates regarded not only his own but also everyone else's epistemic condition to be so impoverished as to ensure that all preferences are equally unwarranted, and every deliberation or decision neither better nor worse, in terms of its agent's justification? Obviously not. In a number of dialogues we find Socrates himself taking action (at least of the quotidian kind) and engaging with others in ways that seem critical only insofar as those others seem to be guilty of a presumption of wisdom about what Socrates regards as "the most important things" (*Apology* 22d7). We do not see Socrates questioning people's choices when it comes to everyday matters. More importantly, we have at least one dialogue in which Socrates at least seems to be engaged in a deliberation about what most of us would regard as an important moral decision. Although it may be debatable whether or not Socrates had already fully made up his mind about what he would do, at least the tenor of Socrates' discussion in the *Crito* makes it sound as if Socrates is genuinely involved in thinking through the question of whether he should stay and be executed or leave and go into exile, as his friend has encouraged him to do. By the end of the dialogue, a decision is reached and we know that this decision was not later reversed. But the dialogue does not rely on anyone claiming to have adequate knowledge of justice, and so we may assume that whatever counted as a reason in this case managed to do so without deriving from such knowledge.

Moreover, we can also find, scattered about in the early dialogues of Plato, examples of things that Socrates seems happy to regard as adequate reasons for actions, but which, again, make no claim of having their basis in the agent's knowledge of the good. Some examples of this qualify as having a religious basis. So, for example, Socrates thinks that his choice of a life of philosophizing is justified on the basis of "oracles and dreams and in every way in which divine providence has ever ordered a human being to do anything whatever" (*Apology* 33c6–7). Notoriously, in response to what he experiences as an intervention from his *daimonion*, Socrates will always cease and desist from whatever he experiences the "sign" as opposing.[24] Readers might reasonably wonder, in the face of such evidence, just how Socrates could suppose he was in a position to determine that his experiences of such things *really were the effects of divine intervention in his life*, as opposed to some alternative we might imagine, but to this question there is no explicit reply to be found in our texts. For my purposes here, it is enough to note that information Socrates believes he has reason to think derives from a divine source will count to him as enough of a ground to warrant action. That is not especially surprising, since Socrates also seems to think that "the god is wise" (*Apology* 23a5–6), and so any information that derives from divinity is actually grounded in knowledge.[25] Accordingly, even if Socrates' own access to this source is not itself an instance of the kind of knowledge that Socrates claims to lack, it seems that Socrates is inclined to suppose that the source itself does have that knowledge. Hence, it is reasonable for Socrates to act in accordance with such knowledge, even if the knowledge is not his own.

We can also find other examples in our texts of decisions that Socrates makes (or else that Socrates observes others making), which he seems to be prepared to grant as justified. One group of these that have particular importance in Socratic philosophizing would be the sorts of examples that he selects for use in what are called his *epagogic* arguments, where Socrates draws inferences from examples that are supposed to be representative of some point at issue.[26] Although Socrates is never willing to accept a list of

---

[24] See *Apology* 31c8–d3, 40a4–6, 40c3–4, 41d6; *Euthydemus* 272e4; *Euthyphro* 3b5–7; *Republic* VI.496c4; *Phaedrus* 242b8–9, 242c2; discussions and analyses of this peculiar aspect of Socratic life abound, but see especially most recently Destrée and Smith 2005; Ehli 2018; Lännström 2012.

[25] Here, too, more questions arise, but the texts will provide no explicit answer to them: on what basis Socrates thinks he is justified in believing that the god is wise, or that gods do not provide misleading "oracles and dreams," and so on. Rather than speculate about Socrates' theology here, I will simply note that Socrates functions in the dialogues as if something he can link to divine intervention will qualify as a justification for action.

[26] For which see, especially, McPherran's most important 2007 study. One of many examples of this type of argument may be found at *Euthydemus* 279d8–280a4, where Socrates uses the examples of

examples as an adequate answer to his "what is F-ness?" questions, he is quite willing to use individual examples of F-ness that he and his interlocutor can agree on, as tests for attempted definitions, or as indicators of what will need to be included within the scope of a successful definition. What justifies Socrates' use of these examples is never stated in our texts, but scholars have suggested that "self-evidence, their endoxic status, experience, deduction from premises to which he is committed on the basis of any of the previous three"[27] all seem to be plausible possibilities. If so, then it now appears that Socrates thinks it is reasonable to appeal to quite a wide variety of grounds for justification, even where the origins of these grounds do not enjoy the status of knowledge.

4.13   An Important Text

The *Crito* seems to be the only text in which Socrates is made to appear engaged in an actual deliberation about what he should do on a matter of moral significance. The reasoning in that dialogue is presented to Crito, and is obviously treated as defeasible. Even so, Socrates is ready and willing to go to his death on the basis of that reasoning. The *Crito*, accordingly, gives us powerful evidence that the kind of ignorance Socrates finds in himself is in no way paralyzing, in the domain of practical reasoning or moral action.

There is, moreover, another text that seems to depict an interlocutor who is represented as either still engaged in, or as having already completed, a deliberation on a matter of considerable moral significance: the *Euthyphro*. In that text, Socrates encounters a younger man who announces that he intends to prosecute his own father for murder. The details of the case are quite unusual: in a drunken rage, a worker on Euthyphro's father's farm slit the throat of a family slave. Euthyphro's father captured the murderer and bound him hand and foot and tossed him into a ditch, while sending a messenger to the Religious Counselor to determine what should be done with the man. But the murderer died of hunger and cold before any answer could be received, and now Euthyphro has decided he must prosecute his father for the murder of the murderer. Given the unusual circumstances, and a cultural norm against sons prosecuting their own fathers,[28] Euthyphro's relatives are completely opposed to the

---

flute-playing, reading and writing, helmsmanship, being a general, and being a physician to show that wisdom always makes one more successful. I will have much more to say about this argument in the next two chapters.
[27] Wolfsdorf 2013: 57.   [28] For which see Tulin 1996: 94 and citations.

prosecution. Socrates never explicitly condemns Euthyphro's plans, and instead engages Euthyphro on one of his famous "what is F-ness?" questions, in this case on the topic of piety.

Now, scholars have debated several aspects of what might be going on in the discussion between Socrates and Euthyphro. One topic that has been debated concerns what stage of Euthyphro's (proposed) legal proceeding might be represented in the dialogue. The discussion is clearly indicated as taking place on the porch of the King-Archon's office (*Euthyphro* 2a3). But the text does not tell us whether Euthyphro has *already* entered his case with the King-Archon, or whether he has not yet done so, and is waiting there intending to do so. But these are not the only two options, even if they are the only two that scholars have actually debated.[29] In murder cases, there would actually be three preliminary hearings (called *prodikasiai*) – one per month over a period of three months,[30] and so it is entirely possible that Euthyphro could be on his way to – or from – any one of these hearings on the day of his conversation with Socrates. But for reasons I have given elsewhere,[31] it seems to me most plausible to suppose that Euthyphro had not yet brought his case before the King-Archon, in which case Euthyphro's sudden departure at the end of the dialogue can be seen as an abandonment of his plans to pursue the prosecution of his father, at least for that day (for which see Diogenes Laertius 2.29).

This understanding of what is going on in the dialogue, then, makes at least Euthyphro's situation into one that is effectively a deliberation. Perhaps he had thought he had made up his mind before he took it upon himself to go to the King-Archon's office that day. After talking for a while with Socrates, however, his earlier resolve seems to have weakened and he is now willing either to abandon or at least to postpone his earlier plan. So even if Socrates and Euthyphro don't directly discuss the specific question, "Should Euthyphro pursue this prosecution?", the conversation has a direct effect on what Euthyphro actually decides to do on that day.[32] But this now raises the question that is my focus, only now applied to Euthyphro's case: did Socrates have an opinion about what Euthyphro should do, and on the basis of *what* might Socrates suppose that his opinion would provide a ground for rational deliberation and action?

---

[29] See Beversluis 2010: 176, 184; Burnet 1924: 82; and Tulin 1996: 74–76 vs. McPherran 2002: 107 and Brickhouse and Smith 2004: 10–18.

[30] About which see Brickhouse and Smith 2004: 14.　　[31] Brickhouse and Smith 2004: 14–18.

[32] I am obviously not the first to have noted this. See, for others' statements of this same point, McPherran 2002 and Benson 2013b.

It has recently been argued that nothing in Socratic philosophy – or at least nothing of that philosophy that is given in our texts – would provide any ground for Socrates to make any judgment in Euthyphro's case,[33] or might even supply Socrates with grounds for approving of Euthyphro's proposed course of action.[34] I am not persuaded. On the contrary, I think there are adequate indicators in the text of what Socrates' actual opinion is on this issue, and I also think the text actually gives us what may reasonably be supposed are the grounds that Socrates would regard as justifying his opinion. So let me take up the evidence for these two claims now, in order.

4.14 What Socrates Believes

Socrates never directly states any opinion about Euthyphro's proposed prosecution. Hence, neither an affirmation nor a denial of the proposition, "Euthyphro would do the right thing by prosecuting his father" would strictly *contradict* anything that Socrates says in the dialogue. But, as Paul Grice famously argued some years ago (in several places, but perhaps most famously in Grice 1975), explicit statements of belief and logical implication are not the only ways to find out what someone else believes. Consider an example provided in Davis 2010:

ALAN: Are you going to Paul's party?
BARB: I have to work.

Notice that Barb does not explicitly *say* that she will not be going to the party, nor could one validly derive that as an inference from what she does say. Instead, what she has done is what is called "conversational implicature," and any competent English-speaker would understand that Barb will not be going to the party. As Davis puts is, "If she knew she was going to Paul's party, she might be guilty of misleading Alan, but not of lying" (Davis 2010). A question to ask about Socrates, then, is whether or not he has committed some conversational implicature about Euthyphro's case in anything he says to Euthyphro (such that, even if it would not strictly be

---

[33] See Benson 2013b.

[34] This worry is expressed in Al-Maini 2011: 2, who (wrongly, I think) attributes this view to McPherran 2002 (at 2, n. 3). Al-Maini goes on to argue that "the ensuing discussion [sc. in the *Euthyphro*] provides the justification for accepting the opinion of [Euthyphro's] family" and "the dialogue gives indications that Euthyphro's impiety stems from his refusal to care for the wishes and aims of his father" (Al-Maini 2011: 3). The remainder of my own argument will make clear that I agree with Al-Maini's assessment of what the dialogue indicates by way of Socrates' appraisal of Euthyphro's plan.

a *lie* for Socrates to deny that implicature, it could be regarded as a case of misleading Euthyphro if he does not actually accept what he gives Euthyphro reason to believe about his own position). I claim that Socrates very clearly does provide several conversational implicatures with respect to his own judgment about the propriety of Euthyphro's plans. But let us look more closely at the way Socrates reacts to Euthyphro.

4.14.1   Euthyphro *3e8–4b2*

SOCRATES: So what's your case about, Euthyphro? Are you defending or prosecuting?
EUTHYPHRO: I'm prosecuting.
SOCRATES: Whom?
EUTHYPHRO Someone whom I seem, again, to be crazy (*au dokô mainesthai*) for prosecuting.
SOCRATES: Why? Are you prosecuting someone who can fly away?
EUTHYPHRO: He can hardly fly away; he's already quite old.
SOCRATES: Who is he?
EUTHYPHRO: My father.
SOCRATES: Your father! (*'O sos, ô beltiste;*)
EUTHYPHRO: Absolutely.
SOCRATES: What's the charge, and what is the trial about?
EUTHYPHRO: Murder.
SOCRATES: By Heracles! Surely most people *don't* see how that's right! Indeed, I don't think this would be done correctly by just anyone, but I suppose it takes someone *far* advanced in wisdom.[35]

There are three moments in this exchange that seem to me to indicate that Socrates has an opinionated response to this news from Euthyphro. The first is when Socrates responds to the news that it is Euthyphro's own father who will be the target of prosecution. Euthyphro has already conceded that he seems to others to be crazy for undertaking this prosecution, and so Socrates' shocked response is one we can expect Euthyphro would not find surprising. But even so, there can be no plausible denial that Socrates is depicted as giving a shocked response.

I contend that we should understand Socrates' exclamation, in his first reaction to Euthyphro's news, in a similar way. When people exclaim, it is because they are responding to something in an excited way. What has excited Socrates? The answer to this question is obvious. Why does what

[35] This and all the rest of the translations from the *Euthyphro* that I provide for the rest of this chapter are my own.

Euthyphro has said excite Socrates? It would not do so if Socrates' first response was one of neutrality or calm information-gathering. Instead, Socrates' shock should be assumed to indicate the same reaction we would expect from anyone in that cultural context, where Euthyphro's plan would seem to *anyone* to be (at least prima facie) a bad one. That does not *prove* that Socrates disagrees with what Euthyphro is planning to do, nor does it rule out the possibility that further information would blunt or even reverse Socrates' initial negative reaction. But it seems to me that his reaction simply cannot be sensibly construed as one of either agreement or neutrality, but only as at least an inclination to judge Euthyphro's plan negatively.

The second moment in Section 4.14.1 that indicates at least a preliminary evaluation by Socrates comes after Euthyphro replies that his proposed prosecution will be on the charge of murder. Now, Socrates begins with an expletive ("Heracles!"), but then gives what would seem to be the reason why Euthyphro had begun by admitting that others think what he is doing is crazy: "Surely most people *don't* see how that's right!" Let us ask how Euthyphro should understand this response. Is it that Socrates thinks that most people don't see how what Euthyphro is doing is right simply because most people are ignoramuses and wouldn't know right from wrong even if the truth were right before their eyes? That, after all, seems to be Euthyphro's assessment of the opposition he has received: as he says at 3c4–5, "We shouldn't worry about them; instead, we should take them on." There are certainly times, in Plato's dialogues, when it is Socrates himself who says that a man of sense should pay no attention to the opinions of most people (see, e.g., *Crito* 44c6–d10). Would this be a plausible way, then, to understand Socrates' reaction here – simply as agreeing with Euthyphro that whatever most people say is irrelevant and should be dismissed out of hand? Obviously not. But if not, then what else would Socrates have in mind when he so emphatically agrees with Euthyphro's apparent assessment that what he plans runs contrary to what most other people think is right? As we saw in our assessment of the first moment, this does not mean that the valence of Socrates' reaction is settled or immutable. But even if it qualifies as *only* an initial reaction, the negativity of his reaction cannot be reasonably doubted.

Finally (in what I am calling the third important moment in Section 4.14.1), Socrates says a little more about what he is thinking about Euthyphro's plan: "Indeed, I don't think this would be done correctly by just anyone, but I suppose it takes someone *far* advanced in wisdom." Why, we must ask, would Socrates believe that what Euthyphro is planning would not be done correctly by just anyone? If Socrates sees no (at least prima facie) reason to pass judgment on what Euthyphro is doing, why shouldn't he remain neutral about the question of whether such a plan would be the right thing to do for

most people, in most cases of the relevant sort? It would seem the opposite
should be the case if Socrates is inclined to believe that what Euthyphro is
doing is the *right* thing to do. When Socrates is persuaded that something is
the right thing to do, he seems eager to mandate acting in that way to
absolutely everyone he encounters, whenever he can (see, e.g., *Apology* 29d2–
30a5). On the other hand, if Socrates doesn't (yet) have an opinion as to what
Euthyphro should do, then how could he (yet) have any opinion about
whether or not anyone else could do the same sort of thing, and do well in
doing so? Instead, the message here is obviously that what Euthyphro is
proposing seems to Socrates to be quite wrong, so that what makes this first
impression of wrongness incorrect – if it is in fact incorrect – must be that
there is some very special wisdom at work, available to Euthyphro and not to
"just anyone." In other words, if it should turn out that, as a matter of fact,
Euthyphro *does not* turn out to be "far advanced in wisdom," then Socrates
would regard it as reasonable to suppose that it is no more right for
Euthyphro to do as he plans than it would be for "just anyone" to do so.
But it is not simply that Euthyphro's proposed prosecution would be *no
better* than if "just anyone" were to behave in such a way. Rather, Socrates is
clear that such an act, for "just anyone," would *not* be "done correctly." So
Euthyphro had *better* be "far advanced in wisdom," or else Socrates has
signaled that he will join everyone else in being inclined to condemn
Euthyphro's plan.[36] Again, that does not show that the inclination
Socrates has signaled here is irreversible or immutable. But it makes clear
that there is only one thing Socrates can right now himself imagine that
would modify the direction of that inclination, and that is some "far
advanced wisdom" in Euthyphro that would compel changing the valence
of Socrates' initial – even if still tentative – response. This response, as we will
see, is repeated in different ways each time Socrates directly addresses the
topic of Euthyphro's proposed prosecution.

4.14.2   Euthyphro 4b4–6

SOCRATES: But surely the one killed by your father is a member of your family. Of
course, that's obvious. I suppose you wouldn't prosecute him for the murder
of someone outside the family.

---

[36] Al-Maini (2011: 21): "Euthyphro's inability to show his great advancement in wisdom coupled with
his proceeding with the prosecution indicates his impiety. Socrates' initial incredulity has had its
desired effect, and we have been provided with an examination that casts doubt on the piety of
Euthyphro's actions."

This response immediately follows Section 4.14.1, straight after Euthyphro affirms that he does indeed have the "far advanced" wisdom Socrates had claimed would be necessary for what Euthyphro had in mind. So in Section 4.14.2, Socrates seems to be guessing at what could be a suitable ground for Euthyphro's actions. This extraordinary plan to prosecute his own father, which, as we have now seen, strikes Socrates from the start as at least prima facie culpable, might yet turn out to be acceptable behavior if, as Socrates here imagines, Euthyphro's prosecution is in response to his father's murder of a family member. But Socrates' response here – searching for what might relieve Euthyphro of blame for what he intends – can make no sense if Socrates tends either to agree with what Euthyphro proposes or to feel neutral with respect to the question of whether the plan is right or wrong. Where there is no apparent guilt, there is no need to find exculpation. So here, too, Socrates signals that, unless Euthyphro can indeed provide some excuse that defeats the appearance of wrongdoing, Socrates is inclined to judge Euthyphro's action negatively.

As it turns out, of course, Euthyphro's father did not murder another family member, but Euthyphro rejects Socrates' assumption that this fact should make any difference. Euthyphro's family, of course, think differently, and say that Euthyphro should desist from this proposed prosecution, but Euthyphro brushes aside the reasons his family provided: "They know so little of the divine point of view concerning the pious and the impious" (*Euthyphro* 4e1–3). Socrates replies as in Section 4.14.3.

4.14.3   Euthyphro 4e4–8

SOCRATES: Before god, Euthyphro, do you really think you know so exactly how things are concerning the gods, and about pious and impious matters that when things have happened as you say they have, you're not afraid that in bringing the case against your father, you're not also doing something impious?

By this point in the dialogue, it has become clear what grounds Euthyphro's confidence in his plan: Euthyphro believes that he is "far advanced in wisdom" with respect to piety, and it is this "far advanced" wisdom that allows him to override his family's judgment of what he should do. So Euthyphro does not at all reject Socrates' claim that *only* someone far advanced in wisdom would undertake such a course of action. Rather, he embraces that condition and takes himself to embody the exceptional case required.

Socrates' reaction to Euthyphro's confidence, however, shows that he (very rightly, as it turns out) doubts that Euthyphro really does have such wisdom. And it is clear what Socrates thinks would follow from a failure of wisdom here – Euthyphro should be afraid of doing something impious. But *why* should Euthyphro have such a fear? Socrates does not count himself as having the sort of wisdom Euthyphro claims to have (or at least in the degree that Euthyphro seems to think that he has such wisdom). But Socrates does not normally live in fear of doing something impious – or at least, even if he does acknowledge that he might do some bad things unwittingly, this recognition hardly paralyzes him from going about his affairs out of fear that, for all he knows, he might do something impious. Again, Socrates "is persuaded by nothing but the reason that appears to me to be best when I've reasoned about it," so unless he recognizes some *reason* to think that what he is doing presents some special risk of impiety, we should expect Socrates not to be afraid in general that impiety is a specific or special risk in what he does or intends. Why, then, does Socrates seem to regard Euthyphro as being *at risk* of impiety here? It can only be that Socrates regards Euthyphro as having some (even if only defeasible) *reason* for thinking that what he proposes to do is impious. Socrates makes no claim to *know* that what Euthyphro proposes is impious, nor does he indicate that he regards Euthyphro as knowing any such thing. But the fear that Socrates asks Euthyphro about would be wholly gratuitous and irrational unless Socrates imagined that there was some reason – a reason that Euthyphro himself was aware of – for thinking that Euthyphro's plan was impious. In the next section, I will attempt to show what that reason is, and why Socrates is so confident that Euthyphro is aware of that reason. But it is enough for my argument in this section that we observe in Section 4.14.3 an indication that Socrates regards Euthyphro's plan as at least prima facie culpable and in violation of some reason for thinking the plan is impious.[37]

The same point that Socrates makes in Section 4.14.3 is repeated again in the middle of the dialogue (at 9a1–b2) and then again at the end (15d4–8), so we can look at these two texts together.

4.14.4   Euthyphro 9a1–b2

SOCRATES: Come now, dear Euthyphro, so that I may become wiser, instruct me about your proof that all the gods think that one has died unjustly when he was a worker and became a murderer and was bound by the dead man's

---

[37] Throughout this section, I am arguing against the contrary view argued in Benson 2013b.

master and who died from being tied up before the one who bound him could learn from the Religious Counselors what he needed to do about him. Show me how, on behalf of such a person, it's right for a son to prosecute his father and to bring against him a charge of murder. Come, then, and try to make this clear to me that all of the gods unquestionably agree that this is the right course of action. If you would make this sufficiently clear to me, I'll never stop praising you for your wisdom.

What is the point in Socrates suddenly reminding Euthyphro again about the specific facts of the proposed case against Euthyphro's father? This text, obviously, simply reminds Euthyphro of what is at stake in Euthyphro's claim to be wise with respect to piety. If he has the wisdom he claims to have, then perhaps he can show how that wisdom reveals why he is not culpable in prosecuting his own father in such an unusual case. But if he does *not* have such wisdom, then, as Section 4.14.3 seemed to indicate, he has reason to think he will act impiously. If, indeed, piety is, as Euthyphro has now claimed, what all the gods agree upon, then Euthyphro had better be able to show that all of the gods agree with his prosecution . . . or else. Of course, Socrates does not simply pass judgment directly. The implication of negative judgment nonetheless hangs clearly in the air and reminds the faltering Euthyphro of what the stakes are for him.

4.14.5 Euthyphro *15d4–8*

SOCRATES: For if you didn't know clearly what the pious and the impious are, you couldn't possibly be trying to prosecute your elderly father for murder on behalf of a servant, and you'd fear that you'd be at risk with respect to the gods that you would be wrong in doing this and would be held in contempt by men.

Here again, Euthyphro's failure to reveal his "far advanced wisdom" is taken as putting him at special risk of acting impiously. There would be no reason to be concerned about such a risk in ordinary circumstances, or if Euthyphro's plan did not confront *some reason for thinking that it was impious*. Given some undefeated reason for thinking that Euthyphro's plan is a bad one, we can plausibly infer (other things equal) that Socrates will judge it negatively. Unless that reason can be defeated, Socrates will be "persuaded by nothing but the reason that appears to me to be best when I've reasoned about it." Even if one lacks knowledge, undefeated reasons qualify as grounds for acting or desisting from action.

In each of the texts I have now discussed from the *Euthyphro*, there is a clear conversational implicature of negative judgment by Socrates. The judgment is left as an implicature only, because Socrates is always alert to the fact of his own ignorance, and so is aware of the fact that "the reason that appears to me to be best when I've reasoned about it" might be wholly defeated by some consideration that would flow from some wisdom that is "far advanced" over anything he can bring to a deliberation. In the face of Euthyphro's explicit claim to have such "far advanced" wisdom, Socrates will not simply pronounce judgment, but only indicate what he regards as the position that must be defeated by the one with "far advanced" wisdom. Even so, it is not at all that the proper evaluation of Euthyphro's plan is simply left open, or treated by Socrates as wholly indeterminate.

4.15 Socrates' Reasons

I have argued that there is significant evidence from conversational implicature for thinking that Socrates' initial reaction to Euthyphro's plan is a negative one. Moreover, the valence of Socrates' reaction remains unchanged when – and because – Euthyphro turns out to be unable to provide anything like the "far advanced wisdom" that Socrates and Euthyphro both seem to think would reveal Euthyphro's plan to be a good one after all. But let us now consider what might have counted to Socrates as the "reason that appears to me to be best when I've reasoned about it" with respect to his evaluation of Euthyphro's case. Is there anything in the text that would provide an answer to why Socrates reacts to Euthyphro in the way that he does?

This question turns out to be a tricky one. On the one hand, the text actually does provide what might plausibly be counted as a reason for Euthyphro to desist from his plan, and that is the position opposing that plan articulated by Euthyphro's family, which seems to provide three distinct grounds for why Euthyphro should not prosecute his father:

> [1] He didn't even kill him, so they claim, and [2] even if he did, because the one who died was a murderer, we shouldn't be concerned on behalf of such a person, because [3] it's unholy (*anosion*) for a son to prosecute his father for murder. (*Euthyphro* 4d7–e1; my numbering)

Notice that the three considerations seem to be independent of one another. If (1) is true, then the relatives take it as obvious that Euthyphro's father does not deserve to be prosecuted for murder. But notice the way that the second part of the relative's argument is framed: even if the first consideration were false, it seems that the second is sufficient in itself to provide a reason against the prosecution. And the third seems too general to be taken as dependent on either the first or second considerations, in which case we can understand the relatives as arguing that Euthyphro's prosecution would be wrong (indeed impious) *even if* Euthyphro's father actually had killed the laborer, and *even if* the laborer himself had not been a murderer. In that case, perhaps, it might still be appropriate for *someone* to prosecute Euthyphro's father for murder, but it would not, understood this way, be appropriate for *Euthyphro* to be the one to do it.

If this is correct, then Socrates' mandate always to be persuaded only by the "reason that appears to me to be best when I've reasoned about it" might be supposed to apply to Euthyphro with the arguments of his family ringing in his ears. Unless and until he can provide some *better* reason (presumably via his "far advanced wisdom" about piety) for his own side of this debate, then the considerations presented by his family remain undefeated and thus in effect. But do the family's arguments also give Socrates reasons to reject Euthyphro's plan?

The problem with thinking that they do is that Euthyphro does not articulate his family's arguments until 4d5 ff. Recall Socrates' initial response, quoted in Section 4.14.1, which clearly indicated a negative reaction. But this reaction thus came *before* Socrates ever hears the arguments given by Euthyphro's relatives for why Euthyphro should not do what he plans. Hence, Socrates' own reasons cannot derive from the arguments given by the relatives, nor can his reactions be conditioned on the success or defeat of the relatives' arguments.

We are left, therefore, with two options for explaining Socrates' initial responses – which, again, never seem to change in their negativity throughout the remainder of the dialogue. One option is to suppose that Socrates had some *other* reason(s) to regard (again, at least tentatively) Euthyphro's action as reckless and presumably impious, but which Socrates never manages to articulate in our text. If this is the case, then it seems pointless to speculate about what such a reason or reasons might have been. My own reading of Plato's dialogues does not bring to light enough in the way of evidence for what implications we could draw here, from other aspects of Socratic philosophy, but perhaps some other scholar might do a better job with such an approach. On the other hand, we might not have to undergo such a strain of interpretation. We might instead suppose that the basis for the arguments made by Euthyphro's family was so abundantly available in Athenian culture of that day that it would have counted to "just anyone" as presumptive – so that the family's expression of those arguments amounted to no more than a *reminder* to Euthyphro what "just anyone" in that culture would say about his plan. If so, then Socrates' initial response could be grounded in the same basis as the source for Euthyphro's family's arguments, which would be accepted common opinion in Athenian cultural presuppositions about the proper relations of sons to fathers, piety prescriptions and prohibitions more generally, and what does and does not qualify as murder or justified homicide. I rather suspect that this is the correct explanation of Socrates' initial reaction – and thus why Plato does not see fit to explain that reaction any more explicitly, in which case it would not be the actual *arguments* given by Euthyphro's family that provide the reasons Socrates requires to be persuaded of something, but rather the same reasons as those arguments make explicit. These reasons, it seems, might be defeated by extraordinary circumstances (such as if the person who was killed was a member of Euthyphro's own family), and someone who was "far advanced in wisdom" might be able to identify extraordinary circumstances that normal people (including Socrates himself) might not be able to anticipate or articulate themselves. But since Euthyphro's discussion with Socrates ends up supplying no exceptional consideration that would excuse or justify his plan of action, the cultural presuppositions against doing such a thing remain undefeated, and thus apply to Euthyphro. They also apply to Socrates and seem to provide a very natural explanation of why he reacts to Euthyphro in the way that he does, and why – since they are never defeated in the discussion – Socrates never seems to waver or change his mind about how he should react to what Euthyphro has said about prosecuting his father.

4.16 The Lesson of Plato's *Euthyphro*

I have argued that the Socrates of Plato's dialogues has at his disposal ample grounds for rational practical action, since all that he requires for counting some action as rational is some undefeated reason for thinking that acting in the relevant way is correct. Of course, he is also the champion of "the examined life," and so we can be sure that he would not count someone as rational who made no intellectual effort to question and consider alternatives, even when some reason for action was available. Reasons, at least for those who do not know what is best, are defeasible, and one must use defeasible reasons with humility, and with a certain degree of caution. Most of all, one must always be alert to factors that might defeat some reason one might have. Bearing these things in mind, Socrates need not be paralyzed by his ignorance into inaction. But he would be a man to pass judgment only cautiously and with a certain preparedness for correction and even reversal, on the basis of new reasons. For one who leads the "examined life," then, preferences and preparedness to act must always be tentative and revisable. Even so, tentative and revisable reasons for certain preferences and actions still qualify *as reasons* and, other things equal, would be good enough for Socrates to go about his business. Acting on the basis of the best reasons that one has for making choices and decisions is the best way to practice the craft of virtue, and to become better at it, but such reasoning must always be alert to defeaters. Accordingly, a combination of leading the examined life together with acting in accord- ance with the best reasons available to one promises to bring the best results for self-improvement. Socrates may have known nothing of "the greatest things." But it does not follow from this that he would regard himself as having no good reason to prefer a clean bed.

4.17   Summary and Conclusion

In this chapter, I have tried to explain the various ways in which the primarily ethical focus in Socratic philosophy included several important epistemological commitments and insights. Central among these is Socrates' conception of the human epistemological condition and his characterization as an exemplar of epistemic modesty. The ethical aspect of his epistemology is to be found in his commitment to remediate his own and others' ignorance. I have paid special attention herein to belief- forming processes that Socrates seems to recognize as important problems for the human epistemic condition, and thus have also offered an account of how Socrates thinks that philosophizing can help us at least to moderate the effects of the processes most likely to lead us astray in our ethical and epistemic missions. I then closed the chapter with a close look at some texts that seem to me to reveal a more positive approach to self-improvement – one that is grounded on following the best reasons available to one even when one must operate in ignorance. In the last chapter, I identified an etiology of belief-formation that threatened the kind of reasoning that we must all engage in, every day of our lives: practical reasoning. I concluded there that keeping one's nonrational attractions and aversions in a controlled condition would bring significant advantage to our attempt to improve ourselves. In this chapter, I have looked more closely at the epistemological side: how do we deal with our ignorance and how can we hope to remediate it, if only to a degree? Three distinct requirements for self-improvement have now come to light: (i) keeping the nonrational factors in belief-formation in a controlled condition; (ii) leading the examined life, so that we may always be on guard for mistakes we might be making; and (iii) since even in ignorance, we must make decisions and take action, we should always follow the reasons that seem best to us when we reason about it. To the extent that such reasonings are unobstructed by nonrational factors, and to the extent that we are vigilant about removing falsehoods that might influence our practical lives, we can have real hope of improvement in virtue.

CHAPTER 5

Is Virtue Sufficient for Happiness?

5.1 Prologue

On January 15, 2009, US Airways flight 1549 took off from LaGuardia Airport and within minutes struck a large flock of Canada geese, which shut down both engines. The pilot, Chesley B. (Sully) Sullenberger, in what was called "an amazing piece of airmanship," managed to put the plane down in the Hudson River. All 155 passengers and crew aboard survived. Sully was the last person to exit the downed plane. The Air Force Academy superintendent declared, "He not only showcased unbelievable airmanship, but exemplary character as well."[1] A member of the National Transportation Safety Board described Sully's feat as "the most successful ditching in aviation history."[2]

On the other hand, in an interview for CBS' "60 Minutes," Sully himself described the situation he endured as "the worst sickening, pit-of-your-stomach, falling-through-the-floor feeling" he had ever endured,[3] and later acknowledged that he subsequently suffered from sleeplessness and flashbacks.[4]

We may well imagine that Sully was relieved that no one died that day. But no one – and certainly not Sully – would have described his condition as a "happy" one. Even so, he did well that day.

This is a book about Socrates, however, and not about Sully. But Sully's extraordinary "airmanship" provides an excellent example of my topic in this chapter.

---

[1] CNN 2009. I have chosen "the miracle on the Hudson," as the story came to be called, as my example, because it was so widely reported and celebrated. But I might as well have used the example of Tammie Jo Shults, who on April 17, 2018 piloted an aircraft that experienced an explosive engine failure that sent shrapnel through a window. A passenger was partially sucked out of the hole and died, but Shults was praised for her calm professionalism in safely landing the badly damaged aircraft with no further casualties.
[2] NYPost 2009.   [3] *Tampa Bay Times* 2009.   [4] Hewitt et al. 2009.

5.2 Did Socrates Accept That Virtue Was Sufficient for Happiness?

In several passages in several dialogues, Plato has Socrates say things that would seem either explicitly to affirm or at least to imply that he accepted this principle. For example, at *Apology* 41d1–2, Plato has Socrates boldly declare that "a good man cannot be harmed either in life or in death." It would appear, then, that goodness is sufficient to make one invulnerable to harm, and thus to any loss of happiness. At *Gorgias* 507c1–5, he tells Callicles that "the self-controlled man, because he's just and brave, and pious ... is a completely good man, that the good man does well and admirably whatever he does, and the man who does well is blessed and happy." Here, too, it appears that the "completely good man" would have nothing to fear in life or in death. At *Republic* I, Socrates tells Thrasymachus that a just soul and a just man will live well (353e10), and that "a just person is happy" (354a4).

Perhaps the most detailed presentation of what seems to be the view that Plato attributes to Socrates may be found in the famous protreptic arguments of the *Euthydemus*. In these arguments, Socrates argues for a special relationship between virtue and happiness. In the first argument, he ends up offering two conclusions, which scholars have taken in different ways. The first of these conclusions goes like this:

> So, to sum up, Cleinias, I said, it seems likely that with respect to all the things we called good in the beginning, the correct account is not that in themselves they are good by nature, but rather as follows: if ignorance controls them, they are greater evils than their opposites, to the extent that they are more capable of complying with a bad master; but if good sense and wisdom are in control, they are greater goods. In themselves, however, neither sort is of any value. (*Euthydemus* 281d2–e1)

But in the second conclusion, Socrates appears to be making a stronger claim:

> Then what is the result of our conversation? Isn't it that, of the other things, no one of them is either good or bad, but of these two, wisdom is good and ignorance bad? (*Euthydemus* 281e2–5)

In the second protreptic argument, Socrates reminds Crito of the conclusion they had reached earlier:

> Cleinias and I of course agreed that nothing is good except some sort of knowledge. (*Euthydemus* 292b1–2)

As Terence Irwin has explained, these two conclusions have been interpreted in roughly two ways, one of which Irwin calls a "moderate view," and the other an "extreme view":

> Moderate View: "When he concludes that wisdom is the only good, he means simply that only wisdom is good all by itself, apart from any combination with other things."[5]
> Extreme View: "When Socrates concludes that wisdom is the only good, he means that nothing else is good."[6]

Quite significant numbers of scholars have endorsed each of these two views.[7] The difference between the two views is stark. In one of his most striking passages Gregory Vlastos complained that the extreme view would leave a virtuous person no grounds for preferring to sleep in a clean bed rather than one soaked in vomit.[8] Even so, going all the way back to the Stoics, the extreme view is one that has often been attributed to Socrates, and even Vlastos sides with most of those who accept the extreme interpretation:[9] that Socrates thought that virtue was sufficient for happiness.[10]

But those inclined to the moderate view have noted that worse things can happen to virtuous people than simply having to sleep in a dirty bed. Our world is filled with the potential for truly catastrophic events – for example, events such as airplane crashes, which, as we all know, typically end up as complete disasters. That is why the remarkable outcome of Sully's "amazing piece of airmanship" was received with such adulation for the one who had achieved it.

Socrates, of course, had no knowledge of airplanes or their crashes, but he did live in a very uncertain world, and passages in other texts make clear

---

[5] "When Socrates says that the recognized goods are not goods 'just by themselves,' he means that they are not goods when they are divorced from wisdom" (Irwin 1995: 57).

[6] "When Socrates says that the recognized goods are not goods 'just by themselves,' he means that they are not goods; any goodness belongs to the wise use of them, not to the recognized goods themselves" (Irwin 1995: 57).

[7] Those who have favored the "moderate view" have included: Brickhouse and Smith 1987, 2000, and 2010: 167–189; Ferejohn 1984: 111; Jones 2013b; Kraut 1984: 2111–2112, n. 41; Parry 2003; Reeve 1989: 128, n. 25; Reshotko 2006: ch. 5. Those who have endorsed the "extreme view" include (in alphabetical order) Annas 1999: ch. 2; Dimas 2002; Irwin 1995: 57; McPherran 2005; Russell 2005: ch. 1.

[8] Vlastos 1991: 215.

[9] Vlastos 1991: 217. In Vlastos' view, the virtuous person would prefer the clean to the soiled bed, but even if such a person had to spend the night soaking in vomit, they would still be happy.

[10] Not all Socratics were willing to attribute this thesis to Socrates, however, and even Plato provides some evidence against such an attribution. In Aeschines Socraticus' *Alcibiades*, Themistocles' failure in Athens is said to have happened in spite of his exemplary virtue and knowledge (VI A 50, lines 34–41). The same sort of story may also be found in Xenophon's *Memorabilia*, where Socrates gets Euthydemus to recall stories of wise men (Daedalus and Palamedes) who end up having bad lives in spite of their wisdom (*Mem.* IV.II.33).

that he is aware that very bad things can happen to people, including good people. For example, at *Crito* 47e3–5, Socrates notes that life is not worth living "with a body that is corrupted and in bad condition." He makes the same point at *Gorgias* 512a2–b2. Again, in the *Crito*, Socrates announces his conviction that retaliation is never morally acceptable, and explains that this is the reason why he will not escape from prison. But it would not be retaliation for him to escape if he hadn't been harmed by the jury's decision. Socrates makes it plain enough in the *Apology* that he regards the alternatives the jury might have accepted would be evils he would suffer (*Apology* 37b7–e2).

In this chapter, I will focus mostly on Plato's account in the *Euthydemus*, because it provides the main reasons why scholars have divided on the question of whether Socrates accepted the sufficiency of virtue for happiness. The arguments there have been taken as strong support for attributing the thesis to Socrates, but I'm convinced that it is a mistake to understand them in such a way, for Plato also reveals that Socrates is well aware that our degree of success can be heavily influenced by things outside of the control of even the virtuous person. By the time I'm done, I hope I will have explained not only what the Socratic view is, with respect to the sufficiency of virtue for happiness, but also why there has been such scholarly disagreement about this subject.

I will advance my argument in stages. First, I will show that the protreptic arguments given by Socrates in Plato's *Euthydemus* are framed primarily in terms of doing well (*eu prattein*). I then argue that this focus allows for a better understanding of how Plato has Socrates' position doing well in relation to *eutuchia*, which most scholars have (I think mistakenly) understood in terms of luck. I argue, on the contrary, that what Plato is interested in having Socrates represent is a connection between doing well and *success*. I then apply one of the main theses of this book to understanding these arguments, which seem to me to indicate a recognition that doing well and succeeding are *improvable* – they can be achieved in different degrees. This allows me to reject the interpretation that so many scholars have found so implausible: that virtue somehow indemnifies and immunizes the virtuous person from any harm of any kind. Rather, the connection between virtue and doing well that Plato has Socrates make in the *Euthydemus* is fully compatible with the kinds of cases Plato himself gives of how bad things can happen to good people, even to the point of defeating any chance of happiness for them. The result is that while not accepting the sufficiency thesis, I take Socrates to think that the extent to which one was virtuous would covary with the degree of success that would be possible for a person, in the relevant circumstances. So while I deny that there is no entailment from virtue to happiness, there is nonetheless a strong relationship between them.[11]

5.3 Doing Well in the *Euthydemus*

Scholars have not unreasonably focused on the first two protreptic arguments in the *Euthydemus* to discern the specific relationship that Socrates sees between virtue and happiness.[12] But it is worth noticing that the connection between virtue and happiness is made in virtue of an identification that Socrates makes, later in the argument, between happiness (*eudaimonia*) and doing well (*eupragia*). At the start of these arguments Socrates' focus is on "doing well." Here is how the first protreptic argument begins:

> Do all men wish to do well? Or is this question one of the ridiculous ones I was afraid of just now? I suppose it is stupid even to raise such a question, since there could hardly be a man who would not wish to do well. (*Euthydemus* 278e2–6)

Doing well (or doing right: *orthos prattein*, as at 280a8) is also repeatedly in play when he gives a number of examples of the sort of thing he has in mind: he talks about doing well in flute-playing (279e1), at reading and writing (279e2–4), at piloting ships at sea (279e4–7), at being a general

---

[11] In the literature, the kind of connection I find between virtue and happiness is called a "nomological" one, meaning lawlike and regular, but not exceptionless. I make no claim to originality in finding this sort of relationship between virtue and happiness. Not only have Brickhouse and I argued for just such a relationship in our earlier work, but the same view is also expressed and presented in detail in Reshotko 2006.

[12] It is worth noting that, strictly speaking, the protreptic arguments in the *Euthydemus* are focused more narrowly on the relationship between wisdom and happiness (or, as I shall emphasize, doing well). One can infer the broader relationship to obtain between virtue and happiness only if one accepts the attribution to Socrates of the unity of virtue (for which he argues in other dialogues, but not in the *Euthydemus*). For a discussion and analysis of this Socratic position, see Brickhouse and Smith 2010: 154–167. It might be seen as evidence that Socrates does not accept the unity of virtue in the *Euthydemus* because from 279b4–c1 and then at 281c6–e5 he seems to put the virtues other than wisdom into the category of neither good nor bad. I do not find this a good reason to suppose that Socrates is depicted as not accepting the unity of virtue here, however, because the only way the other virtues could count as neither good nor bad would be if they were not controlled by wisdom (see 281d1–e1); but Socratic virtue intellectualism requires that all of the virtues are controlled by wisdom, and nothing in the *Euthydemus* gives any indication that this intellectualism has been abandoned.

(279e6–280a1), or at being doctor (280a2–3). Happiness doesn't come into the argument until 280b6,[13] where it is said to go along with doing well. Once he has brought happiness in, he refers repeatedly to being happy (at 280b7, d2, d4, e1), only returning to *eupragia* at 281b3 before returning to what he seems to represent as the original claim at 282a1–2. But when he does, he reports the claim as being that we all wish to be *happy*, showing that he understands the argument he has given to apply to that issue. When the discussants in the dialogue return again to the question they had pursued, Socrates once again puts the issue in terms of happiness, rather than in terms of doing well (so see 289d10, 290b2, 291b6, 292c1, e5).

Scholars have rightly seen Socrates as simply treating "doing well" and "being happy" as equivalent in this argument.[14] So they have focused – just as Socrates himself seems to come to focus – on happiness instead of doing well as they have sought to understand the argument. Such a focus has a tendency, however, to distort two aspects of Socrates' argument: (1) as noted earlier, the examples Socrates actually uses are all about doing well and not about being happy in any sense that seems natural to us; (2) moreover, the focus on happiness tends to make scholars miss the fact that Socrates actually says nothing in the argument of any significance about the relationship between being happy and suffering from circumstances that are destructive and also entirely out of the control of the agent. To return to the "miracle on the Hudson," taking the argument to be about happiness gives us the result that Socrates would characterize Sully as *happy* on the day he crashed flight 1549 into the Hudson River. But to call this an "extreme view" seems to be euphemistic, and we expect that Sully himself would be the first one to deny such a claim. No decent person, and certainly not Sully, would find anything happy about the "sickening, pit-of-your-stomach, falling-through-the-floor" horror that he went through on that day. On the other hand, if we take Socrates' argument to be about "doing well" instead of happiness, the result of the argument seems to fit Sully's case perfectly: he did very, very well, and did so, moreover, because he "not only showcased unbelievable airmanship, but exemplary character as well."

---

[13] Irwin has it that the entire argument is always about happiness, from the very start, simply noting that "Socrates identifies *eu prattein* with *eudaimonein*" (Irwin 1986: 90, n. 11). Another example of this quick move from doing well to being happy may be seen in Annas 1999: 35, n. 20.

[14] In one instance he also mentions making someone "blessed" (μακάριος: 290d7) in a way that seems to treat it as also equivalent to these others. It doesn't follow, however, that we should suppose that each term has the same connotations. In fact, my argument is that the active aspect of "doing well" is an essential element in this argument: the focus is on practical activity and not on (even blissful) passivity.

5.4   The Luck Factor

No doubt one important reason why scholars have attributed the sufficiency thesis to Socrates on the basis of the protreptic arguments in the
Euthydemus derives from what Socrates has to say in the first of these
arguments about *eutuchia*, which scholars have understood in a number of
different ways.[15] Most of them have understood Socrates' argument that
eutuchia is not needed in addition if one has wisdom (280b2–3) to show, as
Irwin has it, that Socrates supposed "wisdom guarantees success whatever
the circumstances."[16] As a matter of fact, and with a very important caveat,
I accept Irwin's "strong conclusion" here. But since Irwin takes "success" to
mean the same thing as "happiness," he understands Socrates' argument to
show that Socrates is committed to the astonishing view that the virtuous
person will be happy even in the most devastating and disastrous circumstances. The implausibility of such a view has led many scholars to deny
that Socrates could possibly have accepted it.

As Julia Annas has complained, taking "*eutuchia*" in this argument as
"good luck" results in the argument appearing to be "outrageous."[17] The
LSJ[18] allows that "*eutuchia*" can mean "good luck," but it also offers simply
"success" as a second possible meaning. Were we to understand Socrates as
having "success" in mind when he claims that wisdom is all that is needed,
we would then see that the argument is, as Irwin had it, an argument for the
"strong conclusion" that wisdom guarantees success. But we might now
stop and wonder precisely what Socrates might have in mind when he talks
about "success."

To see what he has in mind, however, is not difficult, since he gives
a number of examples of what he means, as mentioned earlier: it is what we
expect from those who are wise in flute-playing, reading and writing,
piloting ships at sea, being a general, or being a doctor. It would obviously
be "outrageous" to claim that anyone wise in these sorts of things so

[15] The most common translations given in the literature for Socrates' use of "*eutuchia*" in this argument
are "good luck" or "good fortune." Both appear in the translation given in the Sprague translation
that appears in Cooper 1997; Annas 1995: 40, n. 30 has it as "good luck," as does Reshotko 2006: 143,
n. 8. Irwin 1986 and 1995 uses "good fortune," as does Jones in 2013b: 3, though he later clarifies that
he takes the term actually to refer to what he calls "outcome success." Other translations have also
been offered for the term – Russell 2005: 18 has it as "fare well"; McPherran 2005 sees it as
"providence."
[16] Irwin 1995: 56.   [17] Annas 1995: 40.
[18] For novices, this is the "scholarese" way to refer briefly to the authoritative Greek–English lexicon
compiled by H. G. Liddell and R. Scott, and then later much revised and augmented by H. S. Jones
and R. McKenzie. For some reason, McKenzie's assistance does not get included in typical references
to the work.

controls all of reality as to be able to ensure that nothing could possibly go wrong when they engage their wisdom in action. But it is not at all outrageous to think that experts will have the greatest success in what they do *under any circumstances they may happen to encounter*. If a rival destroys the flautist's flute just before a performance, and the only flute available is one that is very poorly made, the expert flautist may well succeed in playing the bad flute as well as it can be played; but the performance itself may still qualify as a good deal less successful than the flautist themself (or their audience) might have wished it would be.

Socrates all but makes this same point when he talks about how the wise pilot manages travel at sea. Socrates asks, "What about the perils at sea – surely you don't think that, as a general rule, any pilots are more successful[19] than the wise ones?" Cleinias answers, "Certainly not" (279e4–6). It is difficult to read this example in the way that seems to indicate the view Annas and Irwin find so unacceptable – but then attribute to Socrates anyway. The portion of the passage that seems to rule out the "outrageous" interpretation is where Socrates talks about the wise pilot's success in dealing with the "perils at sea." It is very obvious to anyone who has ever dealt with the sea that even the most brilliant seamen do not control the weather, nor do they have the kind of omnipotence that would be required to make sea travel risk-free. Indeed, this is precisely what Sully managed on the day of the crash: he performed in a way that demonstrated "unbelievable airmanship." He very much succeeded in what he was able to do on that day, which was to save the lives of everyone aboard even though circumstances that were entirely out of his control (and extremely unlucky) prevented him from doing what he had set out to do, which was to fly to Charlotte and then on to Seattle. So Sully did not succeed in achieving his goal for that day. Even so, what he managed to succeed in doing was justly praised in the highest terms.

Socrates' point, at least in the example of travel at sea, is not at all that wisdom eliminates any risk to those who exercise it, but rather that wisdom will always make one the best equipped to deal with the kinds of hazards and risks that are beyond human control. The wise pilot cannot calm the waters (or clear the air of Canada geese!), but if

---

[19] Translation modified, as per our proposed understanding of the term in play. The Sprague translation given in Cooper 1997 was "have better luck."

anyone can survive in such conditions, it will be the wise pilot who manages to succeed.

5.5 Achieving Virtue

All of the examples of wisdom that Plato's Socrates uses in the protreptic arguments of the *Euthydemus* are examples of skill. This is sometimes called "the craft analogy," and it certainly seems true here that Socrates is thinking of the sort of wisdom in which virtue consists of a kind of skill. Moreover, it is clear that Socrates is arguing for a very tight connection between virtue and doing well, which in this passage is also treated as interchangeable with happiness. As I have already argued in earlier chapters, Socrates is also aware that the kinds of wisdom involved in skills or crafts are not all-or-nothing achievements; rather, they can be achieved in degrees.[20] When Socrates himself concludes the first protreptic argument in the *Euthydemus*, the upshot was supposed to be that "every man should prepare himself by every means to become as wise as possible" (*Euthydemus* 282a5–6), clearly indicating that wisdom is an improvable achievement. We may now consider what Socrates thinks is the relationship between the different levels of virtue and whether human beings can actually achieve happiness. But again, if we step back from thinking of the debate in terms of happiness, and ask whether or not Socrates thinks that an incompletely wise person can do well, we may find that the plausibility of how we answer the question will appear differently to us.

Of course, if we refuse to recognize anyone as doing well if they do not achieve the goals they had reasonably set for a given task, then only those who are both omniscient and omnipotent will be assured of doing well. Too many circumstances go far beyond human control. Moreover, it also seems plausible to say that all even the most completely skilled person can hope to achieve is the best that is humanly possible under the circumstances. So the question about the improvability of wisdom and doing well now becomes: can some degree of wisdom that is not yet perfect still be sufficient to do well enough to count as "doing well"?

Just from a philosophical point of view, it would seem to be unreasonable to hold that anything that falls short of perfection would not yet count

---

[20] Sully himself seems to have understood the point. He was later quoted as saying about the accident, "One way of looking at this might be that for 42 years, I've been making small, regular deposits in this bank of experience, education and training. And on January 15, the balance was sufficient so that I could make a very large withdrawal" (Newcott 2009: 52).

as doing well. The example of Sully applies to this question, too: at least according to simulations run by the United States National Transportation Safety Board, if Sully had reacted to the accident just a bit more quickly, he actually could have landed the plane back at LaGuardia without anyone being injured and without losing the aircraft.[21] Experts agree that the decision would have had to be made extremely quickly, and also agree that most pilots would have balked at the perceived risk of not making it back and crashing into some highly populated area near the airport. Nonetheless, repeated simulations showed that Sully could have done *even better* than he actually did on that day. Even so, the National Transportation Safety Board exonerated Sully's decision to ditch the aircraft in the Hudson River. No one faulted the decision that he did make, despite its imperfection. So, he did well; indeed, very well.

Would Socrates have supposed that something that was good, but not perfect – some achievement that was estimable but that an even better craftsman could outperform – could count as doing well? A refusal to allow Socrates to hold such a moderate position is not supported by the text, and should not be accepted by scholars. We may wonder just how good Socrates would think one had to be in order to count as doing well at all. Since the argument in the *Euthydemus* is about doing well, and the protreptic conclusion holds that we should all seek "to become as wise as possible," it is reasonable to hope that the degree to which we will do well in life will covary with the degree to which we have managed to become wise.

The fact that success comes in degrees allows us also to consider just how bad things might get, and what such cases would show about Socrates' view of the relationship between virtue and happiness. In the *Gorgias*, Plato has Socrates persuade Polus that everything we do is done for the sake of the good (*Gorgias* 468b7–8). As agents, then, it is the good that we strive for and intend. If we fail to achieve what's good – and certainly if we fail to achieve it to a significant degree – we will not do what we want, but will fail to do what we want. Socrates was surely aware that human beings are not omnipotent, and that factors outside of our control could wholly defeat even our very best efforts to achieve anything good. The unpredictable circumstances involved with travel at sea, for example, can be so desperate, indeed hopeless, that even the wisest pilot would perish (with all their sailors and cargo) at sea. In worst-case scenarios, then, does the thesis for which I am arguing entail that such a pilot would nonetheless

---

[21] CBS News 2010.

count as happy? After all, I am attributing to Socrates the view that the wise pilot would do as well as possible in those circumstances. Notice, however, that once the thesis is conditioned in such a way as to grant that circumstances can completely defeat even the wisest pilot, there is no further reason to claim that such a pilot would actually achieve anything that would count as doing well or being happy. Rather, such a pilot would do as well and be as happy as anyone could be in those circumstances, but would plainly fail to achieve even an approximation of what they, as agent, would want to achieve. So, "as happy as anyone could be in those circumstances" could obviously fall far short of anything that they (or we) would reasonably count as actually *happy*. It follows, plainly, that doing as well as possible under the circumstances is *not* sufficient for happiness. Hence, I reject attributing the sufficiency thesis to Socrates, on the ground that his own examples seem to recognize that all human aims and actions can be utterly defeated by conditions that are entirely outside of our control.

If all this is right, then, it follows that the way in which Plato's Socrates frames the protreptic arguments in the *Euthydemus* does not at all simply assume that wise people can, as if they were wizards or gods, either avoid or prevent the kinds of disasters that would certainly make any happiness impossible for a human being, nor do these arguments have to assume that a Socratically virtuous person could somehow adapt so well to such circumstances as to be happy in spite of them. Instead, we should attribute to Socrates the much more reasonable view that wisdom is sufficient only for whatever degree of happiness is possible in a given circumstance. In the worst cases, that may qualify as no happiness at all; but even that most extreme case does not provide a counterexample to the view I have attributed to Socrates.

5.6 The Stoic Socrates

Although it is not my aim herein to consider all of the different ways in which Socrates has been portrayed in works by authors other than Plato, it is perhaps worthwhile to consider one such view – according to which Socrates accepts an extreme version of the sufficiency thesis. In the view I have attributed to Socrates, virtue, and the happiness that virtue supports and affords, is improvable. If one retains the close connection between virtue and happiness, but then rejects (or ignores) the possibility of degrees of virtue, then one will also be committed to the idea that only the one with the most complete virtue can be happy. There may be degrees to which those who fall short may be thought to *approximate* happiness, but none will count as happy; none will qualify as actually doing well. This, it seems, is precisely the Stoic position. Further, the Stoics grounded this view in their insistence on a perfection standard for virtue. Diogenes Laertius reports (7.127):

> They believe there is nothing in between virtue and vice, while the Peripatetics say that [moral] progress is between virtue and vice. For, they say, just as a stick must be either straight or crooked, so must a man be either just or unjust and neither "more just" nor "more unjust"; and the same for the other virtues.[22]

Those who aspire to virtue may enjoy some relative benefit from their efforts; but none but the Sage will qualify as successful and, so, actually happy.[23] The upshot of the Stoic view, then, is the most extreme version of what Irwin called the "extreme view" of what Plato has Socrates say in the *Euthydemus*. In this version, virtue has become *identical* to happiness.

One might wonder how and why the Stoics came to this view of Socrates – especially if I am right about the account of virtue and happiness Plato gives to Socrates. Perhaps other features of Stoicism tempted them to this understanding of Socrates. Certainly their steadfast determinism about the natural world would lead them to regard the things that are not under human control as irrelevant to ethical valuation.

But perhaps the most plausible explanation as to why the Stoics considered Socrates a progenitor of the most extreme version of the extreme view of the sufficiency thesis is just that, as I have emphasized, the actual arguments that Plato gives, and the conclusions he has Socrates reach in the *Euthydemus*, have seemed to many readers to amount simply to direct statements of the extreme view. We might suppose that the many eminent scholars who have interpreted the *Euthydemus* in accordance with the extreme interpretation were influenced by the Stoics. But we needn't simply assume that; in their presentations of their interpretations, the extreme interpretation is represented as making the best sense of Socrates' protreptic arguments. If eminent scholars of our own day have

---

[22] Trans. Gerson and Inwood 1988.

[23] See also Diogenes Laertius 7.106, 7.120, 7.122, 7.128. Particularly illuminating is the Stoic discussion of moral mistakes where a moral mistake is contrasted with a morally perfect action. Moral mistakes are all equally bad and morally perfect actions are complete and, so, not improvable. Hence, the Stoics accept a perfection standard for virtue and, so, happiness. The argument rests on an analogy between truth and falsehood. Just as truth and falsehood do not come in degrees, so, too, for virtuous and vicious actions. See Diogenes Laertius 7.120, Stobaeus, *Anthology* 5b8, 11e, 11g, 11l, and Cicero, *De Finibus* 3.29 and 3.32. It is worth noting that it is entirely possible that the discussion of truth and falsehood is not, on the final analysis, an analogical argument, but to be taken quite literally by the Stoics.

been led to think this, then I see no reason why the Stoics might not have reached the same conclusion. Such a conclusion is not, however, warranted by a close reading of Plato's text.

5.7 Human Vulnerability

In the view for which I have argued in this chapter, preparing to "become as wise as possible" is the best and indeed the only way to succeed in life. Leaving one's efforts to luck is not just irrational; given how much can go wrong that is out of our control, such an approach all but ensures failure. But I have now said many times herein that the aspirational goal of mastery over our lives and all that will happen to us is not humanly possible. What is possible, and what Socrates exhorts us to do for ourselves and those who may depend on us, is to "become as wise as possible," which is to say as virtuous as possible, and thus as happy as possible. Human lives might be exemplary, as I argued Plato treats Socrates' life as having been; but they can be exemplary only as *human* lives, and not even close to what only gods can achieve.

I will have more to say about Socrates' view of the human condition in the next chapter, but for now, I think another aspect of the Socratic view of human life can be better understood – an aspect that I think scholars have mostly ignored, and left unexplained. In several places in our texts, we find Socrates making claims that not only engage with the vulnerability of human life but also indicate his view of how difficult and disturbing this vulnerability can be. Perhaps the best case of such a text occurs in the *Gorgias*. Socrates expresses his view that doing injustice is far worse than suffering it, and Polus reacts with incredulity.

POLUS: So, you think that a person who puts to death anyone he sees fit, and does so justly, is miserable and to be pitied?
SOCRATES: No, I don't, but I don't think he's to be envied either.
POLUS: Weren't you just now saying that he's miserable?
SOCRATES: Yes, the one who puts someone to death unjustly is, my friend, and he's to be pitied besides. But the one who does so justly isn't to be envied.
POLUS Surely the one who's put to death unjustly is the one who's both to be pitied and miserable.
SOCRATES: Less so than the one putting him to death, Polus, and less than the one who's justly put to death.
POLUS: How can that be, Socrates?
SOCRATES It's because doing what's unjust is actually the worst thing there is.
POLUS Really? Is *that* the worst? Isn't suffering what's unjust still worse?

SOCRATES: No, not in the least.
POLUS: So you'd rather want to suffer what's unjust than do it?
SOCRATES: For my part, I wouldn't want either, but if it had to be one or the other,
I would choose suffering over doing what's unjust. (*Gorgias* 469a9–c2)

The first point I want to make about this most informative passage is
that Socrates makes clear that there can be cases of acting justly that are
nonetheless unenviable: the one who puts another to death justly does the
right thing, but acts in a way that is unenviable. Socrates can make this
claim only if he thinks that just action can be achieved in circumstances
that nonetheless do not count as optimal. So it is not only the fact that
catastrophes can happen even to good people that can obstruct the natural
connection between acting justly and being happy. There will also be cases
in which just action is itself only a matter of making the best of a bad
situation, the badness of which was not in the control of the agent making
the best of things.

But let us now turn to the distinction that Socrates makes between
wrongdoing that is punished as opposed to wrongdoing that goes unpun-
ished. At the end of his discussion with Polus (479d7–480d7), Socrates
reviews the different conditions that he identifies in this earlier passage,
saying that those who commit injustice and are punished for it are better
off than those who commit injustice and are allowed to get away with it.
This allows us to consider the different cases Socrates mentions in the
quoted passage as to how and why those that are dispreferred or regarded as
not choiceworthy or enviable are rated in the way Socrates does. The worst
case, according to Socrates, is:

(1)   Committing injustice and not being punished.

Not choiceworthy, but to be preferred to getting away with injustice, is:

(2)   Committing injustice and being justly punished for it.

Socrates' argument for regarding (2) as preferable to (1) is given from
477a7–479d6, and turns on the idea that being in a condition of injustice is
the worst possible way for a soul to be. Comparing this condition of the
soul to having a treatable disease of the body, Socrates argues and Polus
(somewhat reluctantly) agrees that in either case, to be relieved or cured is
better than persisting in the bad condition. But obviously best is not falling
into the bad condition in the first place. As for the case of injustice, "The
happiest," Socrates says, "is the one who doesn't have any badness in
his soul ... and second is the one who gets it removed" (478d7–e2; my
translation).

The vulnerability problem, for all of us, is how to avoid getting sick or infirm. Socrates seems to think that a regimen of physical fitness will help to keep one's body in good condition, and insofar as we wish to be as healthy as possible, we should engage in what Socrates calls the subcraft of the craft of body-care that is gymnastics (464b6). Our mortality, however, ensures that even the most diligent application of this craft cannot guarantee success forever. But mortality is not the only problem, and in this case, the analogy to soul-care does not seem to apply anyway: mortality results in the destruction of the body, but (as the closing myth of the *Gorgias* seems to indicate[24]) death does not destroy the soul. Insofar as the soul can be destroyed, it can at worst only be made incurable from persistent engagement in vice and injustice that is not remedied by punishment. The true vulnerability problem, from the point of view of health, is that there are all kinds of things that can happen to us – even to those of us who are the most vigilant in trying to remain fit – that will damage our bodies: diseases and other conditions that will make us sick, and accidents and injuries that can break our bones and damage our vital organs. This vulnerability, insofar as human happiness requires some level of physical functionality, is the very thing that I have argued shows that Socrates would not have accepted the sufficiency of virtue for happiness. As too many of us have recently discovered, even the best of us is susceptible to infection by SARS-CoV2.[25] Virtue also does not provide immunity to any of an indefinitely many other kinds of things that will sicken us and damage our bodies, in some cases with devastating results that nonetheless don't kill us outright. Socrates surely did not know about all the causes of infection human beings are susceptible to. But he was surely not so foolish as to think that pursuing the highest possible levels of physical and moral fitness brought absolute immunity to illness or disability. The upshot is that even the best of us can be made worse off than those less skilled in virtue, because of factors outside of human control. I believe most of us are aware of this unfortunate aspect of the human condition. I am also confident that Socrates was also aware of it.

---

[24] This is not the place to discuss whether the closing myth of the *Gorgias* represents Socrates' actual beliefs about death and the possibility of an afterlife. For discussion of this question and consideration of the rival theories about this, see Brickhouse and Smith 1994: 201–206 and 2010: 248–258. For my purposes herein, it is enough that in the *Gorgias*, Socrates represents the myth as his actual view of the matter.

[25] Socrates may have had the great plague of 430 BCE in mind. Although the symptoms he describes are quite different, some of Thucydides' description of the moral and social effects of that plague (Thucydides 2. 47–54) are distressingly familiar.

Virtue might not ensure immunity to physical ailment, and such ailments themselves might be sufficient to make our lives not worth living (as Socrates says at *Crito* 47e3–5). Might virtue not at least be sufficient for one to be immune to the risk of becoming unjust? As Socrates says in the *Protagoras*, the craft of measurement "would be our savior" in making judgments of what is actually in our best interests, since that craft "makes the appearances lose their power by making clear the truth, and gives our soul peace of mind" (357d7–e2). By being virtuous – by having the craft of measuring what is good and bad – we can make ourselves immune from either being a wrongdoer who avoids correction or one who gets it – the two worst conditions one can be in, according to Socrates.

This way of thinking about the effects of virtue, however, obscures another reality of human moral vulnerability, which I have now mentioned several times in this book. By leading the examined life, Socrates made himself an exemplar for other human beings to emulate. What he did not achieve, however, was anything close to his aspirational ideal: neither Socrates nor any other human being can attain the kind of mastery of the "measuring craft" that makes the god truly wise. As I argued in Chapter 2, even the best of us, as Plato represents Socrates as being, can only hope to be an apprentice in the craft of virtue. So from the fact that gods might be invulnerable to moral harm, it unfortunately does not follow that human beings can ever achieve such immunity. The topic of this book is how Socrates thought self-improvement was possible. But what can be improved might also be damaged or made worse. It is time to look more closely at that possibility.

5.8 Moral Harm

In Section 3.11, I noted that even as Socrates thinks that all wrongdoing is involuntary (insofar as it harms the agent of the wrongdoing), he also thinks that it is entirely possible to engage in harming others in a way that is voluntary, and I claimed that it was this kind of voluntary wrongdoing that Socrates had in mind when he talked about the kind of wrongdoing that deserves punishment, rather than simply admonishment and instruction (at *Apology* 28a1–8). The latter kind of wrongdoing, for which instruction is appropriate, is where one harms others involuntarily or unintentionally. We might ask here, however, what sort of harm does Socrates have in mind when he says this? Is it just bodily harm, or does he think that wrongdoers can actually make others worse from a moral point of view?

As I argued in Section 3.4, it is clear that moral harm, which Socrates regarded as the worst kind of harm, was not just conceivable, but also quite terribly possible. I quoted *Republic* I.335b6–e1 to show that Socrates thought that harming others in the truest sense was to make them more unjust. The same point is made when Socrates gets Meletus to state explicitly that he intended to accuse Socrates of deliberately harming others. Socrates' reply to Meletus' accusation, also quoted in Section 3.4, is worth looking at again:

> [Socrates speaking] Come now, do you accuse me here of corrupting the young and making them worse deliberately or involuntarily?
> [Meletus] Deliberately.
> What follows, Meletus? Are you so much wiser at your age than I am at mine that you understand that wicked people always do some harm to their closest neighbors while good people do them good, but I have reached such a pitch of ignorance that I do not recognize this, namely, that if I make one of my associates wicked I run the risk of being harmed by him so that I do such a great evil deliberately, as you say? I do not believe you, Meletus, and I do not think anyone else will. (*Apology* 25d6–e6)

A very unfortunate fact of human life is that not only can we be physically harmed, we can also be morally harmed. Socrates denies that he has done this to anyone, and insists that even if he has, he has done so involuntarily, and thus should not have been brought to trial to be punished. Let us now consider just how one could be morally harmed, in Socrates' view.

In a way, the answer to this is just an extension or special application of my topic in the last two chapters (3 and 4), in which I talked about the sources of false belief and ignorance. In a nutshell, because Socrates is a motivational intellectualist, anything that we do as agents will reflect our beliefs about what is best for us at the time of acting. Insofar as our beliefs are the right ones, we will do good things; insofar as our beliefs are incorrect about what is best for us, we will go wrong. Accordingly, one very reliable way to morally harm someone else is to persuade them of falsehoods about what is best for them, rather than getting them to believe the truth. So one's own ignorance can not only lead to wrongful actions for oneself; insofar as that ignorance is paired with persuasion, it can also be made to infect and damage others. As Socrates says of his own case, if he has harmed others at all, it was out of ignorance.

In the last two chapters, however, I talked about an etiology of belief-formation that derives from a process that is our least reliable one in terms of attaining true beliefs, rather than false ones. That etiology, I argued, derives from our natural responses to basic appetitive urges and aversions:

what we are attracted to looks good to us and we will believe that it is good unless some other etiology of belief-formation presents a different view of the matter, and we retain the ability to adjudicate between the two presentations in a sober way. The cumulative effects of wrongdoing, I argued in Chapter 3, make the latter requirement increasingly difficult to achieve: the more we allow our basic attractions and aversions to "make our minds up," the less able we will be to attend to more veridically reliable ways of generating and preserving evaluative beliefs. Accordingly, another way to harm others is to somehow encourage them to become more reliant on this nonrational etiology of belief-formation – to get others to process in ways that are more attentive to gratification of these basic attractions and aversions than to the real value of things whose value they must judge. It is this way of damaging others that Socrates treats with such disgust when he compares oratory and rhetoric to cookery at *Gorgias* 500e5, and it is in contrast with this way of dealing with others that Socrates counts himself as having taken up "the true craft of politics" at *Gorgias* 521d8, which I discussed at length in Chapter 2.

So Socrates understands that people can harm others, and that the harm that we might do to others includes moral harm. We might wonder, however, just how vulnerable to this sort of harm Plato's exemplary human being supposed he was himself. Looking at several texts clearly indicates that Socrates, too, was well aware that he could be harmed in this way. One excellent example of such a text is the one from the *Gorgias* quoted in the last section. I noted that Socrates ranks a wrongdoer who escapes punishment as the worst condition one can be in. Bad, but not as bad as this, is the wrongdoer who has their wrongdoing punished in such a way as to be rid of what makes the wrongdoer act badly. But what really astonishes Polus is what Socrates says at the end of the quotation: Socrates says that if given the choice between suffering injustice and doing it, he says, "For my part, I wouldn't want either, but if it had to be one or the other, I would choose suffering over doing what's unjust" (*Gorgias* 469c1–2).

Remarkably, scholars have had almost nothing to say about Socrates' aversion to being a victim of injustice.[26] Obviously, if we assume that Socrates actually accepted the sufficiency of virtue for happiness and also

---

[26] This is what prompted Joel Martinez and me to consider this issue in detail in our 2018, and my discussion in this section owes everything to that project, where we also discuss several texts that we take to indicate the same aversion as the one made explicit in the *Gorgias*. For the sake of brevity, I have chosen herein to focus mainly on what Socrates says in the *Gorgias*. Later I briefly consider elements of Socrates' second speech in the *Apology*, where he considers a number of possible

supposed that he was fully virtuous, his aversion to suffering injustice would be difficult to explain. After all, happiness, for Socrates, is the sole measure of value: Socrates is not a value pluralist – he does not think that things can be made valuable by any measure other than whether they conduce to happiness. So the fact that being a victim of injustice might be painful, for example, or shaming should not be issues in and of themselves. What would matter to Socrates – and all that would ever matter to him – would be whether or not what he did and the condition he might be in would be a happy one, and to what degree. Socrates seems to think that anything else that we might value only turns out to be neither good nor bad: valuable only when and if whatever these things might be are used wisely, because only when they are used wisely can they conduce to happiness. This, recall, is what Socrates argues in the *Euthydemus* (278e2–282a7).

And yet, Socrates clearly says to Polus that while he would certainly prefer to suffer wrongdoing than do it, if he had a choice, he would not suffer it, either. But why? The answer to this question requires us to engage in a bit of piecing together of other things Socrates says, since I do not know of any text in which he explains explicitly why his own suffering of wrongdoing would be harmful to him. My arguments in this book, however, make concocting a Socratic answer to this question much easier than an "all-or-nothing" view of knowledge, virtue, and happiness would allow. I have urged that we take the craft model of knowledge very seriously as we try to understand Socrates' various positions, and the main feature of this model that I have been calling attention to is that anyone serious about self-improvement will need to practice at the craft of virtue. Victimization can take many forms, obviously, but certainly one common feature of it is that it reduces the autonomy of the victim; it limits their ability to function as they wish. Obviously, this sort of effect is quite evident in the kinds of punishments Socrates says he would prefer to avoid in the second speech of the *Apology* – imprisonment, imprisonment with a fine he can't pay, or exile (37a3–e2) – and it takes little imagination

penalties that might be assigned to him, which he says would harm him. Such considerations either simply conflict with what he later says at *Apology* 41d1–2 about the gods ensuring that no harm comes to a good man, or else must condition our understanding of that later claim. Scholars who seek to make that claim compatible with Socrates' recognition of his own vulnerability to harm have proposed that the later claim is perhaps hyperbolic: to put it in the way I have been proposing in this book, the more virtuous one is, the less vulnerable to the worst kinds of harms one will be. Complete invulnerability to harm, however, is not achievable in a human life – though perhaps such a condition can be a blessing achieved in death or an afterlife, as Socrates seems to suggest in his final speech in the *Apology*.

to see that what all of these have in common is that they would hinder
Socrates' own ability to do what he seems to think he needs most of all to
do to "become as wise as possible," which is to engage in his philosophical
mission in Athens. Without mastery of virtue, one must always continue
in those practices likely to promote it. Being a victim of injustice has the
all-too-familiar effect of reducing or even preventing autonomous action,
and would thus disrupt Socrates' dedication to self-improvement.

But because Socrates does not have the craft of measurement, he also
remains vulnerable to other potentialities that could lead him astray. In the
last two chapters, I discussed how our most basic attractions and aversions
functioned in the formation of beliefs about what is best for us. I argued
that they are highly unreliable etiologies when it comes to forming true
evaluative beliefs. But they are a part of our psychological and cognitive
constitution, and no virtuous practice can simply rid us of their influence
altogether – unless, of course, we should manage to become godlike in our
mastery of the craft of measurement. Socrates was famously more immune
to physical discomforts and influences than those who knew him.[27] But
we should not overestimate this immunity, or suppose that Socrates was
completely above the effects that such damage and injury could cause. Our
attractions to pleasure and aversions to pain can and will lead us to form
beliefs about what is best for us that will often be untrue, unless we have
complete mastery over those attractions and aversions that Socrates seems
to say come only with the craft of measurement. Socrates may be better at
this craft than his peers – an advanced apprentice, if you like. But he still
experiences such things and to the extent that he lacks mastery in the craft
of measurement, to that same extent he is vulnerable to the siren calls of
his very human suite of attractions and aversions. An excellent (and rare)
text that shows Socrates' own vulnerability to one of these nonrational
inducements to bad behavior is given at the beginning of the *Charmides*,
where Socrates describes himself as experiencing "difficulties" when the
young Charmides comes and sits down next to him:

> [W]hen everyone in the palestra surged all around us in a circle, my noble
> friend, I saw inside his cloak and caught fire and was quite beside myself.
> And it occurred to me that Cydias was the wisest love-poet when he gave
> someone advice on the subject of beautiful boys and said that "the fawn
> should beware lest, while taking a look at the lion, he should provide part of

---

[27] This aspect of the way Plato characterizes Socrates is most evident in Plato's *Symposium*, and is also
often a feature of the way Socrates is characterized in the works of Xenophon.

the lion's dinner," because I felt as if I had been snapped up by such a creature. (*Charmides* 155d2–e2)

Socrates' description of his reaction to seeing inside Charmides' cloak clearly indicates that he was not wholly immune to the influence of lust. As he goes on to tell the story, he does manage to behave himself, but his struggle to do so is all the evidence that is needed to show that even Socrates felt the kinds of things that could lead weaker people to go astray. As I said in Chapter 3, it is these sorts of impulses that he supposed needed to be kept in a controlled condition, and we can safely assume (including from his behavior here with Charmides) that Socrates was a very self-controlled person.

But even a very self-controlled person is still a person who experiences pleasure and pain, lust and disgust, and, in general, attractions and aversions. Those who are victimized are often not just hindered in their autonomy, they are caused to have extremes of experiences to which they are especially averse: bad people can do things to others that cause them great pain and torture, and also great indignity. As self-controlled as Socrates is, he would clearly prefer not to suffer such torments, because without immunity to what they can do to the way one generates beliefs, Socrates, too, may be aware of at least some degree of moral vulnerability. Socrates is a man of exemplary gentleness in disposition, and steadfastness in the face of temptation. But we should not assume that these very estimable characteristics made him completely invulnerable to the ways in which others can not only do mischief, but actually do real moral harm to those they victimize.

Given how strongly the texts support the view that Socrates was well aware of human vulnerability to harm, what are we to make of his apparently categorical claim, at *Apology* 41d1–2, that "a good man cannot be harmed either in life or in death"? Plainly, other passages in the *Apology* seem to indicate that Socrates could certainly have been harmed – by imprisonment or exile or any of the other penalties he considers and rejects in his second speech in that work. I am inclined to think, first of all, that the context of this remark should make us just a bit cautious about taking it quite literally. Recall that he says these words as part of an attempt to console the jurors who have voted in his favor. But secondly, and perhaps more importantly, we should not take what he says here in isolation from the very next thing he says: "and his affairs are not neglected by the gods" (*Apology* 41d2–3). If we include these words in our understanding of what he is saying, he needn't be taken to be claiming that a good man is simply invulnerable to harm from others, but rather that good men who are harmed by others can be confident that such harm will be fully recompensed by the gods.

5.9 Summary and Conclusion

In the view for which I have argued herein, there are four key features in Plato's presentation of the Socratic position. First, Socrates' protreptic arguments in the *Euthydemus* should be understood primarily in terms of doing well and not in terms of happiness, even though Socrates treats these as equivalent. My claim is that we should understand this equivalence in terms of doing well, because our own instincts about happiness tend to set higher standards for achievement than Socrates intends in the dialogue. Second, Socrates' remarks about "*eutuchia*" in the argument should not be understood in terms of luck or anything else that is not under our control. Third, Socrates thinks that success and doing well are matters of degree and not achievements that we either have or lack. Socrates thinks that we should all strive to "become as wise as possible" because he thinks that the more wisdom we achieve, the better we will do. He articulates no clear level of success as the minimum for something to count as done well or for one to count as doing well in life. But we can and should suppose that one can do well even if and when one might still be able to do better. This position is well supported by the text, and gives to Socrates a reasonable position on the potential for human achievement. Socrates ties doing well to being happy, and we should now understand that all his argument requires is that one will do as well and be as happy as one can hope to achieve in those circumstances insofar as and to the degree that one applies wisdom to one's efforts. Finally, Socrates also allows for conditions outside of one's control, and not just one's degree of expertise at virtue, to make a difference to the degree to which one can succeed. Our vulnerabilities are not just limited to physical injury or disability; unless and until we can master the craft of measurement, we are also always and inevitably vulnerable to the distortions of appearances and to the cognitive effects of our most basic attractions and aversions. None of us is immune to harm, including moral harm. In the face of this threat, we can perhaps only rely on the gods to ensure that justice is eventually done.

CHAPTER 6

The Necessity of Virtue for Happiness

6.1   Introduction: Are We All Better Off Dead?

In the last chapter, I argued that Socrates did not accept the sufficiency of virtue for happiness. What he did accept, however, was that becoming more virtuous was not just the best but the only path one could take, if there is to be any hope at all for one to have a good life and do well. To the degree that one is virtuous, one will thereby achieve that same degree of happiness, all other things being equal. Factors that are outside of the agent's control may make a considerable difference to whether any happiness is actually achieved or achievable in that circumstance. This connection between virtue and happiness at least allows that human beings might achieve *some* degree of happiness in their lives, in proportion to the degree to which they develop wisdom and virtue.

It is not enough to say, however, that one's degree of virtue will secure that same degree of happiness, other things being equal. After all, if the most anyone can ever really achieve in terms of genuine wisdom remains "worthless" (*Apology* 23b3), as Socrates has the god assess it, then the connection between virtue and happiness I have ascribed to Socrates will have the effect that "worthless" will also describe the best we can hope to achieve in terms of happiness. In this chapter, I return for a final look at Plato's assessment of Socrates as an exemplar for us to try to emulate. Did Plato think that Socrates was happy? Did Plato's Socrates think that any of us could actually be happy? I begin with a passage that some scholars have taken as strong evidence for negative answers to these questions. In it, Socrates seems to suggest that even those who have had the best human lives will actually be better off dead. If he really means that, then it would seem that our prospects for happiness in this life are nil.

6.2 Death Is One of Two Things

One of the most notorious arguments to be found in any of Plato's dialogues is the first prong of Socrates' argument near the end of the *Apology* intended to give the jurors who voted in his favor "good hope" that death is nothing to fear. The passage, at *Apology* 40c5–41a8, concludes that, "if it [sc. death] is complete lack of perception, like a dreamless sleep, then death would be a great advantage" (*Apology* 40d1–2). As one recent commentator on this passage has understood it, "supposing Socrates means the argument seriously, then, puts a ceiling on how happy we can take Socrates to take himself to be: that ceiling is just short of minimally happy."[1] In fact, I think the case could be made that the implication of the argument is even stronger than this. After all, the argument Socrates gives here is fully general: it does not simply go to show that Socrates' own case is one in which annihilation would be "an advantage"; instead, it shows that annihilation would be "an advantage" for *any* human being. Socrates' argument is not a modal one – he does not argue that *it is not possible* to do better than annihilation. But even so, the picture seems extraordinarily grim: "not only a private person but even the great king" would count annihilation better than the vast majority of the "nights and days of his life." The exceptions to this general rule, Socrates says, would be "easy to count" for any human being. The upshot, then, is not one that most of us would associate with the "great hope" that Socrates says he is trying to instill in those jurors who voted in his favor (40c5). Instead, it seems we should all suppose that we will enjoy only a very few nights or days in which we do any better than "fall just short of [being] minimally happy." Socrates then goes on to consider the alternative, according to which the soul goes somewhere else, and rhetorically asks, about this alternative, "what greater blessing can there be?" In this understanding of Socrates' argument, then, it is the human condition to live lives that are, for the very most part, worse than death. Human life is not worth living, because all of us can expect to be better off dead.

But is this really Socrates' view of the human condition? One reason to think that it is derives from another commitment that most scholars have attributed to Socrates. Various passages in the early dialogues (especially the *Euthydemus*) have been cited as compelling evidence for the view that Socrates accepted that virtue was necessary for happiness (VNH).[2] If we

[1] Jones 2013a: 83.
[2] See, for example, Annas 1993, 1999; Irwin 1986; Jones 2013a, 2013b; Kraut 1984; Reeve 1989; Rudebusch 1999: 143, n. 17; Russell 2005; Taylor 2000; Vlastos 1991. To my knowledge, the

accept this conclusion, then we need only remind ourselves of two of the principles that formed the trilemma about Socrates as an exemplar, which I discussed in Chapter 1: (i) Socrates routinely disavows having the sort of knowledge for which he seeks, and (ii) Socrates was an intellectualist about virtue: he regarded virtue as a kind of knowledge. Since neither Socrates nor any other human being had such knowledge, then it follows from plugging this into VNH that although some of us may be less wretched than others, no one is happy.

In this chapter, I propose a way out of this dilemma. On the one hand, I will argue that the way most scholars have understood the texts (which I will henceforth call "the standard interpretation" given the ubiquity of its variations in the literature) is flawed – not required by the texts themselves, and also implausible for reasons that Socrates himself would surely have recognized. I then show that the correct understanding of these same texts requires a significant revision to the standard interpretation that preserves VNH, but in a form never before endorsed by those who have attributed VNH to Socrates. This revised version of VNH, I claim, provides no support for linking that doctrine to the very negative view of the human condition that some have attributed to Socrates on the basis of the argument about death in the *Apology*. Having removed the support of any other putatively "Socratic" view for such a grim understanding of Socrates' argument about death in the *Apology*, I conclude with some observations about what I think is a more plausible (and more positive) way to understand what Socrates intends in that argument.

6.3   The *Euthydemus* Again

Probably the most important passages cited in favor of attributing VNH to Socrates appear in the protreptic arguments of the *Euthydemus*. In the first of these, we find Socrates offering the following argument:

[SOCRATES SPEAKING] "In working and using wood there is surely nothing else that brings about the right use except the knowledge of carpentry, is there?"
[CLEINIAS SPEAKING] "Certainly not."

---

only scholars ever to deny the attribution of VNH to Socrates are Brickhouse and Smith 1994: 123–136 and Reshotko 2006, chapter 7. Obviously, my argument here indicates that my view about the necessity of virtue for happiness has changed; what has not changed, however, was the reason Brickhouse and I gave for rejecting VNH as it was standardly understood: that attribution would entail that Socrates himself was not happy. In my argument herein, I show how affirming Socrates' own happiness is not inconsistent with VNH as I now understand Socrates' commitment to it.

"And, again, I suppose that in making utensils, it is knowledge that produces the right method."

He agreed.

"And also, I said, with regard to using the goods we mentioned first – wealth and health and beauty – was it knowledge that ruled and directed our conduct in relation to the right use of all such things as these, or some other thing?"

"It was knowledge."

"The knowledge seems to provide men not only with good fortune but also with well-doing, in every case of possession or action."

He agreed.

"Then in heaven's name, I said, is there any advantage in other possessions without good sense or wisdom?" (281a1–b6)

It is not surprising that scholars have typically counted this as essentially just an explicit statement of the standard interpretation. As long as we understand what it means for something to be an advantage in eudaimonistic terms, Socrates here seems to be saying that there can be nothing good for human beings "without good sense or wisdom."

As plausible as this reading of the passage seems to be, the way in which scholars endorsing the standard interpretation have understood it is nonetheless defective. To see what may be wrong with the standard interpretation of the passage, let us think a little more carefully about the first comparison class that Socrates considers. In working with wood, we are told, there is "nothing else that brings about the right use except the knowledge of carpentry." Now, we might think of "the knowledge of carpentry" in terms of being a master craftsman, which seems to be an "all-or-nothing" concept: one is either a master craftsman, or one falls short of that achievement. If we take what Socrates says in this passage in this way, which is the way the standard interpretation has it, then we will understand Socrates to be claiming that only the master craft of carpentry brings about the right use of wood. The problem with this, of course, is that it is plainly false. It is certainly true that master carpenters are much more likely to make the right use of wood than those who are wholly ignorant of carpentry. And it is also no doubt true that master carpenters are more likely to make the right use of wood than even fairly well-trained apprentices. But surely Socrates knew that a fairly well-trained apprentice carpenter would do much better working with wood than a complete ignoramus. Rather, we would expect a fairly well-trained apprentice to make the right use of wood much – or even most – of the time. Is this not compatible with Socrates' point in the *Euthydemus* passage? The point would thus be put this way: one would expect to achieve the right use of wood, *insofar as* (or *to the degree that*) one had the craft of carpentry. Master carpenters have the craft to the highest degree; but fairly well-trained apprentices are well on their way to that achievement, and to the extent that they are well trained in the craft (even if they have not yet completely mastered it), we would expect the right use of wood from them. In the understanding of the argument I am proposing, it remains true, as Socrates seems to want to conclude, that there can be *no* advantage without knowledge or wisdom. What my reading allows, however (which the traditional reading does not), is that there can be *some* advantage we can expect, even if we have not yet achieved the highest levels of mastery.

The same point obviously applies to the second comparison case that Socrates offers: in making utensils, knowledge produces the right method. Again, knowledge will always be preferable to ignorance for making utensils; and the more skilled a craftsman is, the more we can expect the right method from them. But there is no reason to convict Socrates of the absurd view that an apprentice who is quite advanced in their training cannot ever be expected to achieve "the right method." How else, after all, would we be able to say of them that they are, indeed, far along in their training (even if not yet at the end of it)?

So if we take Socrates' examples of carpentry and utensil-making in the way required by the standard interpretation, then we convict Socrates of saying something false – and very obviously so. If we take the point to be about what it takes to work wood or make utensils well, where "what it takes" can be appropriately understood to come in degrees, then we will not only not convict Socrates of a bad error, we will also see that his point is an important and plausible one: one will succeed in one's life "missions" only to the degree that and only insofar as one has the requisite skills to pursue those missions intelligently and capably. We can reasonably expect success to the degree that, and only insofar as, we have such requisite skills.

If we take this reading of the passage, then, Socrates' point is that any advantage we are to achieve in life will be due to (and likely in proportion with) the extent to which we achieve what we do through expertise. To the extent that we *lack* expertise, we can reasonably expect not to achieve the advantages we pursue. But we should not suppose that Socrates foolishly believes that without the full and complete achievement of wisdom, we are all doomed to failure and misery.

What, then, are we to make of what Socrates says as this same passage continues?

> [Socrates speaking] Would a man with no sense profit more if he possessed and did much or if he possessed and did little? Look at it this way: if he did less, would he not make fewer mistakes; and if he made fewer mistakes, would he not do less badly; and if he did less badly, would he not be less miserable? (281b6–c3)

To see how this passage gets read by those who accept the standard interpretation, one does not need to look far to find its clear expression: "For someone like Socrates who lacks wisdom, doing less is better than doing more, for doing less provides less opportunity for harm and thereby makes one less miserable. Certainly, to be less miserable is to be further down the continuum towards happiness, but someone properly described as less miserable is not properly described as happy."[3] This understanding of what Socrates says here, however, also seems to me to be both implausible and un-Socratic. It is implausible because it would amount – again, in the example of craft that drives this passage – to the claim that even a fairly well-trained apprentice carpenter should at all costs avoid working with wood, because that way they will not make so many mistakes. The advice we might expect, on the contrary, is to tell the not-yet-master of a craft to "practice, practice, practice!" The standard interpretation of this passage is un-Socratic, I claim, because it amounts to advising everyone who does not already have fully achieved virtue by all means *not even to try* to improve themselves with respect to virtue, because even trying to be virtuous will make us even more miserable than we will be if we simply don't bother (so, contrast *Apology* 29d7–e3, 30a6–b4). That advice, notice, would have blocked Socrates from taking up "the true craft of politics," as he claims he has done.

It is common for scholars also to see the conclusion of this extended argument in the *Euthydemus* as essentially an explicit statement of the standard interpretation, so let's look at this passage now.

> [Socrates speaking] Then let us consider what follows: since we all wish to be happy, and since we appear to become so by using things and using them rightly, and since knowledge was the source of rightness and success, it seems to be necessary that every man should prepare himself by every means to become as wise as possible. (*Euthydemus* 282a1–6)

This passage does not have to be understood, however, as an endorsement of the standard interpretation. It seems, instead, to be an exhortation "to become as wise as possible," and that is precisely the advice we

---

[3] Jones 2013a: 90.

would have expected given the passages that went before it. Socrates' point is certainly *not* that any extent of failure to achieve perfect wisdom is certain to leave us below the threshold of happiness – it is, rather, that we can expect to be happy only insofar as, and to the extent that, we can improve in the kind of knowledge that is "the source of rightness" in what we do. But this hardly condemns those who have achieved incomplete success to wretchedness; it rather promises better and better results to those who strive for such excellence. Socrates' exhortation must not be taken as promising only lesser degrees of misery for those who "prepare . . . to become as wise as possible." Instead, he thinks that this is the way to be happy, and to expect and hope for ever more happiness insofar as we have greater success in our quest to "become as wise as possible."

6.4 Improvable Knowledge and Virtue Again

Socrates' exhortation, at the end of the passage just quoted, is that we should all strive to "become as wise as possible." This exhortation encourages a revised version of the standard interpretation – one according to which the kind of knowledge we should associate with Socrates' virtue intellectualism is *not* a threshold concept, but rather one that is *improvable* in the ways I have discussed in the previous chapters. Socrates' conception of knowledge, within what has come to be known as his "craft analogy," would be one that can be achieved and exemplified *in degrees*. The master craftsman has knowledge of that craft in some very high degree; the apprentice has knowledge of that craft in some lesser degree, and will continue to be only an apprentice (at best) so long as their knowledge does not reach the level required for master craftsmanship. The ignoramus, with respect to that same craft, will have extremely little or none of the relevant knowledge. Since the conception of knowledge that seems to be at work in "Socratic virtue intellectualism" is explicitly characterized as being some kind of craft, this divergence between his (improvable) conception and our own should not come as a surprise: it is a commonplace to regard "know-how" as improvable.[4] Accordingly, we might now suppose that the position Socrates is defending in these passages is VNH, only with improvable versions of virtue and happiness in mind, allowing for different levels of happiness in accordance with the different levels of virtue (knowledge, wisdom).

---

[4] See Ryle 1949: 59.

Now, it would certainly make it easier to attribute an improvable conception of virtue to Socrates if we found him regularly using comparative forms of virtue words (e.g. *sophôteros*, "wiser," or *dikaioteros*, "more just"). Xenophon, for example, tells the famous story of the Delphic oracle to Chaerephon in such a way as to have the oracle pronounce that "no human being was more free, more just, or more temperate" (*Apology* 14), which we are presumably not supposed to understand in such a way as to suppose that literally no one was any of these, and so no one was any more of these than Socrates, but only because we were all so completely deficient. It is worth noting, moreover, that "more free," "more just," and "more temperate" all seem to suggest that Xenophon's oracle regarded each of these traits as improvable. In Plato's dialogues, we find such forms only somewhat rarely in his discussions with interlocutors, and often the appearance of such expressions is not put into the mouth of Socrates. Even so, it is enough, I think, that we do at least sometimes find Socrates using such expressions in a way that indicates he is comfortable assigning different degrees of the virtues to himself and others. So, for a few examples, we find him seeking to discover which of the two friends he is talking to is *dikaioteros* and *sophôteros* at *Lysis* 207d1–2, and pleading with Euthyphro for help in becoming *sophôteros* at *Euthyphro* 9a2.

Socrates also explicitly counted himself as a good man (see *Apology* 41d1), presumably because, as he says, he is convinced he has never wronged anyone (*Apology* 37b2–3). Even if Socrates is always modest about these ethical achievements, we should not suppose that he actually thought of himself as vicious or wretched – for example, as genuinely deserving to be found guilty of impiety, on the ground that his own piety was incomplete, relative to a much higher degree of that virtue than he might have wished he could have achieved. Such cautiously positive self-appraisals, too, give us further insight into just how deficient Socrates thinks he is with respect to the kind of wisdom needed for happiness. In response to the famous oracle to Chaerephon, Socrates' first reaction was to puzzle that he was aware of having "no wisdom great or small" (21b4–5). But this first assessment seems to be reappraised at least slightly more favorably when he comes to appreciate that, even if he knows nothing worthwhile (*kalon kagathon*: 21d4), his examinations of others reveal to him that he is indeed wiser than others who think they are wise but are not (see *Apology* 21d3). Socrates plainly does not think his "human wisdom" (*Apology* 20d8, 23a7) amounts to anything very worthy, especially relative to the (presumably complete) wisdom of the god, whom he declares to be really wise (*Apology* 23a5–6), presumably thus indicating the highest level of wisdom, far beyond the relatively insignificant level he has achieved himself. In contrast, Socrates' "human wisdom" is "worth little or nothing" (*Apology* 23a7). Even so, as his discussion here in the *Apology* shows clearly enough, he is actually wiser than all or at least most other human beings, and that turns out to be a significant benefit to him, at least relative to the others who are so terribly unaware of their lack of wisdom.

One consequence of this revision to the attribution of VNH to Socrates, however, is that the thesis can no longer just of itself serve to explain the very bleak view of the human condition that seems to be given in the problematic text with which we began. That is, the explanation of why Socrates would believe that annihilation would be an advantage to everyone can now not be given in terms of the VNH having the consequence that, as Jones put it, "puts a ceiling on how happy" human beings can be, and "that ceiling is just short of minimally happy" (2013a: 83). If some lower level of virtue is, however, all that is necessary for (some appropriate degree of) happiness, and such incomplete virtue is something achievable by at least some human beings, it would seem that the "ceiling" for those who do achieve that degree of virtue will be higher than "just short of minimally happy." Whatever we may think about Socrates' assessment of death in the *Apology*, then, we will not be able to count what he says there as evidence for the standard view of VNH, as it has been taken to be.

I have argued thus far that Socrates should not be understood as saying that all deficiencies of craft or virtue are equal, but that we should, instead, aspire to ever higher levels of the kinds of skill that constitute virtue. So it does seem that Socrates accepts that there can be improvable levels of achievement, in our quest to become virtuous, and that these different levels will afford different levels of happiness – as opposed to merely different degrees of wretchedness, all of which fall "short of minimally happy."[5] I am now arguing that Socrates counted craft, virtue (or wisdom), and the knowledge in which virtue consists as improvable conditions, and so would be prepared to deem the achievements in skill of anyone who had at least become reasonably proficient in that domain as examples of "having the craft," even if to a lesser degree than that had by the master. So when Socrates exhorts us to seek to "become as wise as possible," we should take this exhortation to show that he would then count one who had real (but still incomplete) success in that mission as actually being wise, but only to a degree – at least as long as there remained higher levels of wisdom not yet achieved. Moreover, as I will go on to show, it seems clear that Socrates

---

[5] Again, see Jones 2013a: 83.

would count such a degree of achievement as making the one who had achieved so much as being happy – not merely less wretched than most.

6.5 Virtue and Happiness in Other Dialogues

The *Euthydemus* is probably the dialogue most often cited in support of the idea that Socrates supposed that there was a necessary connection between virtue and happiness, but other passages may also seem to indicate such a connection. Perhaps one such passage may be found in the *Charmides*.

> [Socrates speaking] "There is one additional thing I want to know: which of the kinds of knowledge makes one happy? Do all of them do this equally?"
> [Critias speaking] "No, very unequally."
> "Well, which one in particular makes one happy?" ...
> "By which one knows good," he said, "and evil."
> "You wretch," said I, "all this time you've been leading me right around in a circle and concealing from me that it was not living knowledgeably that was making us fare well and be happy, even if we possessed all the kinds of knowledge put together, but that we have to have this one knowledge of good and evil. Because, Critias, if you consent to take away this knowledge from the other kinds of knowledge, will medicine any the less produce health, or cobbling produce shoes, or the art of weaving produce clothes, or will the pilot's art any the less prevent us from dying at sea or the general's art in war?"
> "They will do it just the same," he said.
> "But my dear Critias, our chance of getting any of these things well and beneficially done will have vanished if this is lacking."
> "You are right." (*Charmides* 174a10–d2)[6]

It is easy enough to see why some scholars have taken this as evidence for the standard interpretation of VNH, according to which the conception of knowledge at work is a threshold conception, rather than improvable.[7] But it should not now be difficult to see why I am inclined to resist such a reading. Should we suppose that all hope of being cured by someone who is well along on but not quite finished their training as a physician "will have vanished" if we must find our fate in their hands, rather than the

---

[6] Translation slightly modified by removing gendered terms and changing "science" to "knowledge," which is the more usual translation of "*epistêmê*." It is plain that Socrates is talking about the kinds of knowledge that are constitutive of crafts in this passage.

[7] So Jones comments, "Here Socrates tells us that we require the knowledge of good and evil – which just is moral knowledge or virtue – in order to 'fare well and be happy.' Without it, our chance of doing things 'well and beneficially ... will have vanished.' This is an explicit claim that virtue is necessary for happiness" (2013a: 92).

master physician's? Or do the apprentices in cobbling and weaving not *at all* "make shoes" or "produce clothes," respectively? Is there no hope that an apprentice pilot will keep us from "dying at sea"? As I understand this passage, Socrates is neither stating nor implying any of these very implausible claims, but should instead be taken quite literally when he says that the good effects of the crafts would vanish if (and only if) the skill involved in that craft were also to vanish. He is certainly not saying that there can be no partial skills, or that partial skills will be not be good enough to produce anything good! So again, his (hopefully now-familiar) point is that we can only expect good results to the extent that and only insofar as there is skill applied in the pursuit of those results. That, moreover, is a completely plausible thing to say, and so it is no wonder that Socrates' interlocutors (including Critias, here) readily accept it when Socrates makes such a claim. It may be that we do not count apprentices as yet qualifying as physicians, or cobblers, or weavers, or pilots, despite the fact that they could serve our interests in each area much better than those who are wholly unskilled. But at a certain level of achievement and proficiency, we would count them as having become craftsmen, even if we continued to think that some craftsmen had achieved higher levels of mastery than others. From the fact that some weavers are better than others, it does not follow that the inferior weaver is not really a weaver after all.

Another passage that has been taken as evidence for the standard interpretation of Socrates' commitment to VNH appears in the *Laches*.

NICIAS: I have often heard you say that every one of us is good with respect to that in which he is wise and bad in respect to that in which he is ignorant.
SOCRATES: By heaven, you are right, Nicias.
NICIAS: Therefore, if a courageous man is good, it is clear that he is wise.
(*Laches* 194d1–5)

I agree that this passage clearly indicates a Socratic commitment to VNH. But the standard conception of this commitment, again, runs afoul of Socrates' mission to improve people by getting them to care more for wisdom and virtue than for such things as health, wealth, and reputation. Socrates' mission, as I understand it, is to help people become happier via such improvement; it is not simply to make them less miserable thereby. But if this understanding of the mission is correct, then we must not understand what Nicias says about Socrates here in the *Laches* as committing him to the view that we are not good *at all* unless we are completely wise, and that because we are all, as a matter of fact, at least as ignorant as Socrates, then we are all bad – including Socrates himself! Along the same lines as I understood the other passages I have surveyed thus far in this chapter, I would suggest that the correct understanding of what Nicias says about Socrates is that we are all good to the extent that, and only insofar as, we are wise, and bad to the extent that, and only insofar as, we are ignorant. This, again, is why we should strive "to become as wise as possible," so that we can also be as *good* as possible, which is how Socrates puts what I take to be the same point at *Apology* 39d8. Moreover, I think there are good reasons to think that Socrates is (at least very nearly) "as wise as possible" because of the way he has lived his life.

6.6   Just How Skillful Is Skillful Enough?

I have argued thus far that Socrates' recognition of the improvability of skill opens up the possibility that self-improvement can have the potential to get us to a point where we will go above and beyond being "minimally happy." But there is more to this issue that needs to be said in order to secure that positive result. The question I wish to consider now is, I claim, as important as any question that might be asked about the conception of virtue as being like – or actually being – a craft or skill: just how skilled does one need to be in order to qualify to Socrates as a case of someone having that craft or being skilled? In terms of virtue, my question becomes: just how virtuous does one have to be to qualify as having virtue or being virtuous?

Motivating the asking of this question are a few aspects of the craft analogy that, I argue, have been inadequately explored by scholars. The first aspect is one that I have already talked a lot about in this book, which is the improvability of skills: when it comes to having a skill or being skilled, some are better or more skilled than others. But there is another aspect of the craft model of knowledge that I think needs more attention now: skills seem to have what I am going to call differences of "demandingness." Some skills are very undemanding in the sense that what they require is both straightforward and quite simple. Other (more demanding) skills are much more complex and seem to require not just one very simple ability or requirement, but many that are interconnected, some or all of which may themselves require very high levels of mastery in order to count as being achieved at all. Perhaps related to the differences of demandingness in skills, it also seems true that in order to qualify as skilled or having a skill will require different degrees of adeptness for different skills: in order to have some skills, only very low levels of adeptness are required. For others, much higher standards must be met. What I wish to show now is that

Socrates was aware of each of these aspects and how they might apply to the issue of having virtue and being virtuous. So I now turn to the issue of the demandingness of craft: just how adept does one need to be in order to qualify as having a craft at all – of counting as having the relevant skill, at least to a degree?

6.7 Degrees of Demandingness in Skills

In Chapter 1, I considered a passage in the *Gorgias* in which Socrates gets Callicles to agree that life-saving skills, such as swimming (511b7–c9) and helmsmanship (511d1–e3), are in fact quite uncomplicated and in any case, as he puts it there, nothing "grand." One might think, by contrast to these, that the skill of virtue should be conceived as requiring quite high conditions for one to satisfy, to be counted as one who has that skill at all.

> Someone who learns enough to successfully execute one task related to house-building may not have the skills to execute some other tasks. And since the sub-tasks of house-building are not merely additive, but interdependent, failure to execute some tasks well may not only fail to add value to the house, but might even undermine the good to tasks that were, considered just on their own, well-executed. Someone who knows how to put up straight walls, but does not know how to lay a stable foundation does not get things half right, but rather all wrong. . . . So it is with a life. (Jones 2016: 100)

This is an important point. Swimming may be an extremely undemanding skill – one can plausibly claim to have the skill even if one's level of mastery is quite low. But many skills require a great deal of not just technical mastery but also quite a variety of specific skills that are interdependently required in order for the superordinate skill to be achieved at all – and each of the subordinate skills may themselves require considerable technical mastery. Jones' example of one who attempts to build a house but has no mastery of the subskill of laying a foundation is not a housebuilder, but a failure: they do "not get things half right, but rather all wrong." So housebuilding is what I am calling a very demanding skill. To be a housebuilder at all, one needs to achieve quite high standards of technical mastery. Jones takes it as just obvious that the skill of virtue is like this: highly demanding in terms of complexity and technical mastery.

While it might seem just obvious that whatever skill(s) Socrates thinks virtue must involve will be highly technical and demanding ones, it seems to me that the matter is worth careful consideration. At the very least, if it really is Socrates' view that the demands of virtue are so great that neither

Socrates nor anyone else can meet those demands to any meaningful degree, this has depressing consequences for Socrates' view of the human condition. To put it the way Jones does,[8] the Socratic view of the human condition is remarkably bleak: he thinks that all of us will be better off dead, and the only "progress" we can hope to make in life is to end up less wretched than we might have been, but never actually happy.[9]

So just how technically demanding does Socrates think the skill of virtue would be? Despite the urgency of this question in terms of assessing Socrates' view of the human condition, the available evidence for hypothesizing an answer to it is neither abundant nor as direct as we might like it to be. In what follows, I want to consider two questions that seem to me to be related to this urgent one, and I propose that the answers to these questions promise to give us some insight (and some optimism) about what Socrates thinks about our realistic chances of happiness. The first of these questions concerns just how demanding we should think virtue is, as a skill. The second is about the degree to which one would have to have significant mastery in virtue to qualify as virtuous at all.

6.8   The Teachability of Skills

The main arguments of the *Laches*, *Protagoras*, and *Meno* concern the question of whether or not virtue is teachable. Other skills, Socrates insists, are teachable, and so it seems as if virtue, too, should be teachable. But in each of these dialogues, this thought hits a snag. If virtue is teachable, where does one find a teacher? Those who profess to be teachers of virtue – for example, Protagoras – quickly prove, under Socratic cross-examination, not to have the knowledge they would presumably need to teach this skill. In talking about the skill, they say things that indicate they do not know what they are talking about. In each of these dialogues, Socrates and his interlocutors founder on the question of the teachability of virtue, because they find no teachers of virtue who can prove themselves to be experts.

In the *Laches*, one of the opening moves of the dialogue concerns the question of whether fighting in armor is a genuine skill, and Laches expresses doubt. If fighting in armor were a genuine skill, not only would those who care the most about war be especially eager to learn this skill, but also those who claimed to teach it would themselves be very distinguished in actually performing the skill. But, Laches notes, the alleged teachers of this skill do not go to Sparta to teach it (*Laches* 182d8–183b7), but they also

---

[8] Jones 2016.   [9] See especially Jones 2013a.

never prove to be anything special in actual warfare: "not a single practitioner of fighting in armor has ever become renowned in war" (*Laches* 183c3–4). Laches goes on to recount a particularly foolish and inept display by one of the alleged skill's most famous practitioners, a certain Stesilaus, who managed to make a complete mockery of himself with a weapon (apparently of his own design) that he eventually had to abandon because it had gotten caught in the rigging of an enemy ship passing by (183c8–184a7). Laches concludes his skeptical presentation with a most appropriate observation for us to recall as we consider the skill of virtue and who might teach it to us:

> A man who pretends to knowledge of this sort is the object of envy, so that unless he is outstandingly superior to the rest, there is no way in which he can possibly avoid becoming a laughingstock when he claims to have this knowledge. (*Laches* 184c1–4)[10]

The process is familiar to readers of Plato's dialogues: those who claim to have some special skill in virtue, and who are subjected to Socratic examination, inevitably fail and become laughingstocks.

So why does the skill of virtue prove to be so difficult to learn and so difficult to teach? Jones' proposal might be taken to be that these difficulties are explicable in terms of the technical demands of virtue, which simply exceed beyond our grasp and are only achievable (if at all) by gods. "The god is really wise," as Socrates says at *Apology* 23a5–6, and the oracle to Chaerephon is intended to show that "human wisdom is of little or no value," and the only wisdom anyone can reasonably hope to achieve is the recognition that "he's in truth worthless with respect to wisdom" (all quotations from *Apology* 23a5–b4[11]). This could be taken as Socrates' answer to the question of how and why virtue does not seem to be teachable or learnable: we are simply not the sorts of creatures who can learn or teach it.

Although we can take away from Socrates' remarks here that even the very highest achievements in human wisdom will be utterly unimpressive from the god's-eye point of view, I do not think that Socrates' assessment of human wisdom, relative to divine wisdom, implies a bleak view of the

---

[10] We might now remind ourselves that one of the earlier claims of superiority made by Euthydemus and Dionysodorus was that they were experts on the very skill that Laches regarded as so dubious (see *Euthydemus* 273c7, e3–4). By the time they speak with Socrates in the *Euthydemus*, this expertise has been downgraded to a mere "diversion": they are now, much to Socrates' incredulity, teachers of virtue (273d3–4).

[11] The translations here are those of Brickhouse and Smith 2002.

human condition. What it does imply, instead, seems to me to be compatible with what Laches actually had to say about those who would claim to teach very valuable things: "unless he is outstandingly superior to the rest, there is no way in which he can possibly avoid becoming a laughingstock when he claims to have this knowledge." Since no one qualifies as "outstandingly superior to the rest" when it comes to virtue, there are no true teachers of virtue – only those who deserve to be laughingstocks. But Laches' point, notice, is still compatible with the assessment that some people really are better than others, when it comes to important skills. In the case of virtue, however, it seems that no one is *so much* better than the rest as to qualify as a reliable teacher.

Bu this still leaves us with the problem of not being able to find teachers of virtue. So, how are we to learn it or improve on whatever our current condition might be? The *Laches* offers at least a tentative answer to this question, too: it is possible to learn a craft even without a master to teach it to one (*Laches* 185e7–9, 186b1–5, 187a1). In the *Euthydemus*, Socrates insists that "everyone should prepare by every means to become as wise as possible" (282a5–6), and so perhaps in the case of virtue, we just need to go about the task of developing the skill without having anyone to teach it to us.

This conclusion, however, is very different from what some of Socrates' interlocutors propose about virtue, where the teaching and learning of virtue is compared to a skill that we would normally consider quite demanding. At least twice in dialogues attributed to Plato,[12] teaching and learning virtue is compared with teaching and learning Greek (*Protagoras* 327e3–a1; *Alcibiades* I 111a1). To those of us who have struggled to learn Greek, it is perfectly plain that being able to learn enough to count as skilled in the Greek language qualifies as *very* demanding. But Socrates' interlocutors note that this very demanding skill is taught and learned all the time – so much so that (at least among the ancient Athenians) one couldn't find a teacher of Greek; since everyone was such an expert in that skill, no one especially stood out.[13] Applying this model, Protagoras and Alcibiades insist that learning virtue is much the same: the skill is so widely

[12] One of these is the *Alcibiades* I, whose authenticity is generally accepted these days, despite my own reservations (for which see Smith 2004). Even if it is authentic, it is not clear whether it belongs to the group of early dialogues that are my focus here. I bring it in only because it engages the same claim about teaching and learning language as is given by Protagoras in his eponymous dialogue.

[13] It is curious that this argument is given in the *Protagoras* in the presence of Prodicus, who was supposedly a true expert in Greek. Perhaps the argument only assumes teaching and learning ordinary levels of the skill, whereas Prodicus teaches allegedly higher levels.

distributed among the Athenian people that there is no need to seek for special teachers of virtue. Almost everyone can qualify as an advisor when it comes to virtue (see, e.g., *Protagoras* 322e2–323a2).

If Socrates accepted this – being skilled in Greek – as the most apt analog to the skill of virtue, then the lack of teachers of virtue would not be a problem for its acquisition, since the supposed lack of teachers would turn out to be a superabundance of them. In the *Protagoras*, Socrates does not directly give a reason to regard language skills as a poor analog for virtue. Instead, the argument turns to the question of the unity or disunity of virtue. But in the *Alcibiades* I, Socrates gives an argument for why virtue is not like skill in Greek: people do not have radically different opinions about how to speak Greek; but people have serious and many disagreements about justice and injustice. Those with expertise do not disagree in such ways (*Alcibiades* I 112c2–d2). Hence, the widespread differences of opinion among people count as clear indicators that the skill(s) involved in virtue are very unlike those of knowing Greek. It may be that both sorts of skill are highly demanding. But in the case of virtue, Socrates thinks that the demands of the skill are mostly unmet by human beings. So if one is to learn it, one must develop the skill on one's own and without a teacher. Unlike knowing Greek, there are no teachers of virtue because no one is sufficiently skilled in the relevant way as to be able to teach it.

This outcome, however, hardly presents a more optimistic picture of our chances of being happy in life, nor does it seem to give much hope for Socrates' own condition. From the fact that it is in principle possible to "bootstrap" a skill in some cases, it does not at all follow that one can do this with any skill at all. Jones' objection comes back in force here: if the skill of virtue is one that is highly demanding in terms of technical expertise, then the project of developing it wholly on one's own and without expert guidance looks even more daunting – and perhaps simply impossible. Perhaps one could teach oneself how to swim, but it doesn't seem plausible to think that one could teach oneself rocket science or neurosurgery.

6.9 Revisiting the Demandingness of Skills

But perhaps there is still a path to the view that Socrates is not so pessimistic about the human condition. One way to make a case for a more optimistic view might be to look to our texts to see if there are any demanding skills that Socrates seems nonetheless to think do not require high levels of expertise for one to qualify as having the skill (albeit

incompletely, perhaps), and as (to that degree) skillful. For this, we will do
well to look carefully at what Socrates has to say about the one skill that he
most often likens to virtue: medicine.

Examples of Socrates' thought that medicine and virtue are very much alike
are abundant in our texts. Generally, the way this comparison goes is that
medicine is to the good of the body what virtue is to the good of the soul (see,
e.g., *Crito* 47a12–48a1; *Gorgias* 464b2–c3, 477b3–c2, 478b7–479c1, 480a6–b2,
505a2–b4). From the various ways in which Socrates describes the medical
treatments of his day (especially in the *Gorgias*), he was certainly aware that it
included treatments for physical ailments of complex and dangerous kinds
(such as, for example, inflammation of the lungs – *Laches* 192e6) and often
involved the administration of forms of treatment that one would not at all
want to receive from some nonexpert – treatments, for example, including
prescriptions for medicines to put into a patient's eyes (*Laches* 185c5–8),
cautery, and surgery (*Gorgias* 456b1–4, 480c6–7). Given the complexities of
the human body and all the many things that can injure or sicken us, it comes
as no surprise, then, to see that Socrates so often uses medicine as an example
of how and why experts are the only ones we should look to when some very
advanced skill is needed.

Remarkably, for all the many passages in which Socrates expresses
admiration for the medical skill and for the expertise of its practitioners,
there are almost none where he seems to recognize what we now recognize
about ancient Greek medicine: that it frequently failed to cure patients
and, much worse, was often more dangerous to them than the infirmities it
was intended to relieve. Only once, to my knowledge, does Socrates have
anything at all critical to say about ancient Greek medicine and the doctors
who practiced it: at *Charmides* 156e3–5, Socrates observes that most Greek
doctors are incapable of curing most diseases (suggesting that their inability
was due to their failure to treat the soul and body together).

Applying these considerations to our topic here, we might want to ask
why it is that Socrates supposed that medicine was not only a genuine skill,
but (much more puzzlingly) why he so often spoke as if he regarded
a number of people as actually *having* that skill. By any measure familiar
to modernity, ancient Greek medical professionals had no skill in medicine
at all! Let us look more closely at an explanation that Socrates actually gives
as to why he regards medicine as a skill.

> I was saying that cookery didn't seem to me to be a skill (*technê*), but an
> empirical practice (*empeiria*). I said that medicine, on the other hand,
> has considered (*eskeptai*) both the nature of what it serves and the cause

of what it does, and is able to give an account of each of these. (*Gorgias* 500e4–501a3)[14]

It is a bit tricky to try to figure out just how the contrast between cookery and medicine that Socrates seeks to make here is supposed to be understood. The requirement that one with a genuine skill be able to give an account of how to engage in the operations of that skill cannot be all that is at stake here – after all, it is hardly as if the way to cook some dish is *inexplicable*, or there wouldn't be such things as cookbooks. But soon enough, what is at stake in Socrates' view is made explicit: empirical practices like cookery may have some very settled and well-established routine (*tribê –Gorgias* 501a7), but are concerned only with what happens to bring pleasure, and not with the real good of those served by the chef (501b4–c1).[15] To understand what is really good for those served requires that one know the nature of what is served (in this case, the nature of the body or the soul), and thus also know what is really best for it. Cooks do not know this and do not so much as even attend to such considerations. Physicians apparently do, in Socrates' view.

If we take Socrates' analysis of the difference between medicine and cookery in this way, the contrast he seeks to make may become clearer, but this analysis also puts even more pressure on my question here: if this is what a genuine skill requires, why would Socrates be so ready to concede that (ancient Greek) medicine was a good example of a skill that was (often) achieved in his day?

To go back to the way Socrates makes this contrast, what are we to make of his claim that the (ancient Greek) practice of medicine examined the nature of the body (with an eye to understanding what is good for the body), and could explain its own procedures in those terms? Again, from the perspective of modernity, it is quite clear that the ancient Greek understanding of the body and how it worked was appallingly insecure, to the point of pure quackery. Applying theories of hot and cold, wet and dry, they prescribed treatments intended to restore some alleged imbalance in these conditions. They could also explain why those treatments were well aimed at the result of restoring balances of the relevant properties in the body. But as to whether bodies actually did work, and whether disease processes also worked, in such ways as to be explicable in such terms, it seems that Socrates was ready to accept not just the theories of ancient

---

[14] My translation.
[15] I do not mean to endorse this claim, since I believe that some modern cooking is dedicated to good nutrition. I mean only to report here what Socrates seems to think.

medicine but also the ways in which those theories had implications for proper medical practices. So it is fair to say that insofar as medicine really is a skill, it is one that Socrates and his fellow Greeks almost entirely failed to understand.

Greek ships were actually able to sail across the seas – however precariously by modern standards. Greek construction was crude by modern (and, truth be told, even by some other ancient) standards, but Greek builders were obviously quite able to build things that have endured for long periods of time. The same can be said for all of the other skills that Socrates relies upon in deploying his "craft analogy." The problem with ancient Greek medicine is not just that all of its basic theoretical grounds were either false or irrelevant; many of its actual practices mostly failed as a result of the vast extent of the ignorance and falsity that grounded them.

To insist on the kinds of success that we can now achieve in any of the skills practiced by ancient Greeks is obviously to commit a great anachronism. Even so, the actual skill achieved in Greek medicine, relative to other ancient skills, leaves it puzzling why Socrates would be so ready to acknowledge not just the existence of such a skill, but most importantly to accept and promote the claim that many ancient Greeks actually had that skill.

6.10 Contextualizing the Demandingness of Skills

Let us grant that Socrates recognized that human bodies were remarkably vulnerable to injury and disease, and so also grant that an idealized form of medicine could understand and treat absolutely all of them with such complete success that they could make human beings immortal (that Socrates could imagine a medical skill so advanced is clear at *Charmides* 156d5–6). Accordingly, let us grant that Socrates would regard medicine, at least in this idealized form, as an inconceivably demanding skill. Does it follow that Socrates must therefore *also* believe that no one could have the skill of medicine unless they were far advanced in the mastery of this skill? Plainly not, given his willingness to count some of his contemporaries as being physicians. Rather, it seems that once someone intending to become a physician has fulfilled certain quite minimal conditions with regard to mastery of medicine – relative to its idealized form – that candidate will (despite their lack of knowledge or achievement from the idealized point of view) qualify as skilled, and a genuine physician.

What matters, for something to be a skill for Socrates, is that those who pursue that skill consider "both the nature of what it serves and the explanation for what it does, and [are] able to give an account of each of these." Notice what is actually *missing* in Socrates' requirement. "Consider" is a conative verb: no specific actual positive achievement is required for one to engage in considering something. Moreover, the requirement that one can give an account of one's consideration, and/or whatever results it has actually achieved, also does not set the actual bar for having a skill any higher than the making of an honest and principled effort. What Greek medicine actually did do, despite its meager achievements in Socrates' own time, was focus in a very dedicated way on trying to figure out how the body worked and also on how to benefit patients.

But skills also have to do more than this. In the challenge from Jones (2016: 100), the problem was that the skill of housebuilding seemed to require more than just the satisfaction of what I have called "quite minimal standards" to qualify as an example of that skill. His assessment is surely correct: one cannot exemplify the skill of housebuilding if one's attempt to build a house results in a collapsed ruin. So, too, even skills that Socrates seems willing to recognize as having been achieved by his fellow Greeks will certainly have to achieve some standard of success. For all of its failure to even begin to approximate what I have characterized as "the idealized skill of medicine," Greek medicine was able to treat and even cure some ailments, especially those associated with injuries such as broken bones or dislocated joints.

My proposal is that Socrates' willingness to recognize medicine as an authentic skill was the result of his willingness to accept that it had satisfied two conditions:

(1)   Those who had and used this putative skill had actually attempted to understand the human body and also to recognize at least some causes of both benefits and ailments to it.

(2)   Those who had and used this skill could actually point to the relief or cure of certain conditions that, left untreated, were recognized as likely to cause significant suffering and/or disability.

To be clear, the satisfaction of (1) did not require that the process of understanding the body and the causes of its ailments was even close to complete, and the satisfaction of (2) did not require that Socrates believed that Greek physicians were always or even for the most part successful in treating or curing the many infirmities they encountered. Accordingly, I am proposing that as a matter of fact, Socrates was actually quite willing to recognize that what I have been calling very demanding skills could be achieved to such a degree that he was ready to identify some of his contemporaries as having that skill.

From the fact, therefore, that we can recognize a skill as being quite demanding, and also recognize that Socrates could not have supposed that any of his contemporaries had even come close to mastering all of the demandingness of that skill, it does not follow that Socrates regarded the skill as either unachievable or not yet achieved. Instead, we have at least some evidence – especially in the case of medicine – that Socrates had a contextualized view of what would count as having a skill. To the extent that it had a certain intellectual basis and could also indicate reliable success, Socrates was willing to count the skill as having been achieved (even if not nearly perfected).

6.11 Returning to Virtue

The result of my argument in the last section is an important one for how we should assess what Socrates might have supposed about the actual achievability of virtue. Given not just a conception of an idealized realization of virtue (one appropriate to the gods, perhaps), but also a realistic and contextualized standard, it now seems that it is at least possible that Socrates could regard some level of virtue to be genuinely achievable. But Jones' cautionary argument is not yet superseded, for though Socrates does seem quite willing to recognize some living human beings as having the skill of medicine, he is obviously much less willing to attribute wisdom or any of the other virtues[16] to anyone.

Even so, there are a few indications that his and others' pursuit of virtue might not be condemned to failure, as in Jones' inept housebuilder case. Are there texts that could lead us to believe that Socrates does not think that we always, inevitably, lack virtue to such a degree that we don't even "get things half right, but rather all wrong"?

I think there are, and will conclude my argument by mentioning some of them just briefly (since some of these passages I have reviewed in other chapters at greater length) to indicate why they seem to me to be grounds for a more optimistic assessment of our potential to develop at least enough skill in virtue to count as at least somewhat virtuous – perhaps at least to be

---

[16] I here simply intend to sidestep the controversies about Socrates' commitment to the unity of virtue, and in any case have nothing new to say about it from what Brickhouse and I presented in Brickhouse and Smith 2010: 154–167. Whatever the relationship between the various virtues might be, the only clear cases in which he attributes wisdom or any other virtue to anyone in the early dialogues look to be ironic. But if we do take seriously that Socrates accepts the unity of virtue, then his own assessment of his own wisdom, relative to the others he tests for wisdom, in the *Apology* and elsewhere is an indication of just how little anyone has achieved when it comes to virtue.

able to avoid getting things "all wrong." I doubt that the following is a complete list of the kinds of passages that would support my assessment, but hope at least that the ones I enumerate here will suffice.

Socrates makes a few claims about his own achievements that give at least some evidence of success in his pursuit of virtue. These passages might be categorized into two different kinds: (i) Socrates exhorting others to care most of all for virtue, and then (ii) Socrates claiming of himself some things that indicate genuine success in virtuous activity and achievement.

A couple of samples of the first sort of passages are these:

(T1) *Apology* 28b3–c1: Socrates explains that for a man to be good, he should not concern himself about the risk of death, but only about "whether what he does is right or wrong, whether he is acting like a good or bad man." Without some ability to make such judgments reliably, such a prescription would be otiose.

(T2) *Apology* 30e3–31b5: Socrates the "gadfly" exhorts his fellow Athenians to care most of all for virtue. What would the point of caring for virtue be if the very best we could hope for would be that we would still get it all wrong?

Such exhortations to virtue may also be found in many other passages in the early dialogues. I'll just give two more examples from other dialogues:

(T3) *Euthydemus* 282a1–6: To be successful and happy, everyone should prepare by every means to become as wise as possible. Again, such advice makes no sense unless we have some reliable sense of how to pursue such a goal, and some reason to think that with enough effort, we could also achieve it to some meaningful degree.

(T4) *Gorgias* 480a6–d6: Anyone who has committed injustice should present himself to the judge "to pay his due and get well." But why should anyone suppose that the Athenian legal system actually had the capacity to make people more just? If the best we can hope for is a level of achievement so paltry and flawed as to promise only more error and self-harm, why bother with submitting oneself to "corrections"?

In other passages – and although there are fewer of these in our texts, there are more than I list here – Socrates seems to claim of himself that he has actually done well in the pursuit of virtue that he always encourages others to undertake.

(T5) *Apology* 29b5–7: Socrates contrasts his ignorance of what is in the underworld with his knowledge that disobeying superiors is wicked and shameful. This surprisingly strong claim of epistemic confidence could not be true of one who was hopelessly inadequate with respect to moral judgment and action.

(T6) *Apology* 31c7–e1: Socrates' *daimonion* kept him from engaging in Athenian politics, which he regards as a very good thing, because had he tried to so engage, "I should have died long ago, and benefited neither you nor myself." Socrates seems to think that he has benefited either his fellow Athenians or himself (or both).

(T7) *Apology* 32a9–c2: Socrates risked death by opposing the other members of the Council after the Arginousae affair. He confidently insists that his actions were "on the side of law and justice," whereas the other members "were engaged in an unjust course." It seems that Socrates is a reliable judge of justice and what a just man needs to do, even in very dangerous circumstances.

(T8) *Apology* 32c3–e1: Socrates did not obey The Thirty when they commanded the arrest of Leon. He regards it as obviously true that what they were trying to do was wrong, while his own actions proved that he was unwilling to do "anything unjust or impious." If Socrates is as inept and incompetent in the skill(s) of justice and piety as to count as lacking such skill(s) altogether, then his judgments here qualify as shamefully presumptuous – the same kind of presumption, it would seem, as he finds in those he examines and refutes.

(T9) *Apology* 36d9–10: Socrates contrasts himself with the Olympic victor who "makes you think yourself happy; I make you happy." If virtue is necessary for happiness, as many scholars seem ready to accept,[17] then this claim entails that Socrates also has the ability to make others virtuous – at least enough to be happy.

(T10) *Apology* 37b2–8: Socrates is convinced that he wrongs no one, and thus will not propose a counter-penalty that he "knows very well to be an evil." Both claims would be completely unwarranted unless Socrates has at least some reliable skill in making such assessments.

(T11) *Apology* 41c9–d3: The gods ensure that good men can't be harmed, either in life or in death. If Socrates does not intend to be characterizing himself to the jury as a good man, whatever he is trying to say to them here is pointless.[18]

I will close by simply identifying two additional texts that have seemed to me to make it clear that Socrates regards himself as having at least begun the process of acquiring virtue – as opposed to simply inquiring about it – and also invites us to reflect on just how successful he has been in achieving its acquisition to a significant degree.

(T12) *Gorgias* 521d6–e1: Socrates claims to be the only one among his contemporaries "to take up the true political craft and practice the true politics." In

---

[17] For recent examples, see Jones 2013a, 2016; Smith 2016. I had earlier argued against this claim in Brickhouse and Smith 1990.

[18] Brickhouse and I had earlier (1990) tried to understand this claim while also refusing to make the assumption that it required Socrates to regard himself as virtuous. I now think that was a mistake.

Chapter 2, I argued against the kind of deflationary interpretation of this passage that is required by thinking that Socrates continues wholly to lack the skills he claims here to have taken up and to practice. But I think it is worthwhile here to remind readers that Socrates goes on to explain the way in which he has taken up the "true political craft" and what it means for him to practice that craft. He goes on to say that it is "because the speeches I make on each occasion do not aim at gratification but at what's best. They don't aim at what's most pleasant." The clear implication is that just following this mandate is enough to count as practicing the "true political craft." Moreover, Socrates regards himself as being in a position to engage in aiming at what is best. Socrates can hardly deserve any credit if he inevitably fails to hit his target. To put it again in the terms Jones has rightly insisted upon, it may not be that Socrates gets things at least "half right." But it simply cannot be that he gets things "all wrong." This passage is obviously entirely consistent with what Socrates has to say about his successes in the practices of virtue, in the *Apology*.

Also consistent with what Socrates says in the *Apology* when he contrasts the effects he has actually had on his fellow Athenians (T9) is what he tells Callicles in the next and final passage in this review:

(T13) *Gorgias* 527c4–6: Socrates tells Callicles to follow Socrates' lead, and if he does so, Callicles will "be happy both during life and at its end."

6.12   Becoming and Being Positively Happy

I have certainly not given a comprehensive account of what Socrates thinks about skills, or, for that matter, what he thought about how the "craft analogy" informs his conception of ethics. This would be a project for another day.[19] What I have shown is at least that Socrates recognized a remarkable diversity of skills, with different requirements for what level of success in their acquisition qualified for *having* that skill and *being* skilled. Most importantly, when it comes to the acquisition of skills, we need to remember that such acquisition comes in degrees and not all at once. It is simply not true that either one has a skill or one doesn't; either one is skilled or one isn't. Instead, one develops a skill in stages and qualifies as skilled to the extent that they have practiced effectively enough

---

[19] And no doubt another author. I am aware of at least one who has taken up this task as her dissertation topic: Cecilia Li of the University of Western Ontario, with whom I have had a number of fruitful discussions that have helped me to sharpen my own thinking about this subject. I am indebted to her influence, but do not at all intend to blame her for any errors I have made herein.

to have become to some significant degree reliable in producing the effects of that skill.

Some skills are very simple and seem to be extremely undemanding as far as what will count as having such a skill. Others, however, seem to be much more demanding. I have argued herein, however, that the demandingness of a skill is not a reliable indicator of just how much technical mastery a person must achieve in order to qualify as having the skill at all. Instead, the levels of achievement in such skills will be judged in accordance with more reasonable, contextualized assessments of what may be expected in a given historical circumstance.

Finally, applying these results to the question of the achievability of virtue, which Socrates plainly took to be a kind of skill, I have granted that the relevant skill does seem to be quite demanding – at least from the perspective of idealizations – but have argued that Socrates thinks that he and others have a very real and practical chance of becoming skilled in virtue, to such a degree as also thereby becoming happy. In the case of virtue, Socrates seems to think that the most important impediment to our developing the relevant skill is that we simply don't bother to make any effort to do so. Instead, we pursue money, reputation, or political influence. Socrates' exhortations to people that they should pursue virtue first and foremost would be unnecessary unless others rarely or never did that. By not making this initial mistake – one that short-circuits any chance that one could develop virtue – Socrates takes up the "true craft" of benefiting others, and counts himself as achieving some success simply by aiming at what is best, rather than at what is most pleasant. If we do just that much – concern ourselves to pursue virtue as our first priority and then always aim at what is best – we will have good reason to hope that we may be happy, both in life and at its end.

6.13   Ashes to Ashes . . .

If I am right that the other passages show that Socrates did not accept the very bleak view of the human condition that would follow from a commitment to the standard interpretation, then what are we to make now of the problematic speech in the *Apology* where Socrates seems to indicate precisely such a bleak view of things? I noted earlier that the version of VNH I have attributed to Socrates would not help us to interpret the remarkably bleak picture that Socrates seems to endorse in this passage.

The specific argument, let us recall, proposes that either death is annihilation or it is not, but in either case "there is good hope that death is a blessing" (40c5–6). The argument Socrates offers has not won support among commentators, who have found numerous faults with it,[20] and the very fact that it has seemed like such a bad argument to people is perhaps motivation enough to consider carefully whether and to what degree we should take it as indicating a genuine Socratic commitment.[21] But, as some have also insisted, even if it really is a bad argument, it does not follow that Socrates does not accept it.[22] Even so, I think that what Socrates tells his jurors here should be regarded as a kindly overstatement, at best, and not as a genuine Socratic commitment about the human condition.

Rather than attempt to reconstruct the argument in a way that might spruce it up in its entirety, I think that attending to what Socrates is trying to do with the argument will help to shed light on what he does and does not intend in making it. The argument is offered to a specific audience, one characterized in several ways. First, those to whom Socrates addresses this argument are those "who voted for my acquittal" (39e1), and as "friends" (40a1). Socrates seems to recognize that they might be distraught by the outcome of the trial, on the ground that it condemns him to "what is generally thought to be the worst of evils" (40a8–b1). So he seeks to persuade them, with the argument he subsequently gives, that "What has happened may well be a good thing, and those of us who believe death to be an evil are certainly mistaken" (40b7–c2). Strictly speaking, then, what Socrates needs to do if he is to console his "friends" among the jurors is to give them some reason to think that death is *not* the "worst of evils" and perhaps not even anything bad *at all*. If he can go on and actually give them some reason for thinking that "what has happened may well be a good thing," then so much the better.

Socrates famously compares the "annihilation" option to a "dreamless sleep," and ancient Greek culture lends significant support to such an association.[23] Critics have cried foul when Socrates concludes from this comparison, "then death would be a great advantage" (*Apology* 40d1–2). It is not so clear to me that Socrates' argument is guilty of any greater fault than overstatement here. None of us know, when we fall asleep at night, if we will actually survive the night or wake up refreshed. Even so, Socrates is exactly right to note that when we go to bed at night, even after days we would regard as having been most delightful, we very much welcome the onset of loss of

---

[20] See, for example, Armleder 1966; Roochnik 1985. More charitable assessments can be found in Austin 2010; Ehnmark 1946; Hoerber 1966; Jones 2013a; Rudebusch 1991.

[21] So see Jones: "The passage is familiar not only to scholars, but also to many undergraduates, who have been given the passage as an example of how *not* to argue" (2013a: 82).

[22] Jones 2013a: 82.   [23] See, for example, Homer, *Iliad* 16.682.

consciousness.[24] Excessive fatigue or the desire for relief from some other suffering is not a prerequisite of our having such an attitude. The simple fact is that sleep appeals to us and we typically look forward to it with pleasant anticipation. Socrates' interest in consoling his "friends" on the jury is surely served by reminding them of this fact. We do not need to suppose that Socrates actually intended his jurors to take him quite literally when he goes beyond such a familiar fact to claim that we would count few of our days as "better and more pleasant" than our experience of such repose. The context in which Socrates gives his argument, I am claiming, permits or even encourages such innocent hyperbole.

The other alternative that Socrates offers to his "friends," however, actually lends direct support to the argument I have developed in this chapter. Having shown that if death is annihilation, even then it is nothing bad for the one who has been annihilated, he goes on to give some reason for thinking that the other option, where the soul migrates to another place, would be, as he strikingly puts it, an "extraordinary happiness" (41c4). This wonderful result, Socrates claims, would be achieved for him if he could find himself examining "the man who led the great expedition against Troy, or Odysseus, or Sisyphus, and innumerable other men and women one could mention" (41b7–c2). If Socrates really did accept the standard interpretation, then the only way he could make such a claim would be if he imagines that all of the dead are instantly awarded with complete virtue as soon as they enter the afterlife. But this does not seem to be what Socrates thinks would happen; rather, he indicates that the happiness would flow simply from an opportunity to do with these dead men and women what he has done for so much of his life with living companions and interlocutors. As he puts this fantasy, "Most important, I could spend my time testing and examining people, as I do here, as to who among them is wise, and who thinks he is, but is not" (41b5–7). It could not be possible that there would be both classes of people in the afterlife, unless at least some failed to be awarded wisdom at the doorstep to Hades. Even so, Socrates says, "they are happier there than we" (41c5–6). In the *Gorgias*, Socrates explains in a bit more detail that the dead will be happier because they will have received whatever correction in their souls they need, and, as I have argued, any improvement of that kind will also conduce to improvement in happiness (*Gorgias* 523a1–525c1). In the *Apology*, the greater happiness

---

[24] It is worth noting that Plato depicts Socrates' friend, Crito, in the dialogue named after him, as supposing that Socrates was "spending his time most agreeably" while asleep (*Crito* 43b5). Socrates, it seems, was so untroubled by his impending execution and the injustice that had been done to him that he could still enjoy a good sleep when he was in prison.

of the dead also seems to be assured by the presence of those who Socrates calls "true judges" (Minos, Rhadamanthus, Aecus, and Trimptolemus – *Apology* 41a2–4), and from the fact that the dead do not seem to be vulnerable to the factors outside of our control that can damage our happiness in life. At least no one in Hades will be put to death for doing philosophy (*Apology* 41c4–7). I note, then, that one can take the two alternatives of Socrates' argument together as actually achieving the very goals he indicates as his aims at the outset: the first side actually does give his "friends" a reason to think that death is not a bad thing (for the dead), and the second side gives them a reason for thinking that death might, indeed, be a good thing for the dead.[25]

6.14 Summary and Conclusion

In this chapter, I have explained why we should not accept the standard interpretation of the passages commonly taken to show that Socrates accepted VNH. Even so, I agree that these passages do indicate that Socrates accepts a version of VNH in which the relationship between virtue and happiness allows for degrees of success in both. One must "become as wise as possible" in order to become as happy as possible, for there can be no happiness where wisdom is wholly absent. But even if we can never achieve complete wisdom or happiness, if my argument is correct, by exhorting people in the way he does, Socrates does not offer false hope.

In order to make the hope that Socrates offers genuinely positive, rather than amounting only to the hope that we can become less wretched without actually becoming happy, I spent some time in this chapter looking at a number of things that Socrates says about crafts and skills, to determine just how demanding we might take the kind of skill that really matters for self-improvement to be. I found that Socrates' comparison of virtue to medicine was indicative of how even an extremely demanding craft might allow not just progress in its attainment, but the kind of progress that would be enough for a practitioner to claim actually to have the craft, albeit only to a relatively small degree, relative to a perfection standard of mastery.

I contend that the interpretation I have proposed herein manages to avoid what some have soberly noted is the "disappointing conclusion"[26] that results from attributing the standard version of VNH to Socrates.

---

[25] A very similar picture of the afterlife is given in the closing myth of the *Gorgias*. Although the standard interpretation cannot explain several elements of that myth, it follows from what Socrates says there that everyone really would be better off dead (even if they have been good and thus happy while they lived). See Brickhouse and Smith 1994: 210 for discussion.

[26] Jones 2013a: 97.

Socrates was not, I contend, so bleak about the human condition. Best of all, Plato's early dialogues give us not just the theoretical but also the practical bases that we need to achieve some positive happiness as a result of self-improvement. Human life is, as I discussed in the last chapter, extremely vulnerable to circumstances that are wholly out of our control, and which may defeat and ruin us in every imaginable way. But that does not result in there being no hope at all; self-improvement is necessary for happiness, as I have argued in this chapter. But it *is* possible.

Afterword: Review and Assessment

A.1 Charity in Interpretation

Scholars often advocate for positions they wish to attribute to important historical figures in philosophy, by claiming that their interpretations are more "charitable" than those offered by other scholars. What this usually means is that the interpretation to be preferred offers some philosophical advantage, relative to the alternatives. At a minimum, an interpretation will be more charitable if it finds a way to render the philosopher's position to be at least coherent, if others have claimed that no coherence was to be found. Usually, however, a claim of greater charity means something stronger – it amounts to saying that the position said to be more charitable is supposed to be more philosophically plausible than the alternatives. Ideally, scholars might hope that they can offer an interpretation of some historical philosopher's ideas that actually make them important, plausible, even compelling.

Now that I have completed the strictly scholarly part of this book, it might be interesting to some to consider briefly whether the views I have attributed to Socrates are more charitable than the interpretations I have argued against. Before I do this, however, I would like to remind my audience that aiming at charity in one's scholarly interpretations has to be only a relatively minor desideratum. First and foremost, scholars – if it is scholarship they are really attempting – must do their utmost to interpret their materials in ways that are the most plausible, given what the texts they are interpreting actually say. It is not our job as scholars to "rescue" some historical figure from some error they plainly did make. We might reasonably speculate about how that figure could have avoided that particular error, but charity certainly cannot trump the obvious sense of the text. In writing this book (so far) my attention has been almost entirely on discerning as well as possible what Socrates in Plato's early dialogues

actually meant when he made the statements and arguments that have been
my focus herein. Occasionally, I have noted that I found specific alternative understandings implausible philosophically. Such remarks, however,
have not been the real aim of my inquiry. I will now briefly assess just what
I think the merits of the positions I have attributed to Socrates are. Just
how "charitable" do I think my interpretations have been?

A.2   Socrates' Motivational Intellectualism

I developed one of the views I have attributed to Socrates in this book –
explained mainly in Chapter 3 – in my work with Tom Brickhouse. In
brief, our argument was that Socrates' motivational intellectualism is to be
understood in such a way as to recognize a nonrational etiology for belief-
formation. Briefly, our basic attractions and aversions worked in such
a way as to represent their aims as worthy of pursuit (that is, as something
worth acquiring, for attraction, and for aversion, as something worth
avoiding). Other things equal, when an agent experiences an attraction
or aversion, they will come to believe the value represented by that attraction or aversion: they will believe that they should pursue the things to
which they feel an attraction, or they will believe they should avoid the
things to which they feel an aversion. I have argued that this makes the best
sense of all the things that Socrates has to say about motivation.

What should *we* think about this view? To begin, it is probably worth
noting that contemporary epistemologists do not generally discuss attraction and aversion as etiologies for cognition.[1] The closest contemporaries
seem to get to such an idea is when they (always disparagingly) refer to
the phenomenon of wishful thinking. I expect there is more to be found
about this sort of process in the philosophical and psychological literature
on the emotions, but I confess I do not know that literature well enough to
provide to my readers any indication of where they might find some echo
(or modern rediscovery) of the Socratic insight. In any case, it seems to me
that the idea of such a connection between our most basic attractions and
aversions and the way in which we generate beliefs has, from the time
Brickhouse and I conceived of it as an explanation for things we found
Socrates saying, seemed to me to be very plausible and also allows a much
more plausible account of Socratic motivational intellectualism than others

---

[1] I note, just for three examples of places where we might look to see what contemporaries think about
this idea, that no such etiology of belief is mentioned in Vahid 2009, Dancy, Sosa, and Steup 2010, or
Reisner and Steglich-Peterson 2011.

have offered – since those others either treat our basic urges simply as sources of information or else regard such urges as having no place in the Socratic conception of motivation at all. Were contemporary epistemologists inclined to take the etiology of belief that Brickhouse and I have claimed to find in Socrates, they might also have ways to give the beliefs that are produced in such ways more credence than Socrates seems to give them. For example, fairly sophisticated arguments have been given for the veridical reliability of epistemic processes in terms of their evolutionary fitness.[2] On the other hand, not all human cognitive processes are veridically reliable, and so this could well turn out to be one of the *unreliable* ones, which would match Socrates' assessment.

As for the motivational intellectualism that seemed to Brickhouse and me to require such an etiology of belief-formation, I am inclined to doubt that contemporary philosophers (or psychologists) will find much of value there. Human motivation, it seems, is a great deal more complex and the ways in which people become motivated seem to be a good deal more diverse than Socrates seemed to suppose. In some cases, it is not clear just how much – if anything – in the way in which we practice agency is explicable in terms of purely epistemic states. It also seems unlikely that any contemporary philosophers are likely to revive the Socratic view that denies the phenomenon of akratic action. Having said this, I would note, however, that the way in which we respond to at least our children's actions seems to reflect at least *some* intellectualism: when we see a child who we think has done something wrong, we ask the child what they were *thinking* when they did such a thing. If the child were to tell us that they were thinking all the while that what they were doing was bad, we might then ask them why they did it, if that was really what they thought. It seems that normal parenting often leaves no room for recognition of akratic action.

A.3   The Craft Model

Contemporary epistemology has also paid little heed to the phenomenon of know-how.[3] It does seem to me, however, that this is not a defect in the model Socrates employed, but rather a defect of contemporary epistemology. The relations between knowledge and education are obvious enough. That we expect educators to provide important new skills to their students is also nothing new. In fact, the increasing emphasis on the development

[2] See, for example, Graham 2012 and Evans and Smith 2012: chapters 8 and 9.
[3] An exception is Hetherington 2011. Sennett 2009 also makes a contribution.

of skills, as opposed to the learning of facts, has been embraced internationally.[4] Nonetheless, the philosophical study of epistemology continues to be almost exclusively focused on fact-knowledge. I believe this focus reveals the degree to which contemporary epistemology continues to be driven by Cartesian concerns about skepticism and certainty, and if indeed it is, I would welcome a paradigm shift.[5]

As for whether or not craft is the right way to think about virtue, contemporary philosophers of virtue theory have had mixed responses. Some, perhaps most prominently Julia Annas,[6] have argued in favor of conceiving virtues as skills. Others, for example Linda Zagzebsky, have argued against conceiving of virtues as skills.[7] The virtues and vices of this conception, if I may, continue to be debated among scholars, and were recently the focus of an international conference.[8] But I think it is fair to say that the Socratic conception of virtue as a skill continues to be regarded as at least philosophically powerful. As such, I hope that the account of the Socratic conception that I give herein qualifies as charitable in the sense that it provides a model of virtue that contemporaries should find well worth their serious, even if critical, attention.

A.4 Socrates on the Connections Between Virtue and Happiness

One place I have already clearly made a claim of charity on behalf of the view I attribute to Socrates has to do with what he has to say about the human condition. In the past, I had argued against the idea that Socrates accepted the sufficiency and necessity of virtue for happiness.[9] I had argued against the idea that Socrates accepted the sufficiency of virtue for happiness on the ground that he clearly recognized that very bad things can happen even to very good people, and so even the entirely virtuous person might be simply defeated by things that were entirely outside their – or indeed any human being's – control. Scholars who have defended the view that Socrates accepted the sufficiency of virtue for happiness have claimed that he actually accepted the very implausible view that nothing could defeat a virtuous agent's happiness.[10] Such an agent would be completely

---

[4] See ACT 2000; Partnership for 21st Century Skills 2008; TeachThought Staff 2019.
[5] And have encouraged thought in this direction: see Hetherington and Smith 2019.
[6] For example, in Annas 1995 and 2011.   [7] See Zagzebsky 1996: 106–116.
[8] "Virtue, Skill, and Practical Reason," hosted by Tom Angier at the University of Cape Town in August 2017.
[9] Especially in Brickhouse and Smith 1994.
[10] For a clear example of this version of the sufficiency thesis, see Irwin 1986.

invulnerable to injustice or catastrophe, and even if these should fall heavily on those the virtuous agent loved, there would be no defeat of happiness to the agent as a result. Those who have now read Chapter 5 of this book will realize that my view of this matter has not significantly changed from my earlier work. I do not think that Socrates accepts the sufficiency of virtue for happiness, and I also think that my view of this matter is a great deal more charitable to Socrates than the view that he did take virtue to be sufficient for happiness. The view I have presented herein understands Socrates as believing that, other things equal, one would be happy to the extent that one is virtuous. In that way, the pursuit of virtue really is the best way to pursue happiness, for one's degree of achievement in the former would covary with one's success in the latter. In conceiving of this principle as only applying "other things equal," however, I concede the objections I had offered (with Brickhouse) earlier on the continuing vulnerability of the virtuous agent. My discussion of this topic in Chapter 5, however, goes beyond earlier work that I did with Brickhouse insofar as (having worked on the issue with another coauthor, Joel Martinez) I now think that Socrates also clearly recognized and understood well some of the cases of what has come to be called "moral harm" – the kind of harm that can be done to agents that makes them worse off in terms of their own moral agency. I believe this aspect of my analysis of what Socrates has to say about the connections between virtue and happiness is also a very charitable one, actually attributing to Socrates insights about the kinds of damage that victimization causes that have only recently again been an important focus of philosophical ethics.[11]

During the long period in which Brickhouse and I collaborated on Socrates, we first argued for and then against attributing to Socrates the thesis that virtue was necessary for happiness.[12] We argued against this attribution in 1994 as a result of considering the case of Socrates himself. We noted that he seemed to count himself as happy (which those who have read the final chapter of this book will already know I continue to accept), but we supposed then that his profession of ignorance blocked attributing to him any claim to virtue, given his commitment to virtue intellectualism. Bringing the improvability of Socrates' (craft-)conception of knowledge into focus, as I have done in this book, has allowed me to see the stronger relationship with happiness that the necessity thesis requires, while also

---

[11] For a more recent treatment of this concern, see Card 1993.
[12] In favor of attributing the necessity of virtue for happiness to Socrates, see Brickhouse and Smith 1987 and 1990. Against this attribution, see Brickhouse and Smith 1994: 123–134.

allowing Socrates to have a real share of happiness – one that is proportionate to the ways in which he is wiser (and thus more virtuous generally) than others. Where Brickhouse and I went wrong, I now think, when we saw Socrates as happy but not virtuous was that we were not yet thinking about the possibility that virtue might be achieved in degrees. We accepted – along with so many other scholars who have written on this topic – that, for Socrates, knowledge, wisdom/virtue, and happiness were threshold achievements. Since then, others have agreed with me that we should see Socrates' views about knowledge, wisdom/virtue, and happiness as improvable, but have still contended that all human lives – including Socrates' – fall short of positive happiness.[13] In the final chapter of this book, I argued against this "disappointing conclusion," which attributes to Socrates a "bleak view of the human condition."[14] Since I avoid these results herein (and have argued that the texts support such an avoidance), I regard my results as more charitable than at least one of the significant and well-argued alternatives.[15]

A.5   The Improvability of Knowledge, Virtue, and Happiness

As I indicated when I first took up the improvability of Socrates' model of knowledge in Chapter 1, most contemporary epistemologists do not think of knowledge as achieved in degrees, but as a threshold. Unless and until one reaches the conditions that define the threshold, one will not have knowledge, though one's cognitive condition that is not knowledge might still be conceived as approaching or approximating this threshold. But if we do conceive of the knowledge relevant to Socratic virtue intellectualism as know-how, or skill, or expertise (as craft, in other words), then it seems seeing the achievement of this kind of knowledge as occurring in degrees is part of the model. In this book, I have been working out the entailments of that aspect of the model, and I have

---

[13] Jones 2016.

[14] Both quotations from Jones: the first appears in Jones 2013a: 97, and the second appears in the title of Jones 2016.

[15] Having just made these invidious comparisons of my own results to those achieved by Jones, I should note with gratitude that Jones served as a referee for the National Endowment for the Humanities Summer Stipend proposal, which was subsequently funded and which allowed me to complete this project. My disagreement with his results should not be mistaken for disrespect, and it seems his own disagreements with me also did not prevent him from giving my proposal a favorable review. As Brickhouse and I put it in 1994: "Our critics and those whose works we criticize herein are, in many cases, our best friends. We would not want it any other way" (Brickhouse and Smith 1994: x). With the greatest respect and enthusiasm, I include Jones in this category.

argued that these entailments support several (at least relatively) new views about Socratic philosophy.

My argument, however, has not been that contemporary epistemology is wrong about knowledge. I have elsewhere argued, in fact, for a threshold conception of propositional or informational knowledge.[16] I just don't think this is the model of knowledge that Socrates has in mind when he presents his views about the nature of wisdom and virtue. It seems to me that if I am right about that, then the fact that Socrates treats these as improvable is no challenge to and is not in conflict with modern debates about the nature of propositional or informational knowledge.

As for the improvability of craft, I also think this, too, is simply part of the way we think about know-how, skill, or expertise. In Section A.3 I discussed the philosophical viability of the Socratic thought that virtue must be (at least very like) craft. But now I want to focus on what is really central to the view I have tried to develop herein: the idea that virtue is something we should suppose we can achieve in different degrees. Here, too, I think the view I have attributed to Socrates satisfies our sense of charity in interpretation. To me, at any rate, it is simply obvious that most of the traits that I regard as virtues are achieved by different agents to different degrees. This goes, I think, both for the most basic of our ethical characteristics (for example, personal integrity) and also for those we may regard as pleasing, but optional (such as Aristotle's wittiness – *eutrapelia*) – different people may be credited with actually having such virtues, but to different degrees. At the highest end of the former we find moral heroes and those we regard as exemplars, but we do not suppose that any of us who fail to exhibit personal integrity to an exemplary degree thereby fall short of achieving that virtue at all. Similarly, those who fall short of the sort of wit exhibited by Oscar Wilde, for example, may nonetheless count as admirably witty. I take it as also obvious that the happiness we can achieve in life comes in different degrees to different agents. So here, too, I think that those who have understood Socratic virtue intellectualism in terms of threshold conceptions of knowledge have managed to do real damage to the plausibility of the Socratic view.

To end this book, then, I will gladly say that I wholeheartedly endorse the Socratic view that we will become better people to the degree that we take up his quest "to become as wise as possible" (*Euthydemus* 282a6).

---

[16] In Evans and Smith 2012.

References

ACT. 2000. *Workplace Essential Skills: Resources Related to the SCANS Competencies and Foundation Skills*. Report presented to US Department of Labor Employment and Training Administration/US Department of Education National Education Statistics. Iowa City, IA: ACT. http://wdr .doleta.gov/opr/fulltext/oo-wes.pdf.

Ahbel-Rappe, S. 2010. "Cross-Examining Happiness: Reason and Community in Plato's Dialogues." In Andrea Nightingale and David Sedley, eds., *Ancient Models of Mind: Studies in Human and Divine Rationality*. Cambridge: Cambridge University Press, 27–44.

Al-Maini, D. 2011. "Filial Piety in the *Euthyphro*." *Ancient Philosophy* 31: 1–24.

Annas, J. 1993. *The Morality of Happiness*. Oxford: Oxford University Press.

Annas, J. 1994. "Virtue as the Use of Other Goods." In T. Irwin and M. C. Nussbaum, eds., *Virtue, Love and Form: Essays in Memory of Gregory Vlastos*. Edmonton: Academic Printing and Publishing, 53–66.

Annas, J. 1995. "Virtue as a Skill." *International Journal of Philosophical Studies* 3: 227–243.

Annas, J. 1999. *Platonic Ethics, Old and New*. Ithaca, NY: Cornell University Press.

Annas, J. 2011. *Intelligent Virtue*. Oxford: Oxford University Press.

Apostle, H. G. and Gerson, L. P. 1991. *Aristotle Selected Works* (3rd ed.). Grinnell, IA: Peripatetic Press.

Aristotle. 1924. *Metaphysics*, vol. 1. Trans. W. D. Ross. Oxford: Clarendon Press.

Aristotle. 1935. *Eudemian Ethics*, vol. 20 of *Aristotle* (23 vols). Trans. H. Rackham. Cambridge, MA: Harvard University Press (Loeb Classical Library).

Armleder, P. J. 1966. "Death in Plato's *Apology*." *Classical Bulletin* 42: 46.

Austin, E. 2010. "Prudence and the Fear of Death in Plato's *Apology*." *Ancient Philosophy* 30: 39–55.

Benson, H. H. 2013a. "The Priority of Definition." In J. Bussanich and N. D. Smith, eds., *The Bloomsbury Companion to Socrates*. London: Bloomsbury, 136–155.

Benson, H. H. 2013b. "What Should Euthyphro Do?" *History of Philosophy Quarterly* 30: 115–146.

Beversluis, J. 2010. *Cross-Examining Socrates: A Defense of the Interlocutors in Plato's Early Dialogues*. Cambridge: Cambridge University Press.

Brickhouse, T. C. and Smith, N. D. 1987. "Socrates on Goods, Virtue, and Happiness." *Oxford Studies in Ancient Philosophy* 5: 1–27.

Brickhouse, T. C. and Smith, N. D. 1989. *Socrates on Trial*. Oxford and Princeton, NJ: Oxford University Press and Princeton University Press.

Brickhouse, T. C. and Smith, N. D. 1990. "What Makes Socrates a Good Man?" *Journal of the History of Philosophy* 28: 169–179.

Brickhouse, T. C. and Smith, N. D. 1994. *Plato's Socrates*. Oxford: Oxford University Press.

Brickhouse, T. C. and Smith, N. D. 1997. "Socrates on the Unity of the Virtues." *Journal of Ethics* 1: 311–324.

Brickhouse, T. C. and Smith, N. D. 2000. "Making Things Good and Making Good Things in Socratic Philosophy." In T. Robinson et al., eds., *Plato: Euthydemus, Lysis, Charmides: Proceedings of the V Symposium Platonicum, Selected Papers*. Sankt Augustin: Academia Verlag, 76–87.

Brickhouse, T. C. and Smith, N. D., eds. 2002. *The Trial and Execution of Socrates: Sources and Controversies*. New York: Oxford University Press.

Brickhouse, T. C. and Smith, N. D. 2004. *Routledge Philosophy Guidebook to Plato and the Trial of Socrates*. London: Routledge.

Brickhouse, T. C. and Smith, N. D. 2010. *Socratic Moral Psychology*. Cambridge: Cambridge University Press.

Brickhouse, T. C. and Smith, N. D. 2012. "Response to Critics." *Analytic Philosophy* 53: 234–248.

Brickhouse, T. C. and Smith, N. D. 2013. "Socratic Moral Psychology." In J. Bussanich and N. D. Smith, eds., *The Bloomsbury Companion to Socrates*. London: Bloomsbury, 185–209.

Brickhouse, T. C. and Smith, N. D. 2015. "Socrates on the Emotions." *Plato Journal* 15: 9–28.

Brickhouse, T. C. and Smith, N. D. 2018. "Socrates on Punishment and the Law." In M. Boeri, Y. Kanayama, and J. Mittleman, eds., *Soul and Mind in Greek Thought: Psychological Issues in Plato and Aristotle*. New York: Springer, 37–53.

Burnet, J. 1924. *Plato, Euthyphro, Apology of Socrates, and Crito*. Oxford: Clarendon Press.

Bussanich, J. and Smith, N. D., eds. 2013. *The Bloomsbury Companion to Socrates*. London: Bloomsbury.

Card, C. 1993. *The Unnatural Lottery: Character and Moral Luck*. Philadelphia, PA: Temple University Press.

Carone, G. R. 2001. "Akrasia in the *Republic*: Does Plato Change His Mind?" *Oxford Studies in Ancient Philosophy* 20: 107–148.

CBS News. 2010. "NTSB: Sully Could Have Made It Back to LaGuardia." www.cbsnews.com/news/ntsb-sully-could-have-made-it-back-to-laguardia.

CNN. 2009. "US Airways Captain the 'Consummate Pilot'." http://edition.cnn.com/2009/US/01/16/crash.pilot.profile.

Cooper, J. M., ed. 1997. *Plato: Complete Works*. Indianapolis, IN: Hackett Publishing Company.

Cooper, J. M. 1999. "Socrates and Plato in Plato's *Gorgias.*" In John M. Cooper, *Reason and Emotion: Essays on Ancient Moral Psychology and Ethical Theory.* Princeton, NJ: Princeton University Press, 29–75.

Cornford, F. M. 1933. "The Athenian Philosophical Schools, I: The Philosophy of Socrates." *Cambridge Ancient History*, vol. 6: 302–309. Cambridge: Cambridge University Press.

Dancy, J., Sosa, E., and Steup, M., eds. 2010. *A Companion to Epistemology* (2nd ed.). Chichester, West Sussex: Wiley-Blackwell.

Davis, W. 2010. "Implicature." *The Stanford Encyclopedia of Philosophy* (Fall 2012 Edition), Edward N. Zalta (ed.). http://plato.stanford.edu/archives/fall2012/entries/implicature.

Destrée, P. and Smith, N. D., eds. 2005. *Socrates' Divine Sign: Religion, Practice, and Value in Socratic Philosophy.* Kelowna, BC: Academic Printing and Publishing.

Devereux, D. T. 1993. "The Unity of the Virtues." *The Philosophical Review* 102: 765–789.

Devereux, D. T. 1995. "Socrates' Kantian Conception of Virtue." *Journal of the History of Philosophy* 33: 381–408.

Dimas, P. 2002. "Happiness in the *Euthydemus.*" *Phronesis* 47: 1–27.

Diogenes Laertius. 1925. *Lives of Eminent Philosophers, vol. 1.* Trans. R. D. Hicks. Cambridge, MA: Harvard University Press (Loeb Classical Library).

Dodds, E. R. 1959. *Plato: Gorgias.* Oxford: Clarendon Press.

Ehli, B. 2018. "Rationalizing Socrates' *Daimonion.*" *British Journal for the History of Philosophy* 26: 225–240.

Ehnmark, E. 1946. "Socrates and the Immortality of the Soul." *Eranos* 44: 105–122.

Evans, I. and Smith, N. D. 2012. *Knowledge.* London: Polity Press.

Ferejohn, M. T. 1982. "The Unity of Virtue and the Objects of Socratic Inquiry." *Journal of the History of Philosophy* 20: 1–21.

Ferejohn, M. T. 1983–4. "Socratic Virtue as the Parts of Itself." *Philosophy and Phenomenological Research* 43: 83–95.

Ferejohn, M. T. 1984. "Socratic Thought-Experiments and the Unity of Virtue Paradox." *Phronesis* 29: 105–122.

Fine, G. 2008. "Does Socrates Claim to Know That He Knows Nothing?" *Oxford Studies in Ancient Philosophy* 35: 49–88.

Frede, M. 1992. "Introduction." In *Plato: Protagoras*, trans. S. Lombardo and K. Bell. Indianapolis, IN: Hackett Publishing Company, vii–xxxiv.

Gerson, L. P. 2013. *From Plato to Platonism.* Ithaca, NY: Cornell University Press.

Gerson, L. P. and Inwood, B. 1988. *Hellenistic Philosophy* (2nd ed.). Indianapolis, IN: Hackett.

Giannopoulou, Z. 2011. "Socrates and Godlikeness in Plato's *Theaetetus.*" *Journal of Philosophical Research* 36: 135–148.

Graham, D. W. 1997. "What Socrates Knew." In M. L. McPherran, ed., *Wisdom, Ignorance, and Virtue: New Essays in Socratic Studies.* Edmonton: Academic Printing and Publishing, 25–36.

Graham, P. 2012. "Epistemic Entitlement." *Nous* 46: 449–482.

Grice, P. 1975. "Logic and Conversation." In P. Cole and J. Morgan, eds., *Syntax and Semantics, 3: Speech Acts*. New York: Academic Press, 41–58. Reprinted in H. P. Grice (ed.). 1991. *Studies in the Way of Words*. Cambridge, MA: Harvard University Press, 22–40.

Gulley, N. 1968. *The Philosophy of Socrates*. London: Macmillan.

Hetherington, S. 2011. *How to Know: A Practicalist Conception of Knowledge*. Chichester: Wiley-Blackwell.

Hetherington, S. and Smith, N. D., eds. 2019. *What the Ancients Offer to Contemporary Epistemology*. New York: Routledge.

Hewitt, B., Egan, N. W, Herbst, D., McGee, T., and Bass, S. 2009. "Flight 1549: The Right Stuff." *People* (February 23): 60–66.

Hoerber, R. 1966. "Note on Plato, *Apologia* XLII." *Classical Bulletin* 42: 92.

Hoesly, D. and Smith, N. D. 2013. "Thrasymachus: Diagnosis and Treatment." In N. Notomi and L. Brisson, eds., *Dialogues on Plato's Politeia (Republic): Selected Papers from the Ninth Symposium Platonicum*. Sankt Augustin: Academia Verlag, 60–65.

Irwin, T. H. 1977. *Plato's Moral Theory*. Oxford: Clarendon Press.

Irwin, T. H. 1979. *Plato's Gorgias*. Oxford: Oxford University Press.

Irwin, T. H. 1986. "Socrates the Epicurean?" *Illinois Classical Studies* 11: 85–112.

Irwin, T. H. 1995. *Plato's Ethics*. New York: Oxford University Press.

Jones, R. E. 2013a. "Felix Socrates?" *Philosophia* 43: 77–98.

Jones, R. E. 2013b. "Wisdom and Happiness in *Euthydemus* 278–282." *Philosophers' Imprint* 13: 1–21.

Jones, R. E. 2016. "Socrates' Bleak View of the Human Condition." *Ancient Philosophy* 36: 97–105.

Kahn, C. 1983. "Drama and Dialectic in Plato's *Gorgias*." *Oxford Studies in Ancient Philosophy* 1: 75–121.

Kahn, C. 1996. *Plato and the Socratic Dialogue: The Philosophical Use of Literary Form*. Cambridge: Cambridge University Press.

Kamtekar, R. 2017. *Plato's Moral Psychology: Intellectualism, the Divided Soul, and the Desire for Good*. Oxford: Oxford University Press.

Kraut, R. 1984. *Socrates and the State*. Princeton, NJ: Princeton University Press.

Kraut, R., ed. 1992. *The Cambridge Companion to Plato*. Cambridge: Cambridge University Press.

Lännström, A. 2012. "Trusting the Divine Voice: Socrates and His Daimonion." *Apeiron* 45: 32–49.

Lehrer, K. 2000. *Theory of Knowledge*. Boulder, CO: Westview Press.

Levy, D. 2013. "Socrates vs. Callicles: Examination and Ridicule in Plato's *Gorgias*." *Plato Journal* 13: 27–36.

Liddell, H. G., Scott, R., Jones, H. S., and McKenzie, R. 1940. *A Greek-English Lexicon*. Oxford: Clarendon Press.

Martinez, J. and Smith, N. D. 2018. "Socrates' Aversion to Being a Victim of Injustice." *The Journal of Ethics* 22 (1): 59–76.

May, H. 1997. "Socratic Ignorance and the Therapeutic Aim of the Elenchus." In M. L. McPherran, ed., *Wisdom, Ignorance, and Virtue: New Essays in Socratic Studies*. Edmonton: Academic Printing and Publishing, 37–50.

McKim, R. 1988. "Shame and Truth in Plato's Gorgias." In C. L. Griswold, ed., *Platonic Readings, Platonic Writings*. New York: Routledge, 34–48.

McPartland, K. 2013. "Socratic Ignorance and Types of Knowledge." In J. Bussanich and N. D. Smith, eds., *The Bloomsbury Companion to Socrates*. London: Bloomsbury, 94–135.

McPherran, M. L. 1996. *The Religion of Socrates*. University Park, PA: Penn State Press.

McPherran, M. L., ed. 1997. *Wisdom, Ignorance, and Virtue: New Essays in Socratic Studies*. Edmonton: Academic Printing and Publishing (*Apeiron* 30.4).

McPherran, M. L. 2002. "Justice and Pollution in Plato's *Euthyphro*." *Apeiron* 35: 1–25.

McPherran, M. L. 2005. "'What Even a Child Would Know': Socrates, Luck, and Providence at *Euthydemus* 277d–282e." *Ancient Philosophy* 25: 1–15.

McPherran, M. L. 2007. "Socratic Epagôgê and Socratic Induction." *Journal of the History of Philosophy* 45: 347–364.

McTighe, K. 1984. "Socrates on Desire for the Good and the Involuntariness of Wrongdoing: *Gorgias* 466a–468e." *Phronesis* 29: 193–236.

Morrison, D. R. 2003. "Happiness, Rationality, and Egoism in Plato's Socrates." In J. Yu and J. J. E. Gracia, eds., *Rationality and Happiness: From the Ancients to the Early Medievals*. Rochester, NY: University of Rochester Press, 17–34.

Moss, J. 2005. "Shame, Pleasure and the Divided Soul." *Oxford Studies in Ancient Philosophy* 29: 137–170.

Moss, J. 2007. "The Doctor and the Pastry Chef: Pleasure and Persuasion in Plato's *Gorgias*." *Ancient Philosophy* 27: 137–170.

Nails, D. 1995. *Agora, Academy, and the Conduct of Philosophy*. Dordrecht; Boston, MA; London: Kluwer Academic Publishers.

Nails, D. 2002. *The People of Plato*. Indianapolis, IN: Hackett Publishing Company.

Nehamas, A. 1999. "Socratic Intellectualism." In A. Nehamas, *Virtues of Authenticity: Essays on Plato and Socrates*. Princeton, NJ: Princeton University Press, 27–58.

Newcott, B. 2009. "Wisdom of the Elders." *AARP Magazine* 347: 52.

NYPost. 2009. "Quiet Air Hero Is Captain America." https://nypost.com/2009/01/17/quiet-air-hero-is-captain-america.

Parry, R. 2003. "The Craft of Ruling in Plato's *Euthydemus* and *Republic*." *Phronesis* 47: 1–28.

Partnership for 21st Century Skills. 2008. "21st Century Skills, Education and Competitiveness: A Resource and Policy Guide." www.p21.org/documents/21st_century_skills_education_and_competitiveness_guide.pdf.

Penner, T. 1973. "The Unity of the Virtues." *Philosophical Review* 82: 35–68.

Penner, T. 1990. "Plato and Davidson: Parts of the Soul and Weakness of Will." *Canadian Journal of Philosophy* 16 (Suppl.): 35–72.

Penner, T. 1991. "Desire and Power in Socrates: The Argument of *Gorgias* 466A–468E That Orators and Tyrants Have No Power in the City." *Apeiron* 24: 147–202.

Penner, T. 1992a. "Socrates and the Early Dialogues." In R. Kraut, ed., *The Cambridge Companion to Plato*. Cambridge: Cambridge University Press, 121–169.

Penner, T. 1992b. "What Laches and Nicias Miss – and Whether Socrates Thinks Courage Is Merely a Part of Virtue." *Ancient Philosophy* 12: 1–27.

Penner, T. 1997. "Socrates on the Strength of Knowledge: *Protagoras* 351B–357E." *Archiv für Geschichte der Philosophie* 79: 117–149.

Penner, T. 2000. "Socrates." In C. J. Rowe and Malcolm Schofield, eds., *Cambridge History of Greek and Roman Political Thought*. Cambridge: Cambridge University Press, 164–189.

Penner, T. 2018. "Inequality, Intention, and Ignorance: Socrates on Punishment and the Human Good." In G. Anagnostopoulos and G. Santas, eds., *Democracy, Justice, and Equality in Ancient Greece: Historical and Philosophical Perspectives*. Cham: Springer, 83–138.

Penner, T. and Rowe, C. 1994. "The Desire for the Good: Is the *Meno* Inconsistent with the *Gorgias?*" *Phronesis* 39: 1–25.

Press, Gerald. 2010. "The State of the Question in the Study of Plato." *Southern Journal of Philosophy* 34: 507–532.

Prior, W. 2006. "The Portrait of Socrates in Plato's *Symposium*." *Oxford Studies in Ancient Philosophy* 31: 137–166.

Pritchard, D. 2001. "The Opacity of Knowledge." *Essays in Philosophy* 2: 1, Article 1.

Randall, R. W. and Smith, N. D. 2019. "The Socratic Version of the Opacity Objection." In S. Hetherington and N. D. Smith, eds., *What the Ancients Offer to Contemporary Epistemology*. London: Routledge, 8–24.

Reeve, C. D. C. 1988. *Philosopher-Kings*. Princeton, NJ: Princeton University Press.

Reeve, C. D. C. 1989. *Socrates in the Apology*. Indianapolis, IN: Hackett Publishing Company.

Reisner, A. and Steglich-Peterson, A. eds. 2011. *Reasons for Belief*. Cambridge: Cambridge University Press.

Reshotko, N., ed. 2003. *Socrates and Plato: Desire, Identity and Existence*. Kelowna, BC: Academic Printing and Publishing.

Reshotko, N. 2006. *Socratic Virtue: Making the Best of the Neither-Good-Nor-Bad*. Cambridge: Cambridge University Press.

Roochnik, D. 1985. "*Apology* 40c4–41e7: Is Death Really a Gain?" *Classical Journal* 80: 212–220.

Roochnik, D. 1996. *Of Art and Wisdom: Plato's Understanding of Techne*. State College, PA: The Pennsylvania University Press.

Rowe, C. J. 2003. "Plato, Socrates, and Developmentalism." In N. Reshotko, ed., *Socrates and Plato: Desire, Identity and Existence*. Kelowna, BC: Academic Printing and Publishing, 17–32.

Rowe, C. J. 2006. "Socrates in Plato's Dialogues." In S. Ahbel-Rappe and R. Kamtekar, eds., *A Companion to Socrates*. Oxford: Blackwell, 159–170.

Rowe, C. J. 2007. "A Problem in the Gorgias: How Is Punishment Supposed to Help with Intellectual Error?" In C. Bobonich and P. Destrée, eds., *Akrasia in Greek Philosophy*. Leiden and Boston, MA: Brill, 19–40.

Rudebusch, G. 1991. "Death Is One of Two Things." *Ancient Philosophy* 11: 35–45.

Rudebusch, G. 1999. *Socrates on Pleasure and Value*. New York: Oxford University Press.

Russell, D. 2005. *Plato on Pleasure and the Good Life*. Oxford: Oxford University Press.

Ryle, G. 1949. *The Concept of Mind*. New York: Barnes and Noble.

Sanderman, D. 2004. "Why Socrates Mocks His Interlocutors." *Skepsis* 15: 431–441.

Santas, G. X. 1979. *Socrates: Philosophy in Plato's Early Dialogues*. London and Boston, MA: Routledge and Kegan Paul.

Scott, G. A., ed. 2002. *Does Socrates Have a Method? Rethinking the Elenchus in Plato's Dialogues and Beyond*. University Park, PA: The Pennsylvania University Press.

Sedley, D. 1999. "The Ideal of Godlikeness." In G. Fine, ed., *Plato 2: Ethics, Politics, Religion, and the Soul* (Oxford Readings in Philosophy). Oxford: Oxford University Press, 309–328.

Segvic, H. 2000. "No One Errs Willingly." *Oxford Studies in Ancient Philosophy* 19: 1–45.

Senn, S. J. 2005. "Virtue as the Sole Intrinsic Good in Plato's Early Dialogues." *Oxford Studies in Ancient Philosophy* 28: 1–21.

Senn, S. J. 2013. "Ignorance or Irony in Plato's Socrates? A Look Beyond Avowals and Disavowals of Knowledge." *Plato Journal* 13: 77–108.

Sennett, R. 2009. *The Craftsman*. New York: Penguin.

Shero, L. R. 1927. "Plato's *Apology* and Xenophon's *Apology*." *Classical World* 20: 107–111.

Smith, A. 1998. "Knowledge and Expertise in the Early Platonic Dialogues." *Archiv für Geschichte der Philosophie* 80: 129–161.

Smith, N. D. 2004. "Did Plato Write the *Alcibiades I?*" *Apeiron* 37: 93–108.

Smith, N. D. 2016. "Socrates on the Human Condition." *Ancient Philosophy* 36: 81–95.

Smith, N. D. 2018. "Aristotle on Socrates." In A. Stavru and C. Moore, eds., *Socrates and the Socratic Dialogue*. Leiden: Brill, 601–622.

Stone, I. F. 1988. *The Trial of Socrates*. New York: Little, Brown and Company.

Tampa Bay Times. 2009. "Sully Speaks!" www.tampabay.com/archive/2009/02/08/sully-speaks.

Taylor, C. C. W. 2000. *Socrates: A Very Short Introduction*. Oxford: Oxford University Press.

TeachThought Staff. 2019. "8 Critical Skills for a Modern Education." www.teachthought.com/the-future-of-learning/8-critical-skills-modern-education.

Tulin, A. 1996. *Dike Phonou: The Right of Prosecution and Attic Homicide Procedure*. Stuttgart and Leipzig: B. G. Teubner.

Vahid, H. 2009. *The Epistemology of Belief.* New York: Palgrave Macmillan.

Vlastos, G. 1971. "The Paradox of Socrates." In G. Vlastos, ed., *The Philosophy of Socrates.* Notre Dame, IN: University of Notre Dame Press, 1–21. Repr. from the original version in *Queen's Quarterly* 64 (1957–8): 496–516.

Vlastos, G. 1978. "The Virtuous and the Happy." *Times Literary Supplement,* Feb. 24: 230–231.

Vlastos, G. 1980. "Socrates' Contribution to the Greek Sense of Justice." *Arkaiognosia* 1: 310–324.

Vlastos, G. 1981. "The Unity of the Virtues in the *Protagoras.*" In G. Vlastos, ed., *Platonic Studies* (2nd ed.). Princeton, NJ: Princeton University Press, 221–269.

Vlastos, G. 1985. "Socrates' Disavowal of Knowledge." *Philosophical Quarterly* 35: 1–31.

Vlastos, G. 1991. *Socrates: Ironist and Moral Philosopher.* Cambridge: Cambridge University Press.

Vlastos, G. 1994. *Socratic Studies.* Cambridge: Cambridge University Press.

White, N. P. 2002. *Individual and Conflict in Greek Ethics.* Oxford: Clarendon Press.

Wolfsdorf, D. 2008. *Trials of Reason: Plato and the Crafting of Philosophy.* New York: Oxford University Press.

Wolfsdorf, D. 2013. "Socratic Philosophizing." In J. Bussanich and N. D. Smith, eds., *The Bloomsbury Companion to Socrates.* London: Bloomsbury, 34–67.

Woodruff, P. B. 1976. "Socrates on the Parts of Virtue." *Canadian Journal of Philosophy* Suppl. 2: 101–116.

Woodruff, P. B. 1990. "Plato's Early Theory of Knowledge." In S. Everson, ed., *Companions to Ancient Thought I: Epistemology.* Cambridge: Cambridge University Press, 60–84.

Woodruff, P. B. 2000. "Socrates and the Irrational." In N. D. Smith and P. B. Woodruff, eds., *Reason and Religion in Socratic Philosophy.* New York and Oxford: Oxford University Press, 130–150.

Xenophon. 1985. *Recollections of Socrates.* Trans. A. S. Benjamin. New York: Macmillan.

Zagzebski, L. T. 1996. *Virtues of the Mind.* Cambridge: Cambridge University Press.

Index of Passages

174

General Index

Thrasymachus, 31, 60, 108
Thucydides (son of Melesias), 22
tribê, 147
Tulin, A., 93, 94

Vahid, H., 160
virtue, xi, xii, xiv, xv, xix, 1, 2, 3, 4, 5, 6, 7, 9, 10, 11,
    12, 13, 15, 16, 17, 18, 19, 20, 23, 24, 25, 26, 27, 28,
    30, 31, 32, 35, 36, 37, 40, 41, 45, 49, 57, 62, 64,
    66, 79, 81, 86, 87, 88, 89, 90, 105, 106, 108, 109,
    110, 111, 113, 115, 116, 117, 118, 119, 121, 122, 124,
    125, 126, 128, 129, 130, 131, 134, 135, 136, 137, 138,
    139, 140, 141, 142, 143, 144, 145, 146, 150, 151,
    152, 153, 154, 156, 157, 162, 163, 164, 165
  unity of, 25
Vlastos, G., xiii, 2, 4, 5, 7, 11, 20, 22, 40, 58, 76, 77,
    86, 87, 88, 90, 109, 131
voluntary, 41, 51, 52, 59, 63, 122, 123

White, N., 40
wisdom, ix, x, xii, xv, 1, 2, 7, 8, 9, 10, 11, 16,
    17, 18, 19, 20, 23, 29, 30, 31, 33, 34, 35, 37, 56,
    60, 70, 71, 72, 75, 77, 78, 82, 85, 86, 88, 89,
    90, 91, 92, 93, 96, 97, 98, 99, 100, 101, 102,
    103, 104, 108, 109, 111, 113, 114, 115, 116, 117,
    119, 122, 126, 128, 129, 132, 133, 134, 135, 136,
    137, 139, 140, 143, 144, 150, 151, 156, 157, 164,
    165. *See* craft, expertise, knowledge, skill,
    technê
Wolfsdorf, D., xvii, 33, 44, 58, 76, 77, 93
Woodruff, P., xix, 25, 45, 60, 61, 62, 83,
    85, 88

Xenophon, xi, 2, 5, 6, 7, 24, 57, 58, 84, 88, 109,
    126, 136

Zagzebsky, L., 162

For EU product safety concerns, contact us at Calle de José Abascal, 56–1°,
28003 Madrid, Spain or eugpsr@cambridge.org.

www.ingramcontent.com/pod-product-compliance
Ingram Content Group UK Ltd.
Pitfield, Milton Keynes, MK11 3LW, UK
UKHW020351140625
459647UK00020B/2406